Joyce Carol Oates,
JArtist in Residence

G
1395

April, 1987

Dear father creedy,

To my favorite
(and inveterate!)
reader — with
great affection
and respect.
I'm glad you're
in residence...

Eileen

Joyce Carol Oates, Artist in Residence

EILEEN TEPER BENDER, 1935 -

INDIANA UNIVERSITY PRESS
Bloomington & Indianapolis

To Harvey, Leslie, Sam, and Phil

This book was brought to publication
with the assistance of a grant from the
Andrew W. Mellon foundation.

Manufactured in the United States of America

Library of Congress Cataloging-in Publication Data

Bender, Eileen Teper, 1935–
    Joyce Carol Oates, artist in residence.

    Bibliography: p. 199
    Includes index.
      1. Oates, Joyce Carol, 1938– —Criticism and
interpretation. I. Title.
PS3565.A8Z58   1987   813'.54   86–45474
ISBN 0–253–30483–0
     0–253–20426–7 (pbk)

1 2 3 4 5 91 90 89 88 87

Contents

Acknowledgments

In 1963, a Pasadena newspaper editor gave me a review copy of *Upon The Sweeping Flood* by a new writer, Joyce Carol Oates. I was arrested by the power of these short stories, peopled by American dybbuks and demons and filled with a sense of disturbance both new and uncannily familiar. That first meeting with Oates has led to this study. Understandably, it has involved many others along the way: like the Isolated Artist, the Isolated Scholar is also a myth, for which I am profoundly grateful.

Joseph X. Brennan served as my first reader and reviewer of subsequent drafts. Students have always offered the unexpected: fresh ideas and readings, clippings, stray references to Oates from unusual sources. Several are now friends and colleagues: Claudia Bayliss, Sun Bing He, Sheila Conboy, Cara Chell. A fellow Oates admirer and a fine critic, Ellen Friedman, has proven an especially valuable reader and advisor. The Society for Values in Higher Education has provided a responsive critical audience for my on-going studies, in many ways helping to shape my view of Oates as an artist in residence. Faculty at St. Mary's College and Indiana University at South Bend have made my work easier because of their professional interest. Connie Maher and Georgeanna Caldwell have performed a variety of personal and word-processing miracles, demonstrating new levels of grace under pressure. Perhaps the reader most generous with her time and critical responses has been Joyce Carol Oates herself.

Finally, there are always persons more crucial to such projects than they know. Sam and Sonia Teper, my parents, are responsible for my life-long addiction to literature. Leslie, Sam, and Phil Bender have served as in-house counsel and longer-range contributors. Harvey, my own favorite scholar in residence, continues to inspire me through his love and example.

Introduction

In her twenty years of responding with an artist's and critic's eye to the American scene, Joyce Carol Oates has emerged from an eccentric position as "Dark Lady of American Letters" to become our principal artist-in-residence. That title, of course, is freighted with ambiguity: it suggests both a curious poise and a wry asymmetry, the artist's capacity for empathy and the critic's appetite for antipathy. It is no wonder that Oates herself has been attracted by Blake's idea of "contraries."[1] This perpetual ambivalence is an important key to the phenomenon of Joyce Carol Oates—novelist, playwright, short story writer, essayist, editor, poet, publisher, teacher. For it is the energy generated by these sometimes analogous and at times opposing selves which fuels Oates's ambitious project, now clearly outlined after two decades of conflicting claims and assessments.

In her own words, Oates has always been moved by a desire to consummate a series of "marriages," contracted with full knowledge of potential "infidelities": her profuse and multiform work demonstrates her "laughably Balzacian" hunger "to put the whole world into a book."[2] Universally recognized for her virtually continuous stream of publication, she has assembled an amazing bibliography: since 1963, Oates has published seventeen novels, five plays (which have had notable stage productions), eight volumes of poetry, and literally hundreds of short stories of considerable formal and thematic range. The O'Henry Short Stories awards committee put her in a category of excellence all her own. She has edited an anthology of short fiction, a collection of works on writers and their craft, and a "bedside companion" of ghost stories. She has helped to establish a literary quarterly, *The Ontario Review,* serves as guest editor of the new *Kenyon Review,* and with her husband, manages a small press. At the same time, she has accumulated impressive academic credentials. She has been a professor of literature at the University of Detroit and the University of Windsor; presently, she teaches in the writing program at Princeton University, and is an established critic in her own right, with frequent reviews, scholarly presentations, and articles, including four thematically grouped, book-length collections of essays on classic and contemporary literature and critical theory.

Confronting an artist who attempts so much, some critics and scholars complain about her very profusion, finding her "too prolific."[3] Others find it difficult to move beyond partial estimates or the most general, even grudging acknowledgment of her sheer energy. Yet, as her own comments suggest and as an overview of the phenomenon of Joyce Carol Oates seems to confirm, her work is necessarily wide-ranging and essentially revisionary, produced by a discursive process of immersion, reimagination, mediation, and synthesis. Attempting to make a lie of the "myth of the isolated artist,"[4] Joyce Carol Oates is bent on affirming and rejoining literature and the human community, fulfilling the terms of a residency which is both demanding and open-ended.

Oates's intentions—which, we shall see, are both implicit and explicit in her novels as well as her critical pronouncements—are all the more remarkable because the academic literary community in which she resides seems to place high value on ironic detachment and the separation of the artist from "felt life." "Fragments are the only form I trust," the parodic hero of a contemporary sketch by Donald Barthelme intones.[5] Many of Oates's publishing colleagues are valorized as "fabulators,"[6] word-juggling writers who have uncannily validated Ortega y Gasset's prediction that the artist would turn "waggish" in the modern era.[7] Barth, Barthelme, Nabokov, Gass, Vonnegut, and Pynchon mock fiction's conventions and veer close to self-parody. Abjuring formal coherence and closure, they offer work born of a deconstructive energy as explosive as the bomb-blast which gives our age its sinister name. They are self-consciously academic; they often trade upon their problematic patronage, performing self-consciously before a shrinking literary audience, evermore elitist and cultish. Game-players, they revel in codes and tempt critics with their deliberately obscurantist jargon.

Decades ago, cultural observers warned of establishing such residencies, suggesting there might be a fundamental incompatibility of creative artist and probing critic. Alfred Kazin, for example, warned of a confusion of aims and deflection of purpose. Critics, he felt, would be encouraged wrongly to think of themselves as artists: "Aren't we writers, too?" Heatedly, he defends the traditional and, to him, necessary opposition of artist and scholar, writer and critical reader:

> To the writer reality is something to be transformed—and not by the patient discussion and analysis of impersonal items, but by a creative act. The virtues of scholarship at its best—patience and humility and disinterestedness—are not necessarily the writer's virtues. . . . Above all, the writer does not work with anyone; he is not a collaborator, he is not cooperative. . . .

For Kazin, the academy is an appropriate place for scholars interested in "publication at any price"; for the writer, academic rewards are "harmful . . . they can distract and deceive and soften him up."[8] Artists risk losing their creative freedom, objectivity, and precision; the critic-writer hybrid is unable to function either as author or authority.

Kazin's cautionary remarks now seem prophetic of a change that has occurred in our own critical climate: a renewed interest in the problematic relationship of artist, critic, and text; the double and even at times duplicitous role of the writer-in-residence. The collaboration which was once anathema to Kazin now in fact seems a most appropriate term for contemporary critical discourse, flavored as it is by philosophical speculations and extraliterary theories. As he half-feared, critical texts themselves have become the subject of close reading and exegesis.

Yet today, Kazin's fear has other names. One is "the anxiety of influence," Harold Bloom's phrase for an artist's Freudian resistance to literary fathers, patrons, and coworkers. Another is the growing complaint leveled at art and criticism that seems purely academic: writing, whether minimalist or elaborately contrived, that parades its own facticity; criticism, which has indeed become a metaliterature, and which some readers (John Gardner, Victor Brombert, Gerald Graff) meet with a Tolstoyan condemnation of its esoteric and imperialistic demands. Each new school or manifesto has informed an impressive counterattack; the artist, caught in the crossfire, registers the uneasiness of a parasite in danger of being consumed by its host.

Joyce Carol Oates, in contrast, has consistently affirmed a model of commensalism in which writers and readers nourish each other, sharing in a common artistic endeavor. She believes such a community of discourse exists in the university. Her work is marked by a hospitality to a multiplicity of disciplinary perspectives and philosophical ideas which she finds around her in her academic residence.

Any assessment of Oates must, therefore, emphasize intertextual readings. The present study takes as its primary focus those allusive and multileveled works which the author regards as her most significant texts: her novels. In defining her position in contemporary American literature (and world literature—her fiction is read in translation in many countries, and she has already been mentioned as a Nobel candidate), it will also be helpful to refer occasionally to her other contributions. Oates herself describes "horizontal obsessions" at work while she is completing her novels: a desire to revise, reexamine, and relocate themes and characters that motivates her use of other forms—poetry, plays, essays, and short stories.[9]

Most important of these secondary works of Joyce Carol Oates may be her own critical comments and essays, which in themselves give an account of her own deeply held beliefs about the moral, social, and political role of the artist and the value of literature in our time. In essays and reviews Oates insists that the most ordinary individual is in an important sense an artist. Thus we all live in a community of art; the writer, not only privileged but driven to create literature as well as a shapely life, has a positive obligation to "sanctify the world."[10] Given the enormity of such intentions, it is not surprising to see the size and variegation of Oates's own artistic enterprise.

In the preface to her most recent collection of essays, Oates takes up W. H. Auden's view of the relationship of writer and reader in order to consider and (characteristically) to revise it. Literature, a palpable and mute offering, remains "sacred." Criticism, in contrast, is "profane": derivative, useful. "Why this instinct to interpret?" Oates wonders from the recesses of academic residence. She is moved to account for the incessant need to share, to intellectualize, to provide readings "that will surely be misunderstood or scarcely valued at all."[11] Ultimately she rejects the prevailing model of critic as antagonist; the best critic, she claims here as in many other contexts, is empathic, assimilative, and co-creative. In turn, the artist also is a reader and critic, one element in an ongoing process of creative revision which philosophers call the hermeneutic circle.

The poet Keats attempted to account for Shakespeare's greatness by describing his special gift of empathy. He called the mysterious submission of the writer to the forces set in motion in the work "negative capability." Other artists have testified to the curious ambivalence this capability—this necessity, in fact—creates. When Henry James describes his ambassador as a figure plagued by a double consciousness, he might well have been thinking of his own position as a critic and an artist, simultaneously conscious of the madness of the artistic impulse and the critical desire of the rational intellect to clarify, to objectify art's intention, form, and limits.

Oates's artistic stance—that of mediator as much as individual voice —thus is at once traditional and innovative. She tests strategies of self-effacement reminiscent of T. S. Eliot's call for poetry "standing naked in its bare bones," free of the deliberately artful marks of the poet's personality. She frequently demands an art "not overly intoxicated with the selfness of the self" and thus open to the energies of revision and reconstruction available in "transpersonal experiences."[12]

It may seem more radical to consider Oates a literary feminist. As critic and artist, Oates certainly bears an interesting relation to the contemporary women's movement. She has been subject to accusatory fire from some feminist critics for her comments on androgyny and the portrait of a modern woman awakened by the force of a heterosexual embrace in her novel, *Do with Me What You Will.* Yet despite her own resistance to the label "woman writer," it is clear that she has anticipated and continues to share central feminist concerns. Even in her earliest fiction and critical essays, she attacked what she viewed as perversely masculine ideals:

> Where at one point in civilization this very masculine, combative ideal of an
> "I" set against all other "I's"—and against nature as well—was necessary in or-
> der to wrench man from the hermetic contemplation of a God-centered uni-
> verse and get him into action, it is no longer necessary, its health has become a
> pathology.[13]

In the same vein, she rebuked her male colleagues and contemporaries for playing out "the old, losing, pitiful Last Stand of the Ego, the Self-Against-All-Others, the Conqueror, the Highest of all Protoplasms, Namer and Begetter of all Fictions."[14] The solipsism of post-modern fiction, she further contended, "makes little sense to women, and has as much appeal to them as the self-mutilated priests of old would have had."[15] In her collection of essays on modern literature, *New Heaven, New Earth* (1974), she again voiced her protest at the deforming energies of egocentric art, which has led to a "paralysis of the imagination" for both sexes: "burdened, if male, with the need to conquer and if female . . . terrified of the prospect, seen as inevitable, of being conquered" *(NHNE,* 191).

Thus Oates has always been what Judith Fetterley calls a "resisting reader," arguing against the prevailing masculine stories of our literature and culture. More recently, Oates has come to describe herself as a feminist "sympathizer," offering a well-documented, passionate, and often witty critical response to modern society's "misogynous bias." She also presents her own story in the role of creative artist. Her *A Bloodsmoor Romance* (1982) is a wickedly irreverent and doubly subversive version of the popular, sentimental, nineteenth-century "women's novel," manipulating its own devices: a vaporous and garrulous female narrator and a "ludicrous steamroller plot." More sinister reflections on the grotesque violations of women implicit in literary and social conventions emerge in her mock-Gothic-detective novel, *Mysteries of Winterthurn* (1984). *Solstice* (1985) and *Marya: A Life* (1986) use a more contemporary idiom to voice the aspirations and concerns of the community of women. These novels exploit a wealth of academic resources in order to dramatize the multiple acts of betrayal embedded in traditional literary genres.

She works with similar revisionist energy as a practicing critic, frequently turning to neglected or misinterpreted works by women writers to offer a remedial or corrected vision. In a striking review article, "Images of Women in Twentieth-Century Literature," Oates reopens the work of the celebrated male modernists—Conrad, Lawrence, Eliot, Faulkner—to protest against the same retrograde nineteenth-century misogyny she satirizes in her later fiction:

> A man's quarrel with Woman is his quarrel with himself—with those "despised" and muted elements in his personality which he cannot freely acknowledge because they challenge his sense of masculine supremacy and control. Modernist literature, despite . . . its openness to radical revisionings of the act of "storytelling" . . . exhibits nonetheless most of the received and unexamined values of popular mass culture, so far as images of Woman are concerned.[16]

While she has become more closely aligned with the academy's feminist critique, it is part of a larger focus on selfhood, the central concern of her fiction

—a region beyond parody and sociopolitical invective. In both her creative and critical work, Oates also displays her insatiable curiosity about history, culture, and art—a curiosity not only enriched but indeed abetted by her presence within the university.

Joyce Carol Oates has embarked on a long and ambitious artistic journey, embracing the ambiguities and paradoxes of a complex literary inheritance. She welcomes a collaborator's role; she displays no reservations about taking up both the profane and the sacred obligations of a writer in residence, attempting to balance an artist's sense of possession and inspiration with a critic's remedial and analytic power. This double awareness is evident in her frequent comments about the autonomy of the artistic process, and the critical necessity of the self—whether artist, character, or reader—to take shape, to actualize. It makes her, in a curious way, both self-erasing and self-reflexive. It also gives shape to the paradoxical human journeys dramatized in her novels, in which failure and dislocation seem prerequisite for the fullest expression of human possibility.

It is the intention of this study to consider Joyce Carol Oates as a writer who is always in some sense a critic, and to define her intentions and achievements as part of a larger statement about contemporary American life and letters. The discussion thus will begin with a view of Oates as part of an American literary tradition she at once affirms and attempts to revise. In turn, these comments will serve to preface readings of her novels and their images of self and society. Oates emerges as a remarkable artist in residence, whose work in a sense, is always in progress—open to revision, assimilative and allusive, never purely academic.

Joyce Carol Oates, Artist in Residence

1 Misreadings and Marriages
The "Place" of Joyce Carol Oates

The work of Joyce Carol Oates has proven to be an enigma for critical readers of contemporary American literature. Because she presents herself as a storyteller instead of claiming to be "metafictive," it has seemed irresistible to call her traditional. As she herself recognizes, the critical sensibility enforces such uses of the past. In contrast, the impulses of the artist pull in the opposite direction, toward uncharted territory.[1]

However that tension may register itself in Oates's own art and criticism, it is clear that two decades of Oates readers have found her work especially hard to classify. Since the late 1970s, several full-length studies of Oates's work have attempted to create a more receptive climate for her art. G.K. Waller's study, *Dreaming America,* links her with D.H. Lawrence. Joanne V. Creighton's *Joyce Carol Oates* suggests that reader response theory is useful in coming to terms with the violence in her fiction, thus validating earlier "grotesque" and "gothic" readings.[2] Linda Wagner's *Critical Views of Joyce Carol Oates,* introduced by an engaging if somewhat ironic preface by Oates herself on the difficulty of finding ideal readers, illustrates the diversity of critical estimates of this prolific and popular writer.[3] Perhaps the best of these early studies is Ellen Friedman's *Joyce Carol Oates.*[4] Friedman moves away from more conventional critical categorization to discuss Oates's explicit interest in the psychology of the self, relating Oates's conception of character to the theories of Jung, Freud, and Maslow cited in her essays. A 1984 study of Oates's short fiction by Torburg Norman is the first to put her art into the context of more avant-garde literary criticism, analyzing that enormously varied work through the lens of speech act theory.[5]

Other critics continue in their efforts to put Oates in her conventional literary place. Oates has been labeled a realist and "neo-naturalist," and thus is still frequently compared with Faulkner, Steinbeck, Welty, O'Connor, and Dreiser. Like Faulkner, Oates has attempted to create a social microcosm in which to explore human values; she has also exploited the rural setting of her childhood, "Eden County" near Rockport, New York. Yet Oates's Eden, to which she still returns in the scenes of her fiction, is not a locale with fixed landmarks or a sense of history and tradition; as John Gardner suggests, her fictive landscape is not rooted in specific geography or time. Like Steinbeck,

Oates is concerned with the American migrant. But she finds little redemptive possibility in transpersonal nature itself, and her images of passage are
various and even at times freakish, ranging from racing cars to diving planes,
from pickup trucks to hot-air balloons. When Oates's migrants end their
physical flight, it is because they are paralyzed by repeated assaults. Out-
wardly aphasic, they may nonetheless continue on a torturous and relentless
inner journey. Again, like the American "determinists," Oates is fascinated
by images of closure: the tightening ring of the speedway, chain-link and
barbed-wire barriers, the map's linear grid. Yet her travelers soon discover,
often to their peril, that all boundaries are potentially permeable: Oates's
world is constantly undermined by quicksand possibilities.

Oates has described her affinity with several American women writers.
Like Eudora Welty, Oates describes a universe in which horror can erupt out
of familiar landscape, fed by some irresistible biological imperative. Yet in
Oates's work, there is no trace of Welty's exquisite if anachronistic gentility,
and her county or city or campus is often satirically rather than nostalgically
delineated. Like Flannery O'Connor, Oates may filter her stories through a
grotesque or freakily precocious consciousness, but rarely is it to bear witness
to a supernatural presence. Cripples, misfits, and fat ladies (and the anorexic
alternative!) crowd her scenes, not God-hungry but victimized by their own
internal drives and appetites. Disease in her fiction is fearsome, but displays
the self's terrible vulnerability and mortality, never functioning as an agency
of revelation. In fact, Oates's vision of secular incarnation is closer to Dreiser's than O'Connor's. She is an observer of the natural scene; she can be
moved to lyrical celebration of desire; she has explored the American city as
a magical as well as oppressive presence. But in contrast to Dreiser's strategy
of documentation, Oates prefers intuitive evidence for her recreations of felt
life; documents, when they exist in her work, often seem parodistic, mocking
rather than affirming the intractable texture of reality.

Alfred Kazin, attempting to relate Oates to the American literary tradition
in his study, *Bright Book of Life,* places Oates in the company of American
women novelists:

> The sense of mankind's vulnerability in this age gives special resonance to all
> personal testimony by gifted women writers. By the act of writing well, by their
> acute sense of performance, they somehow put themselves . . . right in the path
> of the disturbance.

In assigning Oates to this group, however, Kazin acknowledges that he faces
certain difficulties. Most of his "Cassandras" display a sense of the "the limitations of their own experience, a sense of being excluded," while Oates
seems to test all limits, dramatizing the sheer multiplicity of American life.
Indeed, Kazin at one point declares that because of the "abundance in her

work," Oates "does not always remind me even of herself"! Her style even more than her subject matter marks her as an atypical Cassandra. "It is rare," Kazin reflects, "to find a woman so externally unconcerned with form." While he gives her little credit for "sensitiveness," he is especially struck by Oates's peculiar empathic gifts, suggesting that "the amazing autonomy" she grants her characters may cause formal problems:

> She is utterly hypnotized, positively drugged, by other people's experiences . . . her mind is unbelievably crowded with psychic existences, with such a mass of stories that she lives by being wholly submissive to "them." She is too attentive to their mysterious clamor . . . to make the right and well-fitting structure.

Ultimately, he labels her a "social novelist," responsive to the "sheer factuality of contemporary life," displaying an "evident love for the scene we Americans make." At best she is a writer whose fiction translates naturalism's traditional scenario into language generated in the dark interior. Indeed, Kazin suggests Oates is "primarily concerned with a kind of Darwinian struggle for existence between minds."[6] Critic Harold Bloom, seeking traces of lineage, also enrolls Oates in the neo-naturalist school, calling her an "ambitious ephebe of Dreiser." On the other hand, Bloom detects Romance in her rhetoric: Whitmanian and Emersonian influences.[7]

If many observers find Oates altogether too prolific and uncontrolled, if the abundance characteristic of her literary production frustrates analysis, if she is rebuked for writing fiction in which too much happens, other critics complain, paradoxically, that she is too conservative. Such readers display their bias for the avant-garde; the question of form which Kazin raises only obliquely is central to their dismissal of Oates's seemingly conventional writing. Ihab Hassan, for example, can find no place for Oates in his own model of current American literature, because she is devoted to the "traditional pieties" of the novel at a time when other American writers have moved into fantasy and "anti-art."[8] For David Madden, too, Oates's work seems anachronistic:

> There is nothing new, nothing avant-garde, camp, pop, absurdist about Miss Oates's stories; reading them is like reading deeply between the hieroglyphic lines of fossils found on lonely landscapes. Her stories offer no isolatable, exploitable elements on which fashion might thrive; nor is the author's personality an exploitable by-product of her work. . . . It is difficult, if not foolhardy, to discuss her stories and novels as literary fabrications. If they have form, it is so submerged in "experience" as to defy analysis.[9]

Michael Wood suggests that Oates's traditional story-telling is "itself a technique of survival, a closed, shaped form set up against a shapeless, leaking world." But however sympathetic he may be, he feels that such strategy can be justified today only if it is self-consciously employed as a literary device: "the form would have to acknowledge its artifice, its estrangement from reality, the degree to which it represents a wish, and not a picture of the world."[10] Yet Oates does not indulge in such metafiction. In one of the earliest essays to take her seriously, Walter Clemons defends Oates's old-fashioned formal strategies on moral if not aesthetic grounds:

> Though she is as aware as anyone of the possibilities of experimentation and as haunted and oppressed as any of her contemporaries by feelings that American life may be "too much," too crazed, too accelerated to be captured in a novel, she hasn't lost confidence in the power of narrative fiction to give coherence to jumbled experience and to bring about a change of heart.[11]

Curiously, while Clemons finds her writing emblematic of a redemptive moral optimism, other readers are disturbed by what they take to be Oates's pessimistic vision. Walter Sullivan complains that she draws us into a philosophical trap. Her radically alienated persona,

> placed irrevocably beyond good and evil, must create himself. This necessity for self-creation is at once his doom and his only avenue to freedom; he must transcend his society and in the process he will destroy himself.[12]

Critics continue to disagree about Oates's formal and thematic intentions. Her work—profuse, abundant, in or out of fashion—poses a special critical challenge. Clearly, traditional criteria will not suffice in coming to terms with her special effects: as David Madden suggests, "aesthetic terms" do not account for her "genius for sustaining the intensity of her vision and for creating such totally alive characters and situations" (Madden, 46).

Seemingly, Joyce Carol Oates's work must be explored on its own terms, both allied with and distinguished from that of her contemporaries. Other social realists are frustrated by the modern scene: Philip Roth, for example, complains that reality leaves him "stupefied." On her part, Oates displays an appetite for contemporary life and an excitement about the artist's prospects:

> Though our turbulent era has certainly dismayed and overwhelmed many writers, forcing upon some the role of propagandist or, paradoxically, the role of the indifferent esthete, it is really the best possible time for most writers—the sheer variety of stances, the multiplicity of "styles" available to the serious writer, is amazing.[13]

Oates has declared her allegiance to "reality" and "story" at a time when an impressive array of contemporary American writers have staged a fabulators' revolt. Defying conventional rules, undermining traditional narrative structures, issuing disparate fragments, these writers—many also in residence—take extraordinary liberties with language and plot; they impose a mocking authority over the admittedly limited and deformed creatures of their own devising. The old fictive character has "shrunk to a point of frightened view" in the literature of fabulation: the author as ventriloquist often refuses to leave center stage, and insists that the audience applaud the ingenuity of the performance. The artist's own autonomy, not that of the character, thus becomes the central preoccupation of much of contemporary writing and the center of critical and academic discourse. Oates, in response, calls such post-modern work inexcusably immoral:

> The stasis celebrated in much of contemporary literature, the erecting of gigantic paranoid delusion systems that are self-enclosed and self-destructing, argues for a simple failure of reasoning: the human ego has too long imagined itself the supreme form of consciousness in the universe.

The egocentric artist, whether male or female, is promoting a perverse "masculine" model. "Suffering, (he) projects (his) emotions outward into everything, everyone, into the universe itself."[14]

She has set forth the terms of her own position unequivocally, using the language of battle. In an essay "Whose Side Are You On?" Oates challenges not only those writers who are producing a literature of "entropy" and "exhaustion," but the critics who cannot believe that a best-selling author can be *good*:

> For many years our most promising writers have lined up obediently behind Nabokov, Beckett and Borges, to file through a doorway marked THIS WAY OUT. How eagerly they have taken their places! If they glance around at the rest of us, who are holding back, they are ready with mechanized scorn: X is too bourgeois; X is too suburban; X is not experimental; X is being read![15]

Ironically, her self-defense may have kept critics from seeing her own experimental intentions. Her view of human character is both original and eclectic, the product of a wide-ranging study of "personality" theory. Jung's idea of a collective consciousness influences Oates's novelistic vision, as does the theory of the "protean" human personality drawn from "Third Force" psychologists R. D. Laing, Robert Jay Lifton, and A. H. Maslow. Oates frequently transforms their terminology into artistic metaphor: many of her characters come "dreaming back" from a downward plunge, groping towards recovery and self-actualization.

Psychology has supplied only part of Oates's picture of selfhood. Gradually, she has moved away from an older autonomous and individualistic ideal to explore a new communal possibility. In the process, she has used the fabulators' own work as intertext: *Childwold,* her novel of adolescence, plays with *Lolita*; *Bellefleur* and *Mysteries of Winterthurn* allude to Márquez; *The Poisoned Kiss* evokes the presence of Borges. The effect is a curious act of reconciliation.

As a teacher as well as a writer in residence, Oates from necessity has taken up a reader's role, complicating her already difficult position. In a recent collection of essays, she describes her double vision with a recognition of its attendant perils. Like one of her own characters, she feels the very contours of individual identity dissolving:

> The practicing writer is . . . not an entity at all, let alone a person, but a curious melange of wildly varying states of mind, clustered toward what might be called the darker end of the spectrum: indecision, frustration, pain, dismay, despair, remorse, impatience, outright failure . . . a concatenation of indefinable states.

She sees this precarious situation as the writer's particular fate and doom: "the artist, perhaps more than most people, inhabits failure." Like Lewis Carroll's Humpty Dumpty, however, Oates makes that word serve her own purpose: failure is the preferable alternative to conventional images of success. Relinquishing rather than brandishing the will, an artist must "fail" in order to become a kind of transparency, in effect exercising the faculty of negative capability. That surrender results not in loss but discovery, an entry into altered states "overlaid with a peculiar sort of luminosity, as if one were, and were not, fully inhabiting the present tense."[16]

Lifting and reweaving the intertextual threads of literary tradition and cultural history, Oates deliberately invokes influences. Oates seems the rapt professor when she suggests in *The Profane Art* that literature demands a loving rather than Oedipal embrace: "We fall in love with certain works of art, as we fall in love with certain individuals, for no very clear motive." As these works yield their secrets to the reader, such intensely personal encounters with texts and their creators may lead to "life-altering" revelations: "One feels distinctly honored, to have the privilege of such moments: to venture around behind the tapestry, to see the threads in their untidy knots, the loose ends hanging frayed."[17] Not only is it *possible* for artist and predecessor to coexist; in Oates's view, their "marriage" is essential.

If critics consider her work too conventional, even "fossilized," this seems a misreading, indeed. "I don't think of myself as one of those writers who is trying to break free of conventions," she declares. "There aren't any conventions really . . . only personalities."[18] Oates's works of fiction, particularly her novels, represent a continuing experiment, an attempt to absorb, revise, and reconstruct narrative fiction, integrating an array of artistic, sociopolitical, and critical perspectives. Hardly "conventional" in an ordinary sense, she exploits an amazing number of conventions in her seventeen novels, reimagining the strategies of regionalist, naturalist, existentialist; creating teasingly familiar frameworks of academic satire, of romance, of the confession, of lyric, of detection, of collage. From our own perspective, Oates's novels may best be read as a representation and refraction of the multiform character of these parlous times.

Her work also offers us a double exposure of modern American life. Her pictures of the foibles of celebrities, the debris of urban ghettos, the fraudulent facades of suburbia, and the ugly secrets of the rural poor display her Balzacian appetites, as well as her debt to Poe and Radcliffe. Documents curl and fray, revealing a realm of night-side and hallucination. Each novel resonates with echoes, the stuff of the literary curriculum, the subtexts of Oates's fiction. In work after work, she alludes to or openly identifies her tutors and "daimons": Milton, Yeats, Kafka, Carroll, Aeschylus, Jung, Dostoevski, Thoreau, Maslow, Mozart, James, Nabokov—a circle as large and varied as Oates's own interest in language and ideas.

Reviewing the novels of Joyce Carol Oates over the past two decades shows the range of her imaginative trajectory and the complexity of her intentions. Her nuclear fable is dramatized in her first novel, *With Shuddering Fall:* a drama of primordial violence, played out in the world of the small American town; a sordid soap-opera tale framed by an elaborate Miltonic myth. These surprising juxtapositions point up a sense of human deprivation and loss; they also demonstrate the author's capacity to weave together multiple texts from literary and nonliterary realms.

She considers the next three novels a trilogy, although they are radically different in form and style. *A Garden of Earthly Delights, Expensive People,* and *them* reinvoke and rework the conventions of the realist, the existentialist/fabulator, and the naturalist. Perhaps reflecting her increasing mastery of the short story form, Oates's later novels become more episodic and "cinematic." Their structure also seems designed to match the erratic motions of Oates's most significant characters, protean shape-shifters who adapt to the slippery texture of reality and struggle with the interplay of plot and paranoia. Her first exploration of this new technique is *Wonderland,* a novel of murderous pursuit and narrow escape, a mad prescription for the sick Viet Nam age. Oates describes it as a traumatic personal passage:

> With *Wonderland* I came to the end of a phase of my life, though I didn't know it. . . . I want to move toward a more articulate moral position, not just dramatizing nightmarish problems but trying to show possible ways of transcending them.[19]

The novel which follows, *Do with Me What You Will,* in one sense a *Wonderland* reprise, also represents a significant departure from the violent closure which marks Oates's first five novels. It, too, is controversial. An unauthorized reading of Kafka's "The Trial," it dramatizes a series of foredoomed attempts to confront patriarchal and racist agencies. (Perhaps inevitably, it drew an intense and negative response from activist and feminist readers.) Pink-jacketed and dedicated (seemingly with great solemnity) to the president of N.O.W., it traces the emergence of a heroine, who, in choosing to throw off the mask of devious female passivity, opens the way for hetero-sexual dialogue. *The Assassins,* Oates's political novel and by some accounts one of her favorites, is an exercise in public and private madness, a narrative climaxed by willful or imagined dismemberment, its loose ends left in the hands of a baffled visionary.

Dedicated to an ideal of open-ended art, Oates frequently revises her own work. Thus, her next three novels take up each of the narrative life-lines of *The Assassins,* testing the viability of its three fractured points of view—artist, lover, and prophet. *Childwold* is the lover's tale, an experiment with multiple voices, a parody of Nabokov's perverse voyeurism, an attempt to recover the lost possibility of adolescence. *Son of the Morning* presents the religious fanatic's singular vision and voice, moving from the wildness of glossolalia to the blankness of normality. *Unholy Loves,* Oates's version of a purely academic novel, is a hybrid, half-parodistic and half-profound, an ex-cursion through the seminar rooms, lecture halls, and libraries which are the habitat of the modern artist in residence.

Appearing almost a decade after the "end" of *Wonderland, Bellefleur* is a playful virtuoso performance by an artist at the height of her powers, a daz-zling display of styles and forms, a cinematic novel indeed, complete with flashbacks and dissolves, exploiting *mise en scene* by embedding a torturous family chronicle with brilliant set pieces. Far from esoteric, it is ingeniously homespun: the author suggests that a crazy quilt, fancifully pieced and open for reassembly and transformation, is the most appropriate model of art drawn out of a world of fragments.

Bellefleur is not, of course, Oates's final statement; like each of her novels, it is both inclusive and prefatory. She continues to be fascinated by the clas-sic reading list. *Angel of Light* is her contemporary revision of the legend of the House of Atreus and its drama of obsessive vengeance: Aeschylus serves as one "ghost writer." She also echoes Thoreau's defense of a native avenger-hero, John Brown. She employs an even more primitive myth to structure her novella of contemporary pagan America, *Cybele.*

Her novel *A Bloodsmoor Romance* is a rich feminist parody of the nineteenth-century conduct book, a critique of patriarchal sensibilities in both society and art. Soon after its appearance, the author began wrestling with the possibilities and limitations of another genre—the detective story. What emerged was a triptych, her anti-detective novel, *Mysteries at Winter-thurn.* In *Solstice,* she returns to the contemporary world to confront the di-lemma of woman as artist. *Marya: A Life* is again autobiographical, the portrait of the artist as a disillusioned female academician, modern in setting and tone. But Oates intends to add two other novels to finish her round of ex-periments in earlier genres.[20]

Wherever her literary itinerary may lead, its lines by now are clear. The novels of Joyce Carol Oates begin with a quest for fact. They test and rediscover the values of the literary and cultural past: they exploit her understanding, as teacher, student, and reader, of the rules of genre and the conventions of poetry and narrative. Like the best of academicians, she also produces statements peculiarly her own. *Wonderland* may mark the end of her darkest journey; it also signals a beginning: her passage into a more spacious fictive universe—the realm of the capacious and variegated *Bellefleur,* her own Balzacian achievement. Using the considerable resources of her residence, Oates again and again attempts projects of synthesis. In her novels and in her criticism Oates continues to fashion a rebuttal to the literati of exhaustion, bearing witness to the vitality of literary art.

Another artist in residence who chooses to keep academic company, Saul Bellow, describes the ambiguity of contemporary life and the corresponding challenge to the artist:

> We know we are part civilized, part barbarous, part triumphant and part ravaged. That is our condition . . . our American and universal conditions. Because we are between the categories, so to speak, because no individual case is quite covered by them, we may enjoy a rich but painful freedom of spirit.[21]

Interestingly, the work of Joyce Carol Oates seems to dramatize the condition Bellow has identified. Her criticism and her imaginative literary expression reflect a curious sense of transition and expansion, the "blur" of genres caused by the interpenetration of old pieties and new visions. Oates has created fiction "between the categories," testing traditional genres not for their reliability but for their elasticity, searching for ways to represent a personality that is polymorphic, part civilized, part barbarous.

Using the devices of realist, existentialist, moralist, and fabulist, working with ideas drawn from history, philosophy, psychology, poetry, and the general culture, Oates has taken fullest advantage of her privileged position. She mines the art of predecessors and contemporaries. In the bewildering profusion and violence of modern times, in the lives of her students, in her own fiction, she finds her subjects. Allusive, assimilative, her novels are profoundly experimental; they are also read. Oates perceives art as an ongoing and open discourse, "a kind of spiritual 'marriage,'" a resource for society's collective aspirations. She thus makes no apologies for either her readership or her university residence.

The chapters that follow will discuss, in sequence, the major fiction Oates has published in the past two decades. Treating her novels as successive experiments in narrative, readings which reimagine "categories," vehicles for personality in process, this study is itself intended to revise the many misreadings of the phenomenon of Joyce Carol Oates.

2 Eden Valley Residence
With Shuddering Fall and
A Garden of Earthly Delights

The work of Joyce Carol Oates seems to court contradictions. Reluctant to share the details of her biography, the decorous Ms. Oates nonetheless teasingly suggests that all of her fiction, however sordid its setting or raw and violent its action, is drawn from her personal experience. That experience is itself marked by enormous contrasts, from her childhood on her grandparents' farm in rural New York to an adult life spent in the sophisticated environment of the academy as a scholar, a prolific writer and commentator, and a prodigious reader of literature, philosophy, and history. Wryly reviewing her background, Oates claims kinship with other eccentric "peasants," prodigies like Heidegger and Jung:

> Part of us is very intellectual, wanting to read all the books in the library—or even wanting to *write* all the books in the library. Then there's the other side of us, which is sheer silence, inarticulate—the silence of nature, of the sky, of pure being.[1]

In the face of this duality, it is no wonder that readers have difficulties reconciling her seemingly discordant impulses: the allusive tendencies of a university professor and the overriding interest in the victimized and inarticulate self which characterizes a social critic.

Indeed, this double consciousness is evident at the outset. While her early critical essays celebrate the sheer variety of our time with an almost messianic optimism, the first novels of Joyce Carol Oates paradoxically present scenarios of elemental obsession, set against an ancient tragic backdrop. The struggles of her heroes and heroines seem foredoomed, reflecting the power of uncontrollable subliminal appetites. In response, Robert Fossum describes the fatalistic design of her early work as a primal double bind:

> Repeatedly, Oates's people crave an order associated with "home" and the loving protection of the father. Repeatedly, this conflicts with a yearning for the "road" and freedom from the father. And both are expressions of a struggle to

control their own lives against the forces of "accident," circumstance, and other people.

Fossum also senses the possible antithetical relationship between Oates's aesthetic and thematic concerns: he goes on to speculate that, perpetually deterred from achieving control, her central characters are very like "failed artists."[2]

It is a provocative thesis, and a useful starting point in dealing with Oates's apprentice work, her first two novels. In *With Shuddering Fall* and *A Garden of Earthly Delights,* control seems a central issue: the rage for order informs her wide-ranging exploration of social history and novelistic form. What may not be as obvious in her early work, but becomes clearer in the context of the fiction and essays to follow, is that Oates views this quest for domination as life-defeating rather than heroic: a dead end. Even her first novels display the death throes of the imperialistic self, as again and again the egocentric hero is brought to a violent finish.

The place of the artful and academic is problematic in the early fiction of this artist in residence. Not surprisingly, Oates's first published novels depend upon a dense and sometimes tangled web of patterns superimposed on one another, drawn from literary art and from related disciplines—psychology, philosophy, history—counterpointing her observation and passionate presentation of everyday events. Clearly, Oates has begun to test the resources of the literary tradition, convinced, as she tells us, of the "biological imperative" of generic literary forms.

But, in what must seem another paradox, while she embraces the traditions of philosophy and literature, Oates simultaneously dramatizes the limits of reigning cultural mythologies. Her first two novels dramatize a double "failure": the failure of both conventional forms of fiction and conventional expectations of heroic action in a world gone mad. Her characters achieve a measure of control, but always with destructive outcomes; the very drive for mastery seems to lead them away from their best possibilities. Thus, even these two apprentice works move far beyond a simplistic scheme of Freudian control, dramatizing the disjunction between ideals of order and the violence of contemporary reality and human history. Her larger project is to awaken the reader to the deathward pull of older systems of value and to set the stage for as yet unrealized human possibilities.

An author's first published work generally holds more interest for the collector or scholar than the common reader. And although Oates has suggested to interviewers and would-be biographers that she had already destroyed two previous manuscripts,[3] *With Shuddering Fall* (1964) bears many marks of a first novel. Ellen Friedman aptly calls it an "ordeal of initiation," characterizing its major themes as well as its relationship to her later fiction:

Oates portrays initiation as a condition which mediates between two types of
anonymity: the anonymity that results from a complete surrender to a religious
or social order and the anonymity that results from revolt, the defiance of the
past which holds the individual's identity.[4]

Oates's first novel also registers the contradictory pressures of her childhood
experience and her academic residence. Resonant with classic literary echoes, it is staged in the tawdry world of rural and small-town America. Rising
to mythic levels of violence, descending to a shuddering fall, the novel presents the reader with an almost bewildering array of thematic and formal issues.

It is not surprising that the critical response has been contradictory as
well.[5] The assessments in the main seem justified. Oates's first novel displays
many signs of literary apprenticeship: David Madden and others identify the
failures of craftsmanship, the almost arbitrary shifts in focus and point of
view.[6] Yet the violent swings of character and plot also convey the force of
Oates's cultural critique. Torn between a savage hunger for self-assertion and
a need for order and communion, her central figures trace an orbital path between acquiescence to authority and rebellion. Oates herself refracts and
shifts her narrative focus in an attempt to mirror her characters' essential dilemma and dramatize their loss of vision. In violence itself, in the play of an-
archical energies, she also seeks a possible locus of human salvation.

Clearly, too, Oates's novel reflects her academic preparation and
continued residence. As Stanley Kauffman suggests, "it is literature born of
literature."[7] Her allusive impulse is also counterweighted by the demands of
political and social realism. Oates deliberately focuses on the lives of characters who lack her own sophisticated resources for self-analysis and expression; their sordid soap-opera dramas are played out against an aesthetic
backdrop which seems at times out of place and at other moments uncannily
appropriate. The major characters are filled with inchoate anger, struggling to
articulate or even understand their own passions and self-disgust. Oates
joins her own vision to theirs, thus setting their stories not against but
within a classic context, a Miltonic scheme: the ordered world of poetry and
allegory.

At both a literal and symbolic level, *With Shuddering Fall* is a chronicle of
human displacement, moving from country to city and back again, tracing
the tragic relationship between Karen Herz—a dream-ridden and beautiful
seventeen-year-old country girl—and Shar Rule, once a neighbor boy but
now a brutal, self-centered race car driver. Karen, betrayed by teasing, rough
classmates and seemingly protective but prurient schoolmasters, has
dropped out of school in an act of negation if not open resistance. Shar has
grudgingly come home to witness his father's dying moments; Karen's father
forces her to participate in the conventional rituals of charity and civility at

old Rule's deathbed. Thus, the two lovers are initially joined by their resentment at their fathers' claims. Shar expresses his defiance and rage at such containment by turning his father's house into a funeral pyre, by driving carelessly and too fast, by attempting to rape Karen, by assaulting and nearly killing her father. Gasping, Mr. Herz begs Karen to avenge him. Lacking the weapons for open aggression but displaying the peculiar passivity that characterizes many Oatesian heroines, Karen stubbornly places herself in Shar's path, baiting him and inviting further violation and abduction.

Joined with him as part of his entourage, Karen is swept into the world of stockcar racing, at first bending to the primal force of Shar's desire. But in an awesome display of passive power, Karen provokes Shar into assaulting her once more and thus, unwittingly, causing the death of their unborn child. When he begs for absolution, she tells him icily, "You make me sick" (*WSF*, 181). Maddened by his guilt and her frigid resistance, he races to a fiery suicide on the auto track. In a reciprocal series of scenes, Karen herself is driven to madness by the mob violence and rioting which follow Shar's death, as well as by the recognition of her own murderous agency and complicity. Finally, in what John Knowles describes (perhaps ironically) as the novel's "peaceful coda," Karen comes home from the mental hospital to rejoin her family and community.

In this first novel, Oates tells what for her is a quintessential American fable, using the approach of a psychological naturalist to reimagine a classical agon, the doom of a hero. She describes her Dreiserian methodology: "You start from what you do know about speed . . . and go on from there. I read a couple of issues of car magazines. And I remembered fairgrounds."[8] At the same time that she strives for a realistic portrayal, she is intent on evoking a mythic surrealistic terrain where love and death commingle, where a primitive life-force works its terrible will. The "American Parable" she identifies in the work of James M. Cain could equally describe the multiple levels of her own story in *With Shuddering Fall*:

> The passion that rises in us is both an inescapable part of our lives and an enemy to our lives, to our egoistic control of ourselves. Once unleashed it cannot be quieted. Giving oneself to anyone, even temporarily, will result in entrapment and death; the violence lovers do to one another is no more than a reflection of the proposed violence society holds back to keep the individual passions in check.[9]

Her novel is obviously intended to serve both as document and moral allegory. It is set in the ruined paradise of "Eden County"; at the beginning, "old Rule" is dying; "Shar" lights the pyre; the lovers fly to "Snyderdale"; Shar dies in a race on Independence Day; Karen returns to Eden and the "Herz" home to be forgiven. A closer reading reveals layers of intertextual resonance: echoes of Blake, Kafka, Melville, Beckett, Nietzsche, Milton, and Meredith. Oates's attempt to blend these voices is ambitious, but the ultimate effect is discordant.

Nevertheless, despite its fundamental incongruities, *With Shuddering Fall* justifies examination for its exposition of Oates's artistic method. To explore the problem of freedom and selfhood, Oates embodies her ideas in the characters and plays them off against one another. The ironies multiply as this sordid drama of realism is juxtaposed against the mythic visions of philosophers and poets. Shar Rule is a literal representation of an American type: the unreflective, egocentric hero-athlete, simultaneously inflated and victimized by the vicarious appetites of the anonymous crowd. But he also functions as a contemporary Superman, aggressive and full of heroic rage; inarticulate, ultimately frustrated, he is doomed to die without issue. "Happy only when in control of some sort: driving his machines, drinking himself into a stupor, seeing the tabulation of his threatened violence on another's face" (*WSF,* 118), Shar is a parodic version of Nietzsche's *Ubermensch*:

> His simplicity, Karen thought, made him dangerous, for to him the world of man was not valued for its uniqueness, nor was human experience judged to be good or evil, nor was sin possible: there was only Shar's will, the deadly whimsical range of his desire. (*WSF,* 119–20)

Indeed, the novel's epigraph is taken from Nietzsche: "What is done out of love always takes place beyond good and evil." At first glance, Oates's intention may seem problematic: while Nietzsche's words justify defiance of social dictates for love's sake, Oates's fictional battle of wills is motivated less by love than by murderous revenge. Yet on further reflection, it is clear that Nietzsche's *Beyond Good and Evil* has profoundly influenced *With Shuddering Fall.* His self-assertive phrases similarly evoke a sensation of ecstatic vision:

> It is precisely the brief little pieces of good luck and transfiguration of human life that here and there come flashing up which we find most difficult and laboursome to evoke in ourselves: those miraculous moments when a great power voluntarily halted before the boundless and immeasurable—when a superfluity of subtle delight in sudden re-restraint and petrification, in standing firm and fixing oneself, was enjoyed on a ground still trembling.[10]

Nietzsche also characterizes the inner violence which seems to charge the actions of Oates's early heroes:

> Measure is alien to us, let us admit it to ourselves, what we itch for is the infinite, the unmeasured. Like a rider on a charging steed we let fall the reins, we modern men, like semi-barbarians—and attain our state of bliss only when we are most—in danger. (Nietzsche, 529)

Thus, in her epigraph, Oates is appealing to an ideal reader, one attuned to the rich frame of academic reference; Nietzsche's tone and style, his very images represent a powerful intertextual influence.

The novel's title is an allusion drawn from Meredith's romantic lyric, "Ode to the Spirit of Earth in Autumn." In the final lines of Meredith's poem, the persona cries out to nature, the "Bacchante Mother," affirming not the human will to power but the powerful seductions of surrender: "Into the breast that gives the rose Shall I with shuddering fall?"[11] Ironically, the very idea of "mother" nature is undercut in Oates's reading of Meredith. The wanton Karen, nurturing death rather than life, is the beckoning flower. Tipping and tilting in the novel's violent gusts of passion, she survives because of her "silent, limp passivity" (*WSF*, 110).

She is a terrifying Narcissus. Staring into the mirror (a frequent preoccupation of many an Oatesian heroine), she sees "a face unrelated to her . . . a mockery of what she was. . . . Inside her, somewhere in her heart, or in her brain, somewhere, was her true self." Her external appearance, dissociated from her authentic identity, is designed to conform to the desires of others, "defined only in terms of what it had surrendered itself to: to claims of blood and duty, to love, to religious ecstasy . . . the universe had contrived her life, her father had planned her birth" (*WSF*, 11–12). But her secret and repressed self generates a monstrous, silent energy. Oates, perhaps more than any contemporary artist, dramatizes this "feminine" power capable of overcoming and destroying the most savage masculine will:

> Karen's gentleness did not soothe him but goaded him—as if deliberately; he felt himself entrapped, falling, incomplete until he gave himself to her. . . . It was as if she had designed herself so: a woman imagining what would attract him, entrap him. . . . (*WSF*, 79–80)

Representing polarities of aggression and submissiveness, Shar and Karen play out a ghastly ritual, stalking each other fearfully and murderously, moving "through their months together in an elaborate dance" (*WSF*, 174). It is a pattern which will recur in Oates's later work, but transformed into more harmonious and loving discourse.

In an analogy to the lovers' bestial circling, Oates describes the man-made mechanical vortex of the track, drawing the contestants toward annihilation as part of a deathly community spectacle. Like a Hemingway torero, Shar seeks a moment of grace under pressure, "lifted above time . . . free of human bondage, of hatred, of jealousy, of anger, of lust, most of all, of love!—free of love!" (*WSF*, 84). Yet Oates makes it clear that he is never a free agent, but an agent of death: his unborn child's, another driver's, and his own. The circular enclosed track, offering only the illusion of freedom, is another allegorical figure, paradigmatic of the death trip of the aggressive and egoistic modern hero.

While Shar escapes the world of human responsibility in a blazing finish, Karen Herz is catapulted back into time, forced to submit to external violence, to suffer—and to survive. Here, Oates is already exploring "third force" psychological theory in her vision of ego-annihilation as a necessary prelude to self-recovery. At this point, however, she concludes that the cost to the self is devastatingly high.

More interestingly, Oates weds the psychological to the religious. In an essay later republished as part of *New Heaven, New Earth,* Oates declares, "the 'Christ' experience may well be interpreted as a psychological event"(*NHNE,* 167). It is a key to the complex vision of her first novel. Oates depends upon religious metaphor in *With Shuddering Fall*—merging psychological, social, theological, and academic or literary concerns—both a reflection and imaginative transformation of her own Catholic background.

Many critics, such as Madden, find the pervasive religious imagery of the novel a bizarre gloss on the secular, violent world of the auto track. It seems more than a peripheral concern to Oates. Shar is the center of garish rites of "mock Communion"; when he offers up his own death, it is only after he is convinced "there was nothing except violence, mutilation, death . . . there was no communion" (*WSF,* 184–86). Similarly, at the novel's end, Karen returns to the scene of her girlhood's "secret ecstasy" (*WSF,* 26), the communion rail, to become the ironic agent of the community's collective spiritual vision:

> They felt love for her . . . for the Karen who had suffered to prove to them the justice of their universe. . . . The sacrifice of the Mass was a distant, calculated ritual, and the perfunctory humility of the priest was for their eyes alone, but Karen's sin and penance and expiation had been real enough, and showed . . . the crushing justice of a moral universe. For this they loved her, though their love was nothing personal. (*WSF,* 220–21)

Through rite and ritual Karen as a child is drawn beyond the prison house of her own flesh into a transpersonal vision. As an adult, she mutely accepts her secular role, as living proof of a just, vengeful, and punishing world.

The pervasive Christian motifs in this novel are thus part of a complex ironic design. They combine in an overarching allusive pattern: an intricate scheme borrowed from Milton's *Paradise Lost,* offering another jarring counterpoint in the realistic narrative. *With Shuddering Fall* is a modern expulsion from the Garden brought on by perverse temptations and masochistic appetites. Eden County is a savagely inverted paradisiacal setting:

> Branches of little stunted trees and bushes locked and interlocked. . . . Winters here . . . were long and brutal and recovery from them always seemed to Karen

a miracle. In the worst days the snow looked like an incredible sifting of earth and heaven, blotting out both . . . reducing them to an insane struggle of white that struck at human faces like knives. Summers reeked with heat, and heaven pressed downward so that the sun had to glare through the skies of dust. Sometimes there would be holocausts of fire in the woods. (*WSF,* 21)

Between this fallen paradise and the fallen human cites of Synderdale and Cherry River lies a bridge—a curious reimagining of Milton's causeway over chaos:

> It was an old rusted bridge, built before Karen was born, spanning the creek with a rattle of boards and high intricate beams that looked like a parodyof a real bridge. It had been struck by lightning many times . . . and though, when she was a child, she had screamed when they approached it, her father had assured her, his hand on his heart and no fingers crossed, that it would never collapse while she was on it. (*WSF,* 38)

On this shaky span, Karen first fights Shar for control, causing an accident that prefigures his fatal crash. Crossing the bridge, Karen also later reenacts the Miltonic pattern of return:

> Karen stared with fascination at the bridge as it loomed up above them. . . . And there was the scarred grass beside the road and the twisted guard rails . . . grass had recovered, grown up straight again and now frozen with the cold, as if nothing had even happened. "Now I am home," Karen said. (*WSF,* 213)

Shar and Karen, a savage Adam and brutalized Eve, reenact Milton's archetypal drama of rebellion, "two people condemned to an eternity in each other's presence, lovers or criminals who had sinned together on earth but who could not understand precisely what they had done, or why, or in what way it was a sin demanding damnation" (*WSF,* 116). Even Karen's rapt self-absorption seems designed as a Miltonic echo. In a recent critical essay, Oates points out that gazing at one's reflection may be more than an image of Narcissus; it could well suggest "Milton's Eve in her surprised discovery of her own beauty," with potential for self-creation as well as self-immolation.[12] Yet, in *With Shuddering Fall,* the creative potential is unrealized.

Perhaps the most curious Miltonic character in this novel is Max, Shar's patron, and surely a fallen angel. He is "imprisoned" (*WSF,* 160) in an alien shape (gluttonous, obese). Because of the actions of this "bloated, insatiable spectator," both Shar and Karen have sudden intimations that they are "lost" (*WSF,* 140–42, 131). Through his sponsorship and ministrations, they fall. And if that is not enough to mark his literary origins, Oates provides more explicit clues. Max even carries a copy of *Paradise Lost* in his back pocket

(*WSF,* 86)! Describing the poem to the motley race track entourage, Max sneers at both the timeless vision and the artistic structure of Milton's work:

> In literature, now, things are different; this long poem I've been rereading . . . temptation, sin, fall, and expiation, all around in a circle, into the garden and out of it, many angels, great blazes of rhetoric and light—an immense scheme of tautological relationships you need never believe in! As if it mattered that there was ever a paradise, or in what way it was lost to us—the only important thing is that we have no paradise. (*WSF,* 127)

This grotesque hybrid—entrepreneur, racketeer, voyeur—tests the limits of verisimilitude, lecturing to what must be a baffled circle of drivers, grease monkeys, and race-track groupies. A bookish and misplaced academic, Max insists upon the disjunction of human reality and the work of art:

> All an expression of something else—an imitation, a metaphor. . . . But life is not like that, your life is not being created for you out of a mind. Your life is not a metaphor for anyone or anything. Your life is not a metaphor for anything beyond it. (*WSF,* 127)

Max is indeed a quintessential fabulator, who, with satanic majesty, insists upon the fundamental irrelevance of the "beautiful poem." But Oates presents this elaborate vision in order to discredit it. In response, she deliberately forces the great poem and her realistic drama into the same metaphoric space in order to show the paradoxical convergence of canonical art and ordinary life. Even in her first novel, Oates is testing the novel's capacity for synthesis.

With Shuddering Fall can best be viewed as the proving ground for Oate's primary obsessions: her concern with the self's inchoate, often destructive, but irresistible energies; the more intricate and problematic relation of the artist and society. She is also consciously attempting to recover a traditional vision for the modern age—in this case, what she has described in critical essays as Milton's "totalitarian" but heroic attempt to fuse an aesthetic scheme with a representation of experimental reality.

This early novel also provides an index to the Oatesian character. Her powerfully conceived fictional creations seem to strain *against* the designs of art. Shar dramatically breaks out of his Adamic role by his suicidal act. Despite the final images of reconciliation, Karen also continues to struggle against the tightening Miltonic circle, at first through the escape of madness. Her breakdown and recovery win approval from her Freudian analyst, another parody figure—impatient with other patients "imprisoned" in their illogical irrationality. He approves of the "logic" of her condition, and is even more impressed by Karen's "self-cure," her "magnificent will power" (*WSF,* 208–9). But beneath her certified sanity there are glimmers of an imp of the perverse. Karen is torn with dark fears: "My mind is wrong, put together wrong. Am I to blame for that? Can I help my mind?" She finds no sure footing in Eden County after all: "It is insane to look for meaning in life," she thinks, "and it is insane not to" (*WSF,* 223). In the last scene, gazing at the prayerful congregation, she meditates cunning and obscene seductions. Milton's grand design of temptation, sin, fall, and expiation is unraveling at the novel's end, partially undone by the nature of reality itself; deconstructed by a probing revisionary author.

Oates revisits the dark valleys of Eden County in her second novel, *A Garden of Earthly Delights* (1967), and readers once more offer contradictory responses. Rose Marie Burwell approves of the novel as an ingenious and consistent "moral allegory," noting in detail the fictive parallels to the painter Hieronymus Bosch and his nightmarish triptych to which the title alludes.[13] In contrast, Walter Sullivan begins to articulate a strident critical resistance to Oates's designs. His voice rising in anger, he argues that it is imperative for literature to dramatize linear causal relationships: "Days lived under any kind of ordinary circumstances form a pattern and this pattern helps establish the texture of a novel. Motivations develop . . . aims are pursued . . . consequences are suffered. But these are ends that Miss Oates will not seek in her work." What is worse, he finds, is the author's "tendency to let her people go insane"; a tendency that he insists invalidates her work:

> This is not the place to examine such a view of human morality, but I do submit that should it gain complete hegemony it will be the death of art. Literature requires action that is morally significant, which means that characters must be at least theoretically free to choose for themselves. . . . Once a suggestion of lunacy is allowed to intrude, then doubt is cast over all the procedures of a novel.[14]

While Alfred Kazin is also sensitive to the elements of contingency and irrationality in *A Garden of Earthly Delights,* he offers a different interpretation of Oates's moral vision: "there is a sense of the shifting, turning unexpected combinations and permutations of the human fancy as our only real freedom."[15] What Sullivan sees as an amoral and irresponsible position, Kazin understands better as Oates's route of deliverance.

To track her journey, it is useful to compare the commonalities of Oates's first two novels. Both describe narrowing avenues of human freedom, the frequent incursions of violent, irresistible forces, the tantalizing but elusive promises of mediation. Both novels dramatize the myth of a lost and debased Eden, and show the desperate strategies of the figuratively and literally dispossessed. Irrational forces influence the actions of Karen Herz; they also terrorize the characters in *A Garden of Earthly Delights.* But as Kazin perceives, the very accidental texture of modern existence may represent the hope of escape for the self caught in the stampede of time.

There are also telling contrasts between the two novels as Oates begins to revise her own conceptions and test new formal strategies. *With Shuddering*

Fall unfolds in a series of concentric circles: Milton's world and that of the racer, the beloved, the patron, the psychiatrist. Also structured by a series of accidents and violent collisions, *A Garden of Earthly Delights* is a narrative about migrants propelled *out* of the human circle, competing for survival itself, denied both communion and return.

Oates thus deliberately and almost playfully works out her "horizontal obsessions." Offering variations on her own scenes and themes, she echoes and revises Shar's flaming auto crash in *With Shuddering Fall*. Her second novel begins with a highway accident, the wreck of a truck carrying a load of migrant workers along a rutted Arkansas road toward a harvest of shame:

> It wasn't the first accident this driver had had. But they never got used to the sudden lurching, the squeal of the brakes, and that hushed instant when everyone's heart paused—then the crash itself, this time not bad. The truck tilted sharply, but no one moved. They did not move for a few seconds. Then the children began to cry, the woman shouted for help, and everyone woke up—another crash. (*GED*, 4)

Oates introduces the novel's antinomies: the male and female in deathly and loveless combat; the rivalry between the driver and the driven. For the men, even minor highway accidents are charged with a welcome significance; they mill around the wreck "with an air of festivity" (*GED*, 2), apparently disappointed that no one has been killed. The novel's first narrator, Carleton Walpole, grumbles to himself, "nothing ever happened" (*GED*, 6). But for the women, such accidents set life's irresistible energies violently into motion: a daughter, Clara, is born prematurely to Walpole's screaming wife on the tilted truck bed, screened from his tormented view by a wall of women. Again, Oates exposes the punishing sexual conflict between restless, uprooted men and the women who, trapped by biological necessity, glower at them in crazed passivity.

With Shuddering Fall describes the violent catapult and ultimate return of a self circumscribed by emotional, familial, and communal forces; an arc analogous to Milton's grand design. The possibility of reentry is sharply delimited by social and economic realities in Oates's second novel. Her characters feel that the landscape itself is "turning to sand and falling away" beneath their feet (*GED*, 18). Carleton longs for his former community and land but knows "he could not get to them no matter how urgently he desired them" (*GED*,17). Traditional ties seem fatally severed; attempts of the vagrant self to achieve control, stability, or a cessation of hostilities eventuate in frustration, death, or madness. In this seething, explosive environment, form seems ephemeral and arbitrary while "plot" is invariably threatening.

The first section of this novelistic triptych, Carleton Walpole's story, is better seen as a preamble for the events depicted on the central panel: the narrative of Clara, the child born in the aftermath of accident, a brutalized, half-literate Eve. Her journey begins when, as a child, she hitchhikes from the migrant camp to a nearby town. Even at this point in her life, she senses her innate sexual power. Riding in the cab of a truck, she is unwittingly seductive; like an inchoate artist, creating a character, a persona not her own: "She seemed to be doing something, keeping something going. . . . Then she . . . lost control. . . . She was a child again" (*GED*, 67). Clara's metamorphic imagination is at work as she escapes from the bewildered and dazed truck driver and moves gleefully through the automobile junkyard at the edge of town:

> The cracks were like spider webs, like frozen ripples in water. Clara stared and stared, and what she saw got transformed into new, strange things. A piece of rubber was a snake, sleeping in the sun. A scraped mark on a car was a flower, ready to fall into pieces. In a yellowed car window was a face that might have been under water . . . it was her own face. (*GED*, 69)

But once she is inside the town and subject to the terms of necessity and time, the magic dissolves and delight is succeeded by betrayal. Humiliated by her poverty, unable to buy a simple gift for her brother, she suddenly knows "she would remember this moment all her life . . . the colorful toys, her sweaty fingers closed about the dime, the saleswoman's pity" (*GED*, 73). She walks through the streets lined with white picture-book houses and her dreamy self-reflection (she seems another "Eve") explodes into bitterness: "Clara's face felt as if it were breaking up into pieces" (*GED*, 76). Vengefully, she steals an American flag from one of the neat white front porches. The act of petty theft is again explicitly symbolic; it also marks her coming of age and sets the tone for her future vengeful and cunning actions. Years later, Clara remembers "that street, that house, that flag" (*GED*, 206), and feels that all the tumultuous events of her existence have followed inexorably "from one moment, from her catching sight of that flag hanging by someone's porch" (*GED*, 210).

From that moment, indeed, Clara begins to resist the motion, fluidity, and shiftiness of life; seizing the flag is her first effort to grasp something tangible for herself. In the migrant camps, children are familial property, pitifully vulnerable to drunken and incestuous fathers, part of "a world made up by someone else, controlled by someone else, herded around on buses" (*GED*, 139). Motherhood is reduced to biological retribution. Clara gladly exchanges this life for the stability of a tawdry town bearing an incongruous Wordworthian name (another of Oates's characteristic and ironic academic touches):

> Tintern was permanent. It had always been there, it was settled deep into the ground and so it would remain. This permanence was easy for her to see in the dime store, because there merchandise stayed on counters for months in exactly the same positions; you could get used to anything that way. (*GED*, 142)

But while she escapes her father's control, she cannot engineer her own liberation; women like her mother have taught her there was "nothing else in the world . . . except to give themselves to men . . . and to hope afterwards that it had not been a mistake" (*GED,* 147). Thus she runs from one man, Carleton, to another, her lover Lowry, believing he was the "kind who took over and got you where you needed to go" (*GED,* 132). Yet he, too, is a fugitive self: what Clara takes for autonomy is closer to irresponsibility. After their brief hours of love, Lowry takes flight from his own furies and shadowy pursuers, leaving Clara pregnant and desperate.

As her only defense, Clara must weave a devious sexual snare. Fighting down her instinctive revulsion, she seduces Curt Revere—bearing an emblematic name, part of the landed gentry of Eden County—making him believe he is the father of Lowry's child. Clara muses wryly that he "fell in love with me the way another man falls into a swamp" (*GED,* 235). Her own motives are loveless and unambiguous. She does not want her child to be "just an accident" (*GED,* 209), or, like her own father, "hopeless because he could not control anything" (*GED,* 163–64). As the trap closes on Revere, she thrills at her own power: "All her life she would be able to say: Today she changed the way her life was going and it was no accident" (*GED,* 223).

It is clear that it is not "lunacy" (Sullivan's charge) which fuels her actions, but its opposite: a calculated drive for mastery, a free choice curiously related to her unfulfilled early artistic predilections. Attempting to "bring all those accidents into control" (*GED,* 213), Clara defies the adventitious, the contingent, the nonrational. Yet her resistance is ultimately more problematic than heroic. Oates again suggests that in the very rage for order, Clara forecloses the possibility of transformation and transcendence, trapping herself in her own design. Her strategies of self assertion, like her artistry, then, are infernal.

Perhaps the most destructive moment of resistance in the novel occurs when Lowry returns to Clara years later. She is still Revere's mistress, living with her son (Swan Walpole/Steven Revere) on the outskirts of town, awaiting the death of his invalid wife. Shaken by the unspeakable horrors of world war, Lowry appeals to Clara out of his love and need, begging her to share his dream of a pastoral existence far from any combat zone. Overcoming her own love and longing, Clara rejects Lowry in favor of the security she expects from Revere—not only for herself but for Lowry's child. Clara and Swan finally indeed cross the bridge over the Eden River and move into the Revere house.

The third section of the novel focuses on Swan's way. Although the honorable Revere has kept his promise, even favoring Swan over his own sons, the subliminal forces Clara has repressed emerge in the novel's terrible denouement, taking destructive and perverse forms. In a series of "accidents," Swan shoots and kills his stepbrother Robert, and—his matricidal aim deflected by Clara—kills his stepfather, Revere, achieving his own freedom only in suicide. The shock drives Clara to the asylum; in contrast to Karen Herz, however, she has lost the will necessary to engineer a cure.

In this second novel, then, Oates re-imagines and revises her own nuclear fable. Like Karen Herz in *With Shuddering Fall,* Clara Walpole commits what for Oates is the unpardonable sin: she hoards her individual power; she resists and denies the appeal of human love. Like Karen, too, Clara is driven into virtual catalepsis by the violence which explodes around her in the wake of that perverse choice. The characters in *A Garden of Earthly Delights* experience a downward spiral of expectations, a diminution of creative powers and redemptive possibilities. Oates's deepening pessimism can be seen in her treatment of the very mediating agencies which offered some promise to the self in *With Suddering Fall*: nature, religion, family. In *A Garden of Earthly Delights,* each seems to exacerbate the pervasive sense of dispossession.

Drawing again on a range of sources and analogues, Oates underscores her bleak reportage with an array of artistic references. Much of the novel's intensity can be credited to the influence of Bosch. The landscape in Oates's first novel is an infertile wasteland; in this second novel, nature teems with vile and corrupt forms of life; the "garden" of the title is more a realm of terror than of earthly delight. Clara and Lowry make love on the banks of the Eden River; when Clara looks down at the water, she is struck by "its film of sleek opaque filth" (*GED,* 179), and when she wades through the river's debris, a bloodsucker fastens onto her bare foot. The pastoral vision, given form by centuries of poets, also exerts its influence upon this novel. A dream of nature informs the hopes of the landless. Carleton imagines that he is a cut above his fellow workers because his family owned land in the past (*GED,* 52); Lowry longs for a future on a farm in British Columbia (*GED,* 273). Oates invokes Flannery O'Connor when she describes Swan's "strange mystical love for this inherited land that was almost a terror in his blood" (*GED,* 416). Yet, in her view, the pastoral dream and the sense of mystical awareness are radically undercut by a countervailing myth of human bestiality.

In the same way, religious rites and practices have lost their supernatural promise for the itinerant self: children glimpse a stamped holy medallion accidentally gathered up in gambling winnings (*GED,* 60–61), and are betrayed by the hypocrisy and prudery of proselytizing churchwomen. The child in Clara longs for the absolution and purity given form in the whitewashed town church; but once inside its doors, she is conscious instead of a suffocating atmosphere of guilt:

> The air was crowded and breathless with these sobs of guilty people, and the melody they made was one Clara understood better than she had understood the words of that song.

> She understood something then: that these people had done something bad,
> something wrong, and that they would never get over it. (*GED*, 100)

The members of the congregation seem also impoverished, barren; the ingenuous Clara thinks God was "probably watching other people who were
more interesting" (*GED*, 99). After this disappointment, she moves to receive secular communion offered after the service in a roadside tavern. When
Lowry takes her from that sordid scene and baptizes her, cleaning away the
dirt of the camp with soap and bucket, Clara easily confuses her sexual response with "godly" visitation:

> Her brain was pounding with terror. She had never done anything like this, had
> never gone so far. She felt driven by the same God that had possessed the min-
> ister, making his voice shrill and furious at once, making his legs jerk him about
> on that platform. God had torn out of that man's mouth sobs and groans of des-
> peration. Clara understood what he must have felt. (*GED*, 110–11)

Oates's critique of religious institutions thus deepens in *A Garden of
Earthly Delights*. Interestingly, she reimagines the final communion scene
she described in *With Shuddering Fall*. As Revere's mistress, Clara finds herself the object of covert attention when she attends the funeral of her friend
Sonya who has been strangled by a deranged lover. Karen Herz is envisioned
by the congregants as a secular agent of redemption. Clara feels trapped in a
more implacable universe:

> These people could look at her today without any special hatred, believing that
> she was . . . destined to be punished for anything sooner or later. And it did
> happen, Clara thought, that you were punished sooner or later. It happened
> whether you did anything wrong or not. (*GED*, 250–51)

For Clara, the community of Tintern does not offer even a parody of romantic love or poetic justice; it is a world which rejects the fiction of transubstan-
tiation in favor of facts:

> The minister talked . . . wheedling and prodding them into thinking about a
> strange invisible world of God that was somehow simultaneous with this world
> but never found in it, until she wanted to cry out to the man that he should shut
> up.
>   No matter what he might say, trying to turn facts into something that
> sounded better, Sonya was dead and that was that. (*GED*, 251)

Just as religious ceremonies are virtually meaningless in the migrant's
world, the family has also lost its mediating function. The Herz family in
With Shuddering Fall remains throughout the novel a locus of value, security, and love, offering a refuge of sorts in the final scenes. In contrast, the
Walpoles and Reveres might have come from R.D. Laing's casebooks. Nur-

turance is a deceptive myth; in reality, the family imposes a template of violent repertoires on the hapless children. Family life becomes a "protection racket": the weakest are vulnerable to assault. The concept of lineage itself seems a delusive but reigning myth for Oates's rootless migrants: names are their only means to avoid total engulfment. For Carleton Walpole, the affirmation of one's genealogy takes the place of prayer:

> Late at night, when the camp was finally quiet, he would whisper names to himself; names of family first, then distant relatives, then neighbors, then distant neighbors, stretching back for years, hundreds of miles, to astonish him with the number of years he had been alive on earth. Only when he felt that he had named everyone, and that he knew where he was among them, could he fall asleep. (*GED*, 29)

But if Carleton's litany provides a momentary stay against the world's confusion, it also liberates his deathly, combative impulses: "just saying the word 'pa' sent more strength into his body" (*GED*, 38). Defending his family pride, Carleton kills a fellow migrant ("Walpoles ain't no hillbillies," he cries). Ironically, in the very act of clearing his name, Carleton becomes a wanted man, a fugitive. In turn, he relentlessly pursues his runaway daughter Clara out of a confused sense that she is meant to serve as his posthumous vehicle: "He wanted her to remember his name . . . there was no one else to remember these things" (*GED*, 126–27). But he dies alone, en route, moving from country to city, his name and mind and memory erased by wracking pain.

For Clara, in contrast, ancestral names have no magic. Female, she must rely on borrowed surnames; she seeks a new name which will give her security. On her flight, Clara discards the Walpole name ("Just Clara. I don't have any last name," she tells a mailman [*GED*, 230], although her full name is listed on Swan's birth certificate). When Lowry (always identified by his surname only) taunts her, "You don't even have a last name any more, kid," she retorts fiercely, "I'll get one then" (*GED*, 137). On behalf of her child, she seizes a name and waves it like a stolen flag: "Revere." That emblematic American name promises property rights for her unborn son; Clara is confident it will make him "a person . . . who would control not just isolated moments in his life but his entire life, and who would not just control his own life but other lives as well" (*GED*, 227). In a passage which stands in a curious relation to Oates's vision of art, Clara dreams of a great tapestry of namers and name-bearers, a Whitmanesque procession:

> From Revere . . . she got a picture, gradually, of a vague web of people, the generations mixed together and men present . . . simultaneously with their grandfathers . . . it was like a great river of people moving slowly along, bound

together by faces that looked alike and by a single name. How wonderful to be
born into this name and to belong to such a world. (*GED*,233)

Again, Oates will develop this image in the maps, atlases, and diaries of
later fiction. Here, Clara's strategy misfires. "All your life you'll be a Revere!"
she cries to her son (*GED*, 301); yet Swan is convinced from the first that it
is a bogus baptism: "He said his name, Steven Revere, and then a quieter
voice said his real name, which was Swan Walpole" (*GED*, 372). For Swan-
Steven, names *are* "magical" (*GED*, 394) in the sense that they are accursed.
His own double name signals a fatal self-division, a split that widens into
madness and hallucination, intensifying a final, punishing, murderous rage.
Swan's patrimony is neither "Walpole" nor "Revere"; it is the malediction
uttered by his real father, Lowry, on the single occasion of his return.

Oates remains concerned about the politics of the family. Unaware that he
is cursing his own child, but embittered by Clara's refusal to come away with
him, Lowry sneers at the small and terrified boy, "You're going to kill lots of
things . . . I can see it right there—all the things you're going to kill and step
on and walk over" (*GED*, 281). As Clara never forgets her theft of the flag,
Swan can never shake off Lowry's prophecy. From that moment, he thinks of
himself as "a killer who had not finished with his work but was waiting for his
deed to rise up in him" (*GED*, 417). In Oates's world of contingency and
change, such psychological influences take on the quality of classical fate:
Swan lives to act out Lowry's appalling scenario.

Again, this novel is a literary hybrid: a work of social realism woven out of
a less substantial fabric of allusion. Oates's triptych is densely stippled with
Yeatsian images of feathered visions, clamorous wings, diving predators and
unwitting prey, "hawks of the mind." Yeats is in fact one of Oates's poetic
mentors, an influence both compelling and disturbing to whom she often refers. "We resist him," she declares in an early critical essay in the *New York
Times* "as we resist going insane, losing the strength of our egos."[16]

Oates seemingly finds Yeats irresistible in *A Garden of Earthly Delights*.
Yeatsian metaphors serve as emblems of Swan's inner division, embodying
the mysterious warring forces within his imagination. It is the godly flock,
"The Wild Swans at Coole," aloof, detached, and powerful, that Oates seems
to invoke when Clara gives her son his curious, private, and highly-literary
name:

> I thought of what I would call the baby if it was a boy. I would call him Swan
> because I saw some swans once in a picture, those big white birds that swim
> around—they look real cold, they're not afraid of anything, their eyes are hard
> like glass. On a sign it said they were dangerous sometimes. (*GED*, 295)

But Oates's reference is once again ironic. Clara's charm is powerless to save
Swan from Lowry's curse. The boy is driven by a different image, "a presence

. . . descending over this house like a bird circling slowly to the earth"
(*GED*, 197); Lowry's malediction is symbolized by another Yeatsian echo,
ugly hawks with "fetid breath" (*GED*, 291, 297), which hover over their
earthbound prey. Swan himself feels he is a victim in a landscape teeming
with violence, struggling against winged assailants as vainly as Yeats's Leda:

> In his brain there was a bird fluttering to get out. He was aware of it in his most
> helpless, frantic moments, or when he was exhausted. Its wings beat against the
> walls of his head, pounding along with his pounding ears, and would not give
> him peace. (*GED*, 352)

All his life, he is moved to strike and kill by "something fluttering and mad"
(*GED*, 437).

Yet metaphors, as Max is made to observe in *With Shuddering Fall*, are
both more and less than life. In a critical reflection, Oates describes Yeats's
artistic struggle as if it were her own personal dilemma as well: the problem
of ever finding literary forms which can do justice to multivarious, teeming
life. "It is reality itself, the impersonal and gratuitous, the ever-changing, the
unheroic, that cheats him of a final form. . . . The most a poet can hope for is
a kind of equanimity with the powerful chaos of nature" (*EI*, 186). An artist's
dream of "final form," the grand design, is simultaneously evoked and paro-
died in the Miltonic structure of *With Shuddering Fall*. In *A Garden of
Earthly Delights*, Oates goes still farther: she seems to dramatize the failure
of "various claims of the artist, the supposed controller of will." If Yeats
poses a crucial question for the poet in his "Leda and the Swan," Oates imagines his answer: "The answer is 'no,' Leda cannot 'put on his knowledge with
his power'" (*EI*, 186). Efforts to transcend the limits of mortal existence
through art seem both alluring—and foredoomed.

In the bestial world of *A Garden of Earthly Delights*, art itself becomes a
metaphor for paranoia rather than a vehicle of control. In a darkened movie
theatre, Swan finds frightening representations of his own powerlessness:

> Swan stared at the actors acting out their parts on film. . . . Out of those mouths
> words came involuntarily. . . . They did not think and so everything was drawn
> out of them relentlessly. They had no choice. Someone had written the words
> for them to say and so they said them, they fulfilled their roles. . . . Swan did not
> understand why watching them made him so uneasy . . . he might have been
> watching himself on the screen and waiting for the terrible moment when he
> would have to speak his lines. (*GED*, 428)

The first of Oates's intellectual and academic prodigies, Swan tries to suppress the powers of his creative intelligence; he apes his mother's illiteracy
and deliberately avoids libraries, the perilous "garden of men's minds"
(*GED*, 12–13). Yet there is no way out of the mind; Swan cannot free himself
of his book-ridden past:

I don't know who made me the person I am now but I have this strange idea it's someone who's watching me right now, I can feel that person staring at me . . . he made me come alive and is following it through to the end, and I can never get free. . . . I don't want to be a character in a story, a book. I don't want to be like someone in a movie. I don't want to be born and die and have everyone watching—reading along. Everything decided ahead of time. (GED, 432–33)

The certainty that he is the hero of a monstrous fiction seems to markSwan as schizophrenic: "He felt like one of those actors in the movie he had seen, speeding on into the dark without especially thinking, confident that someone had written out the words and actions for him to fulfill" (GED, 435). A robot-self, he becomes an agent of destruction. Oates has not only created metaphoric equivalents for human madness. In a short story, "Plot," she describes a realm familiar to Borges, and the dilemma of an artist caught in his own trap as life uncannily imitates art:

What made him pause was the knowledge that if he wrote something terrible he might have to fulfill it; might have to make it come true. But what other possibility of salvation would there be for him, except this writing of the scenario of his own life? (Scenes, 230)

Oates thus draws on a range of bookish reference to describe the ontological terror of the divided self in her earliest published fiction. In her essays, she presents her alternative, declaring that the artist's true vocation is not that of fabulator, but of mediator, negotiating between systems of value. In the dynamic interplay of worldly experience and literary signs and stories she hopes to discover "scenarios" of survival. All art ought to be "moral, educational, illustrative," Oates insists in a rare autobiographical reflection; "it shows you how to survive . . . that someone managed to get through."[17]

Yet despite this show of optimism, her first two novels offer little hope beyond bare survival for her characters. The network of literary allusions only heightens the atmosphere of loss and fragmentation. In With Shuddering Fall, Milton's paradisiacal scheme begins to skew in a world ruled not by divine plan but by subconscious drives. In A Garden of Earthly Delights, she transforms the beating wings of Yeats's circling hawks into terrible images of human obsession and subconscious predisposition.

In her essays, Oates is consistently critical of Yeats's artistic stance. Turning from traditional cosmology, creating a realm of myth and fantasy, Yeats, mistakenly in her view, suggests that the artist is both fabulator and Prometheus, required to "make and remake the world." Accepting the grimmer terms of ordinary life, Oates offers no such romantic ideal in A Garden of Earthly Delights. Her inchoate artist, Swan, can end his agonies only through patricide and self-destruction; the displaced person can never return to a garden of earthly delights. However alienated, Karen Herz had rejoined the human community. But in this novel's final pages, Swan's mother Clara sits in a mental institution, a burned-out case, left to watch flickering caricatures of the American dream:

> She seemed to like best programs that showed men fighting, swinging from ropes, shooting guns and driving fast cars, killing the enemy again and again until the dying gasps of evil men were only a certain familiar rhythm away from the opening blasts of commercials, which changed only gradually over the years. (*GED*, 440)

Oates's second novel thus follows the evolutionary pattern of twentieth-century American literary realism, employing documentary strategies to fashion an ironic critique of modern life. Clearly, her allusions to Yeats are subversive: his Leda is ravished by transhuman appetites; her Clara is seduced by tawdry advertisements. But her irony works both ways: the mythic weave of poetry unravels in the violent pull of ordinary existence. Oates has begun her own search for telling signs of metamorphosis, avenues of revision, ways to address the tragic discordance of literature and reality.

Oates's first two novels both can be viewed as deliberate experiments, testing the resources of poetry and classic symbolic conventions. They also show her obsessive concern with the fate of the half-educated and inarticulate, men and women without her academic privileges or imaginative gifts who attempt to give their lives some meaningful design. Oates works with live models; she also plays with images and narratives from her beloved "books in the library." Out of the same curious double consciousness—that of empathic observer and passionate intellectual—she tries her hand at two radically different literary genres in her next two novels.

3 Fabulation and Documentation
Expensive People and *them*

Oates's first novels are dramas of the self pushed to the breaking point, drawn inexorably toward a violent ending, or left lobotomized, permanently disfigured by the interpenetration of their inner being by the outer world. No wonder, then, that Oates uses apocalyptic language in describing both contemporary life and the realm of her fiction: "This . . . era levels personality," she declares in her first critical collection, *The Edge of Impossibility;* "a 'deluge of experience' breaks over us and within us, destroying limits" (*EI,* 186). The artistic forms she has thus far employed, the literary mythologies that echo in her early work, and even the designs of the greatest poets are not sufficient to resist the modern confusion.

In her next two novels, Oates seeks new ways to resolve the conflict of self and world. In the process, she also tests dimorphic literary conventions which are part of her twentieth-century American academic inheritance. One exposes the limits and dangers of private authority. The other focuses upon socioeconomic forces and external constraints. *Expensive People* (1968) is Oates's playful "existentialist" experiment, a cagily academic novel which takes the form of a confession from the psychic underground of a precocious fabulator-*manqué*. Her next novel, *them* (1969), works self-consciously within naturalistic conventions, recognizing and dramatizing the deterministic forces of nature and society, exploring familiar American territory.

Oates shows herself not only an adept parodist but a good reader as she manipulates these virtually opposite literary strategies. One novel is overtly comic, satiric, shaped by the associations and disgressions of a witty and articulate but claustrophobic self. The other, thorough relentless linear chronicle, presents the searing history of a family caught up in urban violence. One novel dramatizes the self-absorption of a supreme egoist, an isolated prodigy, a manic voice emanating from a grotesque fleshly casing. The other illustrates Oates's own definition of naturalism: art which "dramatizes the struggles of those to whom the self-questioning of the isolated ego is still a future horror." *Expensive People* represents the point of view of a "dissociated" modern self, seeking "to escape the wearisome confines of its own ego"; *them* treats "the economically disenfranchised . . . seeking an 'ego,' a selfhood, a permanent identity that will make them human" (*NHNE,* 100).

It is important to note that Oates is not simply imitating traditional schools or genres. Rather, she seems to be rethinking their history and philosophical implications as a scholar, critic, and teacher. Interestingly, in these two novels Oates uses literary existentialism and literary naturalism as if they were reciprocal artistic strategies, playing with their obvious contrasts of shape, voice, and tone. Thus, the novels treat many of the same themes: the relentless play of accident, the threat of violence and madness which undercuts the modern self's autonomous pretensions. In both, Oates underscores and focuses sharply on the crippling double bind of family relationships—reflecting her growing receptivity to the new humanistic psychology, as an expansion and revision of prevailing Freudian models of the self. In the same vein, both novels deal with the facticity of such labels as sanity/insanity, reality/nightmare, fiction/fact. In these experimental novels, Oates not only tests the limits of novelistic form; she documents the human struggle for freedom in contemporary society and the problems that struggle poses for the artist in residence.

To evoke a lost world of harmony and value, her first two novels were set in a rural landscape, "Eden County." But Eden is the monstrous joke of *Expensive People,* the pseudo-paradise of suburban "Fernwood." Dante is evoked with a knowing smirk, as the narrator Richard Everett exclaims breathlessly,

> Ah, to tell you these things would be to write another *Paradiso,* and we writers are better equipped to write of the Inferno and Purgatory. . . . Before the rare beauties of the wealth of America a writer can do nothing. . . . Little orchards, little cars . . . gray tweeded businessmen hopping out the side doors, faces flushed with happiness and close antiseptic electric shaves. . . . (*EP,* 121)

Fernwood is a fraudulent man-made Eden, designed as a denial of time and change and mortality. Imperfection is disguised in the El Dorado beauty salon; puppies are instantly and conveniently replaced by doubles should their deaths occur; and both the opulent mansions and the expensive people who inhabit them are oddly interchangeable. Apparently awestruck, Everett describes the scene:

> If God remakes Paradise it will be in the image of Fernwood, for Fernwood is Paradise constructed to answer all desires before they are even felt. Heaven and earth converge like two friendly halos of perfume, overlapping, sinuous . . . and there is never any contrast between what is said and what is done, what is done and what is intended, what is intended and what is desired. (*EP,* 122–23)

Oates here mockingly erases—and simultaneously suggests—the inner division of twentieth-century "hollow men." As Everett's tale unfolds, Fernwood's gilded edges begin to tarnish, revealing the meretricious reality beneath this suburb of words.

In striking contrast to Oates's first two novels in which the author's academic predilections are overshadowed by the violence of the lives she dramatizes, *Expensive People* is an act of fabulation: a book of explicit verbal trickery and conceits, exploding in a barrage of puns and arch allusions. Oates also teasingly inverts her own previous schemes. In the denouement of *A Garden of Earthly Delights,* Swan, unable to kill his mother, turns his weapon on himself. When Oates reruns the same scenario in *Expensive People,* the child has succeeded: the novel's opening words are "I was a child murderer." Swan is labeled a patricide; this narrative purports to be the first-person memoir of a self-styled matricide, a parodic "underground boy," who has killed Nada, his mother, and is now eager to confess his crime. Ironically, Richard's desire for justice is frustrated by the cabal of adults who have designed the suburban realm. One by one, they convert Richard's true confession into hallucination, undercut his reliability as narrator, and ultimately denude his action of its moral or existential significance.

Expensive People thus offers a variation on a Dostoevskian theme: the individual's search for power—even for criminal authority, a self-designed, gratuitous source of meaning in a world where traditional value systems are defunct. Albeit with mockery, it also describes the life sentence of freedom, the high cost of remaining at large. "There's nothing more terrible than to commit a crime and still be free," the narrator blubbers to one of a series of consulting psychiatrists; "there's nothing more terrible than to be a murderer without a murderer's punishment" (*EP,* 254). Yet the therapists and literati, this culture's lay priests, coolly rationalize the impassioned confession, diagnosing it as Oedipal delusion, frustrating the boy's rage for order and retribution. Richard must face a terrible absence.

Throughout the novel, aching with a "peculiar hollowness," he attempts quite literally to fill the void with food: "the softness of bananas, the hardness of peanut brittle, the pliant cool sanity of lettuce!" (*EP,* 255). Richard is another of Oates's grotesque gluttons—and the funniest, although Sullivan dismisses him caustically: "a tale told by a slob."[1] Several other commentators including Kazin have suggested that Oates's pervasive images of gluttony make up a social critique; Friedman finds them a metaphor for the "glut of things . . . in this spiritually-bankrupt period."[2] Interestingly enough, one source of this reading could be Richard Everett himself:

> I should have told you of the pies, both fresh and frozen, the custard cups, the ice-cream cones, the strawberry and cream tarts, the chocolates, the mints, the fine sweet cake Nada sometimes made (from a mix). . . . I should have reprinted menus from the most exclusive restaurants, and from the country

clubs, and from Nada's kitchen, to give you not simply a sense of my sinking into a slough of food but an idea of social conditions as well. (*EP,* 227)

Borrowing Richard's superficial sociological interpretation, many critics also miss Oates's more central artistic and philosophical concerns. Her characters' prodigious alimental orgies are emblematic of their insatiable appetites for self-determination. In *Expensive People* (and in much of Oates's later work), overeating is a paradoxical gesture of self-assertion: Richard's mind is defying his body in a bizarre attempt at suicide. One of Richard's uncles has already taken this bulemic escape route:

> He decided to kill himself by forcing food down his throat and into his bursting stomach, eating his way through a room full of food. Admirable man! . . . I like to think of that supreme moment when he broke through the slippery, stubborn wall of his own stomach and entered eternity at once. . . . (*EP,* 31–32)

Gluttony in Oates's novels has interesting academic dimensions. In *Expensive People,* Richard makes the association between eating and literature: "You think only food excites me, my readers? . . . Food means nothing but words mean everything!" (*EP,* 181–82). Oates has done her own scholarly research: her narrator allies himself with an entire school of literary gluttons— Juvenal, Sterne, Churchill:

> History gives us these weird writers whose scribbling must in itself have been a kind of grossness, but not enough to satisfy, coming to London or Paris or Rome or New York, anywhere, to fill their stomachs and brains with whatever was handy. (*EP,* 190)

Oates evokes the visceral pathos of Kafka's hunger artist in these tragicomic gustatory images.

Expensive People is in this sense a work of waggery; the novel is droll and bookish, offering flashes of Nabokovian delight. The allusions are unassimilated, playful, bald. Yet, as Oates declares elsewhere, such parodic mockery can be a danger sign,"an act of aggression" (*EI,* 7). Here, it expresses her wry discontent with academic residence. Self-referential, self-congratulatory, the intellectual clique she describes feeds on its own language, negating life's moveable feast.

Ironically, Richard Everett's very life is a perverse imitation of existentialist art. In her study of this novel, Alice Martin appropriately regards Richard's frequent dramatic bouts of vomiting as a child's version of existential "nausea."[3] There are many echoes of Kafka as well as Sartre: Richard sees a "shy cockroach" (*EP,* 81) and soon is meditating on metamorphosis (*EP,* 86), literally changing his own form by fleshly accretion. Richard alludes to "sad dark Russia"; Dostoevski may well have influenced this vision of crime and punishment, these notes from the underground. Richard's literary name-dropping also includes references to Rousseau, Flaubert, Genet, Proust, Dickens, Tolstoi, Stendhal, Hemingway, Faulkner, Mann—all of whom are brought in to authorize his own "angst."

Oates also invokes F. Scott Fitzgerald. Richard's mother (and victim?), Nada/Natashya Everett, is a feminine Gatsby, a character perhaps endemic in American fiction. She has fought to remake not only her world but herself, obscuring the vulgar origins of "Nancy June Romanow," attempting to defy time: "I am Natashya Everett and I am out of history" (*EP*, 214). After her disappearance and probable murder, her sour and saddened parents come forth to expose her real identity and exchange the gorgeous myth for the dimmer terms of mortality (*EP*, 249–50).

Fernwood parties cater to academic appetites. Unaware of the threat posed by their son the sniper, the Everetts mingle gaily with their allegorically-named friends: the Spoons, the Bodys, the Bones, Dr. Hugg, the Voyds, the Veals. The latter are subjects of a hilarious exchange. Nada learns that the Veals have been killed in a plane crash. With Fernwoodian imperturbability, Elwood Everett remarks, "Well, we should invite them over. Thelma was very nice to you. . . . Maybe we should wait awhile before having them over though" (*EP*, 160). The dialogue sounds like a scene from Ionesco as Oates parodies the fabulator's comically foreshortened perspective.

Martin identifies Thomas Nashe as the "unfortunate traveler" to whom Richard/Oates teasingly alludes (*EP*, 87), and finds the picaresque adventurer the inspiration for this novel.[4] But Oates also has a different scheme in mind. In *Expensive People*, Oates reimagines the myth of Daedalus—the prototypic fabulator—and Icarus, an even more "unfortunate traveler," destroyed by his willful disobedience and the hypnotic and dangerous illusion of art. The classical references are everywhere: the Everetts live on "Labyrinth" drive; Fernwood is a "maze" harboring an insatiable, murderous assailant. Most importantly, Richard himself is a son trapped in a fatal dream of flight:

> I felt as if I were trying to fly with wings soaked with sweat, feathers torn and ragged, falling out. . . . Me, the child, the shabby angel pumping his wings furiously and weeping with shame; Nada, the mother, digging in her heels and cursing me on. I kept struggling up into the sky, my eyes bloodshot and my heart just ordinarily shot, waiting for the end. (*EP*, 48)

The Icarus of this age is sent aloft but ludicrously exposed, antiheroic, graceless, vulnerable to the tug of earthbound forces while the skyward lure of art threatens his literal existence.

Expensive People thus moves from parody to parable: a parable of the dilemma of the contemporary artist. Richard Everett hopes to control the rising disorder of the world, to halt the erosion of values, to stem the rising terror of ontological insecurity. His strategies are not merely playful. Paradoxically, he must murder his mother to keep his world intact: "I would rather see her die than lose her" (*EP,* 85), he decides. In his intensely private sphere, fiction displaces fact, and "reality" must be deliberately designed:

> I have no patience with accidents. I don't want whimsey or lies, blunders, trivia. I want the real thing. The real thing: a crime of murder committed with all premeditation by a child in full possession of his own wits, with a certain minimal level of intelligence. (*EP,* 10)

In many ways, *Expensive People* is Oates's most academic work of fiction. In *With Shuddering Fall* and *A Garden of Earthly Delights,* school literally and figuratively provides a temporary refuge for the young and questing self. Oates makes even more telling use of the classroom setting in *Expensive People.* The authorities at Richard's school, Johns Behemoth, certify to his intelligence after testing and retesting; Richard displays his capacity for volitional action by vomiting on his records. But he is conditioned more strongly to be a good student. As narrator, he attempts to go beyond ordinary assignments to design the "posthumous future" for his novel in a set of witty book reviews: *The New York Times* ("more sentimentally electric than tragically enlightened"); *Time Magazine* ("Everett sets out to prove he can out-smartre Sartre"); *The New Republic* ("the would-be novelist who would reduce complex sociological material to a thalamic crisis"); a fashionable psychological quarterly:

> *Expensive People* is . . . valuable as a fabulous excursion into the realm of the orally obsessed. Food abounds in this memoir. . . . Those of us who have read Freud (I have read every book, essay, and scrap of paper written by Freud) will recognize easily the familiar domestic triangle here, of a son's homosexual and incestuous love for his father disguised by a humdrum Oedipal attachment to his mother. (*EP,* 133–36)

Oates thus proves herself adept at the fabulator's game even while she parodies it. Again, her purpose here is not only to sport on lexical playfields, but to expose the terror that lies beneath the fabulator's egoistical display. As we have seen, attempts to control a continually shifting, dissolving reality are destined to be defeated by the arbitrariness of human perception. Thus, Richard complains of his situation:

> I have a story to tell, yes, and no one else could tell it but me, but if I tell it now and not next year it will come out one way, and if I could have forced my fat, heaving body to begin this a year ago it would have been a different story then. And it's possible that I'm lying without knowing it. (*EP,* 7)

In a "footnote" to the reader, he cries out, "The experience is there, the reality

is there, but how to get at it? Everything I type out turns into a lie simply because it is not the truth" (*EP,* 31). Trapped in the prison-house of language,
Oates's would-be author is driven to the edge of impossibility.

In this lampoon of avant-garde writing, Oates uses another fabulator's
trick, the story-within-the-story, to its best advantage. Interrupting his narration, Richard presents a story supposedly written by Nada Everett, "The Molesters." A tale of child abuse and rape is told in three successive versions, to
demonstrate the alterations of reality caused by shifts in time and point of
view. "The Molesters" is in fact a fascinating palimpsest. The ingenuous
narrator-victim of the opening pages is at ease in a sunlit realm of sensual
perception, but is incapable of dealing with the violence that erupts out of the
world of time and experience. The narrator of the second story is more hesi-
tant and tentative. Finally, in the third inscription, an older, more sophisticated narrator is fatally out of touch with the forces of nature that might have
redeemed the original account and the "teller" as well. As one further touch
of irony, "The Molesters"—by Joyce Carol Oates—*actually* appeared
months earlier, in the journal named as Nada's publisher in this novel.[5]

Complicating the reader's dilemma here, Richard himself proves an unreliable exegete, interpreting the story as a document of his mother's infidelity. Like the perverse Nabokovian narrator in *Pale Fire,* he sees fiction not as
a transparent thing but as a mirror of his own egoistic and infantile suffering:
"Nada wrote the story to exorcise the guilt she rightly felt for abandoning me
so often" (*EP,* 180). Yet in another turn of the screw, this interpretation sends
Richard into existential fear and trembling. "There are some of us. sick
people and madmen, who should not be shown symbolic matter," he
cries. In the words that follow, Oates again represents him as a crippled modern Icarus: "Pictures, designs, words, are too much for us. We fall into them
and never hit the bottom; it's like falling and falling into one of your own
dreams" (*EP,* 181).

Richard's agony is the central irony of the novel: he is progressively reduced from artist-hero to a minor character, changing from controlling narrator into a fictive personality in a work literally ghost-written. *His* major
character (and ostensible victim), Nada Everett, is ultimately immortalized
as the arch-fabulator of *Expensive People:* self-absorbed, cultivating the "private sphere mystique" with a vengeance. "Have I ever mentioned," Richard
notes with evident relish, "Nada's total lack of interest in politics, in events,
in reality?"

> She might have believed her brain too finely developed to be overloaded with
> the trivia of daily reality, daily suffering. Her brain was instead stuffed with
> books. What was "only real" couldn't be very important, and I have to confess
> feeling this way myself. I have caught her solipsism from her. (*EP,* 85)

Such egoism is attractive, influential, contagious. It is also, Oates seems to insist, criminally irresponsible and dangerous. Simultaneously exploiting and vacating her authority, Nada puts Richard into a Laingian double bind, condemning him to a schizophrenic's existence. Significantly, Nada justifies her selfish, heartless treatment of her child in the name of freedom:

> "Don't give me that solemn weepy look through your glasses, my friend, I don't particularly care to be called Mother by anyone. . . . I'm trying to hold my own and that's it. No *Mother,* no *Son.* No depending on anyone else. I want you to be so free, Richard, that you stink of it. You're not going to blame me for anything."

Desperate for continuity and authority, Richard whimpers, "Who should I blame then?" Nada's response, in another of the novel's oblique puns, seems self-incriminating: "Nobody," she declares (*EP,* 188). Although Richard continues to deny that his mother is the "evil genius" who has made him her "ingenu-narrator," the truth of the matter is that she *is* the culpable fabulator, in control even beyond the grave. The novel's most interesting document is an excerpt from Nada's "sacred" notebook, an outline for an unwritten story, "The Sniper," which proves uncannily predictive:

> The climax will be the death of X, but one must get past. The trouble is getting there . . . and getting past. As in any first-person narrative there can be a lot of freedom. . . .
>
> "comic nihilism"
>
> Idea for a short novel: the young man . . . leads two lives, one public and the other secret. buys a gun. frightens people, doesn't hurt them. I can stretch this out to three episodes but no more, fine . . . then the fourth . . . results in the murder: planned all along though maybe he didn't know it. (*EP,* 116–17)

Reading on, Richard feels possessed; from this point, he lives out Nada's scenario.

Expensive People thus dramatizes many of Oates's central themes and horizontal obsessions. The designing author assumes control with terrible risks for the surviving reader, as Oates deftly exposes the paradoxical hazards of fabulation. Abandoning what is "only real" for a garden of bookish delights, Nada becomes the author of her own death! Her murderer-son, irresistibly under her influence, insists he has

> the fierce consolation of knowing that whatever I did, whatever degradations and evils, stupidities, blunders, moronic intrusions, whatever single ghastly act I did manage to achieve, it was done out of freedom, out of choice. This is the only consolation I have in the face of death, my readers: the thought of my free will.

Yet the novel's last words undercut that boast: "I must confess," Richard nervously reveals, "that there are moments when I doubt even this consolation" (*EP*, 255).

Oates's curious third novel, which begins with a brash declaration of autonomy, ends in whining self-doubt. In the process, Oates has matched wits with a host of artistic precursors and modern colleagues, exploiting the terms of her residence. *Expensive People*, her version of fabulation, tracks the descent of a contemporary Icarus, drowning in seas of counterfeit art.

In her next novel, *them*, Oates radically shifts her stance. As she leaves the suburbs to document the naturalists's sordid urban scene, she also pushes beyond the limits of first-person perspective, inventing a series of third-person narrators. This strategy has moral as well as aesthetic implications. As John Barth suggests, the self-conscious narrative act itself mirrors life in a shifting and treacherous public world. He defends the fabulator's pose on those grounds: "when the characters in a work of fiction become readers or authors of the fiction they're in, we're reminded of the fictive aspect of our own existence." Oates, in contrast, is impatient with "novels which imitate the form of the Novel, by an author who imitates the role of Author."[6] Richard Everett, imitating authorship, becomes lost in a maze of his own devising, capitulating to the madness of the private sphere, an unreliable narrator clinging to fiction's flimsy disguise. But in the contemporary world, Oates seems to say, we may already have too many reminders of the fictive quality of life.[7]

Thus, Oates offers affidavits of literal truth in her naturalistic novel: "This is a work of history," she declares in the introductory author's note. Characteristically, however, she is quick to define history on her own terms. It must arise from a "personal perspective . . . the only kind of history that exists" (*t*, author's note).

Richard Everett presents a savagely comic contrivance in which the fall of man often seems reduced to a pratfall. He derives his existential reality, his very identity, from the act of writing: "My body is just a vessel or instrument I am using, as this typewriter is an instrument I'm using, and when I am finished with this memoir I will be finished with this body" (*EP*, 197). He is also a character invented by Nada, another fictive writer. In *them*, the real author, Joyce Carol Oates, is introduced to the reader as an artist-medium, the vehicle for a true story drawn from personal history. Interestingly, she draws upon her experience as an artist in residence:

> In the years 1962–1967 I taught English at the University of Detroit. . . . It was during this period that I met the "Maureen Wendall" of this narrative. . . . Her various problems and complexities overwhelmed me . . . so much material had the effect of temporarily blocking out my own reality, my personal life, and substituting for it the various nightmare adventures of the Wendalls. Their lives pressed upon mine eerily, so that I began to dream about them instead of about myself. . . . Because their world was so remote from me it entered me with tremendous power, and in a sense the novel wrote itself. (*t*, author's note)

One critic, L. E. Sissman, finds it hard to regard Oates's documents— testimony, personal letters—as genuine history; *them* to him is seen "as in a dream," rather than an objective and "explicit" presentation.[8] Oates herself emphasizes the hallucinatory quality of these revelations: "My initial feeling . . . was, 'This must be fiction, this can't all be real!'" But she goes on to declare,"'This is the only kind of fiction that is real'" (*t*, author's note). She intends in her fourth novel to testify to a horrifying reality, the "sordid and shocking events of slum life," just as her third novel is meant to reflect the artifice of suburban existence.

Like *Expensive People, them* dramatizes the self's struggle for order and control in a world apparently controlled by ferocious antagonists. But here Oates questions the fate assigned by the literary naturalist to the poor and the powerless. Assimilating the visions of poets and psychologists, she reimagines the deterministic designs of Zola and Dreiser:

> It seems to me that the greatest works of literature deal with the human soul caught in the stampede of time, unable to gauge the profundity of what passes over it, like the characters of Yeats who live through terrifying events but who cannot understand them; in this way, history passes over most of us. (*NHNE*, 105)

In *them*, the fictive and the factual merge, obliterating such convenient categories. Only at one level is *them* a socio-economic document, "about poverty in America"; at a deeper level, she tells us, it is a psychodrama about the "awakening of levels of consciousness."[9]

The subtitle of *Expensive People* is "Children of Freedom" (*EP*, 125). In contrast, Oates introduces the Wendalls, the central figures in *them*, as "Children of Silence," like "sea creatures—drawn helplessly together" (*t*, 15), stammering, literally requiring the services of a novelist-translator to make some sense of their lives. Unlike "expensive people" who can draw freely on extensive repertoires of language and metaphor, these are the anxious poor whose dreams are shaped not by the classic curriculum but by cheap celluloid fictions and two-dimensional comic-book representations: the Lone Ranger (*t*, 65), "Alan Ladd in Shane, Marlon Brando" (*t*, 99), and other "enviable heroes of books and movies" (*t*, 111).

The world the Wendalls inhabit is similarly tawdry, and dominated by infernal mechanistic energies which send men and women "spinning out of control" (*t*, 129) like helpless toys:

> A woman in a laundromat in Detroit only appears to be in control of the machines! A woman in a car only appears to be in control! Inside, her machinery is as wobbly and nervous as the machinery of her car, which may have been slammed together by someone . . . mutely angry . . . on the assembly line at Chrysler. (*t*, 93)

In such a world, it is no wonder that characters exhibit withdrawal symp-
toms; threatened by external forces, they find even their own physical selves
alien and treacherous.

Oates once called the British psychotherapist R.D. Laing "one of the sanest
persons" she had ever met.[10] Oates's *them* is in many ways informed by
Laing's analysis of human personality. Her typical character, like his typical
patient, is a "divided self," a secret, invisible, watchful presence, a "mental
observer, who looks on, detached and impassive, at what the body is doing
or what is being done to his body."[11] In this novel, the public and private
realm, the vantage points of "us" and "them" for Laing, are fatally out of key.
Maureen Wendall, her mother Loretta, her brother Jules, and her uncle
Brock also represent what Laing would call the family "protection racket."
The Wendalls seem pursued by vengeful furies, haunted by the public spectre
of poverty, depression, urban decay; but the real violence in their lives is domestic. Reaching for love, they are betrayed and victimized by their mutual
need. The family *is* a refuge of sorts; but it also generates irresistible energies,
legacies of belief and behavior that successive generations are fated to reenact. Paradoxically, it is simultaneously a locus of value and the most menacing secret agent.

The novel's opening pages demonstrate the politics of the family (also
Laing's chief concern) in a violent succession of events. Another of Oates's
Eve figures, Loretta, stands looking into the mirror, imagining herself in a
glamorous scenario which seems more real than her brother Brock's threatening presence at the supper table:

> She felt like a heroine in a movie, confronted by a jealous husband in the
> kitchen while outside the camera is aching to draw back and show a wonder-
> land of adventures waiting for her—long, frantic rides on trains, landscapes of
> wounded soldiers, a lovely white desert . . . the mysteries of English drawing-
> rooms cracking before the quick, humorless smirk of a wise young woman from
> America. . . .
>   Brock was staring at her. She watched as his jaws ground the food she'd made
> for him. (*t,* 15)

Such celluloid fantasies are ephemeral at best. Only a few pages later, Brock
has murdered Loretta's lover (Jules Wendall's father). Trembling, she feels
betrayed by her dreams and by mortal flesh itself, no match for a mechanical
metal weapon which had a "power greater than the man behind it" (*t,* 31):

> Her hatred burst upon her . . . for men always disappointed you, there was no
> hope to them, nothing. . . . Loretta stood in a hazy, vivid hatred. . . . It was the
> heaviness of the body she hated too. . . . What had been so hot and sweet earlier
> that night was now heavy with death, and the fact that death had come so fast
> and without any struggle showed how little you could trust the body, even the
> body of a man, arms and legs and chest and belly, all of it useless. (*t,* 30–31)

In a brilliantly controlled series of short episodes, Loretta has been thrust from a world of promise and romance—the world of "us"—into a world of alienation, of "them." Her first impulse after this jarring rebirth is to find a gun of her own. The pattern of betrayal, disillusionment and vengeance is acted out over and over in this novel. Seduced by fitful dreams, made acutely conscious of their mortality, the characters belatedly attempt to arm themselves against a hostile environment.

Thus, Oates has shifted her scene far from the glittering fakery of Fernwood (in *them,* it is obliquely glimpsed as a Grosse Pointe suburban mirage). She is also far from Eden Valley. The Wendalls, like the Walpoles, have no fixed address; but they are *urban* migrants, drifting from upstate New York to the streets of Detroit. The city is always an imposing force for the literary naturalist: but Oates has revised the genre to conform to mid-century America. To the Loretta of the opening scene, the city is a magical realm, its streets a "carnival" of wonders (*t,* 22). By the novel's conclusion, the city has become a nightmarish "carnival" of race riot and pillage (*t,* 447) and Loretta muses bitterly that it is "a carnival that had gotten stuck" (*t,* 469). At that point, she has survived by sheer pluck two brutalizing marriages, the degradation of one daughter and the catatonia of another, and the near-murder of her son. In her last appearance, she stands not before a mirror but before a flickering television set. Unlike Clara Walpole in *A Garden of Earthly Delights,* she is not hypnotized by counterfeit heroes. Instead, viewing her own son's manic gestures on the screen, understanding that he, too, is a killer, she is left weeping, but "with dignity" (*t,* 474): the tenacious core of herself somehow survives.

But *them* is not only Loretta's story. Oates again exploits the triptych: *them* has three foci. It is also the story of the Wendall children, Jules and Maureen, curiously complementary selves. Jules at first is jealous of his sister's "slow, stubborn, passive power"; Maureen is as envious of her brother's autonomy, mastery, creativity. For her, Jules is a kind of artist, "a magician; he could create things with his hands, in the air, outlining them again and again in swift, skillful strokes. Maureen . . . could create nothing" (*t,* 67). Soon, however, Oates peels back the young woman's docile mask. Maureen's passivity becomes a wanton invitation not to love, but assault. Jules's magic, his "reverence for power" (*t,* 68), somehow also incites the world's destructive energies.

Both sister and brother hoard a secret dream of themselves, at variance with both physical appearances and society's estimate. Jules seems caught up in the masculine American heroic myth, longing to be "a commander of some sort. A general, an admiral, a minister of war" (*t,* 81). He imagines an environment appropriate to such exaggerated self-assertion: "a wilderness, land out West; a golden sky, or perhaps a golden field of wheat . . . mountains

... rivers ... something unmapped" (*t*, 93). But that American Eden is only available in Jules's inflamed romantic vision. In reality, he and his family survive "like the weeds that grew to a height of three or four feet right through the sidewalk's cracks, struggling upward. . . squeezing around the rubble . . . permanent though they had no consciousness" (*t*, 449–50). He moves out of the city limits at the bidding of one of the novel's "expensive people," (not Nada this time, but a lovely and loveless girl, Nadine). Yet once on the open road, Jules finds to his horror that the archetypal golden land has been scarred and subdivided:

> This was not the country. It was not the city either. Raw, gaping hunks had been cut out of the earth—in preparation for a shopping plaza maybe—and trees were overturned, dried out. He was truly in a foreign country. He was a stranger. (*t*, 278)

One by one, the storybook images of American life are debunked: "the freedom of trucks and trains" (*t*, 87); the "godly and magical" distances their drivers cover (*t*, 81); "free and floating" aerial maneuvers in the Detroit skies (*t*, 241); the golden key of wealth; the luxurious abandon of sexual love—all are revealed as delusions born in dime novels. As a boy, Jules thinks of himself "as a character in a book being written by himself, a fictional fifteen-year-old with the capacity to become anything. . . . He could change his name. He could change his looks in five minutes. He could change himself to fit into anything" (*t*, 97–99). Like Richard Everett, Jules seems to have a certain gift for fabulation. But reality alters his "fiction" and his self-styled heroic plan; the drag and threat of human relationships undercut his optimistic assertion of freedom. However far he runs, he cannot erase his sense of connectedness: "The affection of other people was like a fishook in Jules" (*t*, 279), qualifying his motions and choices.

Again, the craft of fiction becomes a metaphor for the self's struggle for identity and control. Like Swan Revere, like Richard Everett, Jules at first senses he has lost the power to write his own story, and Oates describes him succumbing to the reigning paranoia: "My life is a story imagined by a madman!" (*t*, 255). Indeed, his existence displays all the craziness of pulp fiction; standing in a drugstore, he unwittingly reads his own history in *Detective Annals*: "My Baby's Father Was Killed in My Arms!" (*t*, 280). He is cast in the role of the accomplice in a fictive thriller when he assists an erstwhile patron, Bernard Geffen; he seems enmeshed in a gothic *Frankenstein* fable when he serves as a paid guinea pig in a medical experiment. He continues to feel he is "the hero of countless stories" (*t*, 370)—all selected from the reading lists of Joyce Carol Oates.

The story which most obviously structures Oates's naturalistic narrative is drawn from a more academic reference: *An American Tragedy*. Like Clyde

Griffiths in Dreiser's novel, Jules emerges from poverty to be patronized by a wealthy uncle, taking his cousin's place in the business; also like the hapless Clyde, he falls victim to his own sexual drives and the allure of a glamorous heiress. When he sees the beauteous Nadine in a crowded restaurant after months of separation, his uncle looks at him and remarks (in another more obvious reference to Dreiser's work), "Kid, you look like somebody sat you in the electric chair" (*t*, 333). Characteristically, most of Oates's literary allusions are oblique, fragmentary, inverted: she subjects them to alteration, weaving them into her own story. Thus, unlike Clyde, Jules does not become a murderous agent in this love affair; rather, he is himself the victim. No mental or moral coward aspiring to tragic stature, he is instead the survivor of a bad melodrama.

As it is in Dreiser's work, human love is an ambivalent force in *them*: pulsing and dangerous, promising enchantment, threatening annihilation. Jules feels his will "flattened out" (*t*, 276) in his earliest encounters with Nadine; he longs to be "the carpet beneath her feet" (*t*, 258–61), and agrees to help her escape her own gilded prison. But she betrays and abandons him, leaving him in a sordid motel room, delirious and ill. Nonetheless, when they meet again, Jules again drops his resistance. In an ironic replay of the novel's opening scenes, he becomes the target of a concealed weapon, almost fatally wounded by Nadine's surprise sadistic attack: "The spirit of the Lord departed from Jules" (*t*, 380) the narrator intones, and Jules's quest for love seems over.

For Maureen Wendall, love is equally life-threatening and problematic. While Jules is a central figure in a latter day American tragedy, she is a soap opera heroine. She wants to whisper to the rebellious Jules, "give in" (*t*, 124); she "thought it was all crazy, this worry about being kicked around, when all you had to do was recoil with the blow and start to cry as soon as possible" (*t*, 118). Buffeted cruelly by "them," Maureen longs for stasis and security. Jules dreams of playing war; Maureen imagines herself playing house:

> Maureen, having no hardness to her, crept in silence among them and waited for the day when everything would be orderly and neat, when she could arrange her life the way she arranged the kitchen after supper, and she too might then be frozen hard, fixed, permanent, beyond their ability to hurt. (*t*, 125)

Yet such dreams also include a peculiarly feminine mode of domination, which Oates describes from her own academic perch as playing school:

> In her mind she shouted commands, like a soldier; all the kids obeyed her and lined up. . . . She made them read their lessons one by one. Her heart would begin to pound, thinking of the captive childen and herself watching over them, guarding and bullying them. (*t*, 127–28)

In the midst of this violent and searing drama, Oates presents the university as a peculiar haven. Within its confines, Maureen is an acquiescent protégée of other authoritarian mentors: demanding nuns, accusing librarians, dogmatic teachers of literature like "Joyce Carol Oates." In this realm, too, the house of fiction offers a promise of control over the real world of contingency and loss. "The world of this novel was real," Maureen thinks, reading Jane Austen, while "her own life . . . could not be real" (*t*, 182). Living in poverty, she feels "the only richness was in books" (*t*, 182). All too soon, this worshipful response is transformed into an Oatesian pun: when Maureen turns to prostitution to buy her way out of the Wendall household, she hides her earnings in a volume of poetry. Her hoard is ultimately discovered by her frustrated, incestuous stepfather. Maureen can no longer retreat into academic residence; she is beaten almost to the point of death and certainly to the edge of madness.

Thus, both Maureen and Jules find not only their fantasies of freedom but their very lives threatened and virtually obliterated by brutal human assaults from those with whom they are most intimate. As their defenses dissolve, both lose consciousness, undergoing a death of the spirit very like a Laingian regression. Yet each takes quite a different path toward recovery and new identity.

Maureen's is the deeper dive. She is plunged into catatonia, almost classical schizophrenia. Like the artist-glutton Richard Everett, Maureen Wendall uses food as "something to fill up her entire body" (*t*, 293); for her, however, it is a means of anesthesia rather than defiant self-assertion. Interestingly, her life is reassembled through narrative: the stories of her uncle, Brock, who mysteriously reappears in the family circle; the letters from recuperating Jules. As Maureen slowly comes back to life, she also comes to regard literature as a vehicle of human betrayal. In an ironic twist, Maureen angrily turns on her teachers, writing heated letters to "Miss Oates" to protest against academic malpractice: "The books you taught us are mainly lies I can tell you. . . . The world can't be lived, no one can live it right. . . . You write books. What do you know?" (*t*, 319–20).

This interruption in the narrative of *them* is, as one critic suggests, "a concrete mode of mediation between the world inside the novel and the world outside."[12] It also stands in curious relation to the narrative break in *Expensive People*: the intrusion of Nada's short story in what purports to be Richard Everett's true confession. Each is a dramatic formal disjunction, an apparent challenge to the authority of the dominant novelistic voice. Each demonstrates the permeable membrane between the world of fiction and the world of fact. Tellingly, the consequences within each novel are quite different. Richard is overcome by the power of the story within his story, though he struggles manfully to misread—and thus make it his own. Maureen Wendall, in contrast, uses the occasion to defy "Oates" (who has, incidentally, failed her in the course), and takes control of her own real future by plotting a pulp fiction escapade: to fall in love, win security, assume a new identity, and gain even a measure of sly vengeance on Oates in particular and academics in general by seducing her current English teacher, Jim Randolph. She prepares to rewrite her life as a banal college novel.

Randolph is a pathetic caricature of an academic in many ways, an Oatesian pedant. Like a member of the Behemoth faculty, he is deluded by a sense of his own professorial autonomy: teaching, he thinks he is "in control and . . . exerting power over these strangers" (*t,* 402). He assigns what he believes are objective, value-free exercises: "What is wrong with this sentence?" (*t,* 399). Again, Oates satirizes the academic scene with an extended play on words. For the teacher ultimately submits to his *pupil's* devious "sentence," leaving his own wife and family, fulfilling Maureen's dreams of order and feminine design, finally imagining himself as a character in a magazine story or a murder movie (*t,* 407, 411).

Maureen herself continues to resist the images of "high-brow" fiction. As she tells "Oates," a stock scenario is good enough for her:

> I don't ask to turn into you but to see myself like this: living in a house out of the city, a ranch house or a colonial house, with a fence around the back, a woman working in the kitchen, wearing slacks maybe, a baby in his crib. . . . Every cell in my body aches for this! My eyes ache for it, the balls of my eyes in their sockets . . . my God how I want that house and that man, whoever he is. (*t,* 315)

Ironically, as Maureen attempts to give her life a manageable shape, Oates suggests she has stepped into another equally restrictive, formulaic drama *not* of her own making—a "Harlequin" romance. At the beginning of *them* it shapes the story of dreaming Loretta: "One warm evening in August 1937 a girl in love stood before a mirror" (*t,* 9). In April 1966 the dreamer is Maureen: "A girl in love is standing before a mirror, very still" (*t,* 383), a character in a story already written. Her own version is different from Loretta's: it has a deliberate, willed quality. "*I will fall in love,*" Maureen commands her image, "*I will make him love me*" (*t,* 387). Yet the mirror also reflects her own entrapment and desperation.

In constrast, the recuperating Jules sees his mirrored reflection as that of "a stranger, possibly an enemy." After his own dark night of the soul, he moves to a college job, reamed-out, virtually lobotomized, rootless, but granted the immunity implicit in residence. In another of Oates's ironic thrusts at the modern university, he exploits the institutionalized beneficence of the late sixties, receiving federal money to represent the urban poor on campus. He plays his assigned role shamelessly, bullying a coed into serving his supposedly primitive sexual appetites, drifting irresponsibly in the city streets.

But in spite of his retreat, Jules is suddenly swept into a *Walpurgisnacht* flood of looting, arson, and gunfire—the shocking world of events that invades the campus environment in the form of the Detroit race riots. His private self is reborn in violent spasms; Jules recovers his spirit, his old intoxication with life and love, his sense of engagement. Before the public insanity ends, he himself becomes a looter and, almost irrespective of his own choice, a killer. Engaged in a deadly struggle with a policeman in a smashed flowershop, "not to blame for anything," he aims a stolen gun at his armed assailant, unwittingly replaying the murderous encounter years before between his own father and his uncle Brock.

Curiously, although he is a minor character, Brock's figure haunts the entire novel; his apparently contradictory but impetuous actions offer a mocking reprise of the Wendalls' history. By killing Jules's father, he sets the events of the novel in motion; he also serves as Maureen's guide back into life from the underworld of madness. During his lengthy vigil at Maureen's bedside, the story he tells about his own experience is, in another ironic twist, a parody of the myth of the American outlaw. Brock narrates his failure as a would-be suicide: he has tried to stage his own death in a bank robbery shootout. Unintentionally, he succeeds as a bank robber. Subsequently, however, he is picked up and sentenced to prison for crimes he has *not* committed (*t*, 303–5). Brock's narrative could be the scenario of a zany comic film, a triumph of the absurd which underscores the fictive aspect of everyday life.

But the real victories in *them* belong to Maureen and Jules, who live out more realistic alternatives. However difficult it is to call the novel optimistic, Oates points out that her characters in *them* achieve some measure of success: "the fact about them—which reviewers seemed never to mention . . . is that they all survived."[13]

Oates thus insists that the violent events of the novel are not signs of defeat but are meant to offer hope. In the case of this brother and sister, hope goes beyond mere survival. In the last scene, Jules visits Maureen in an apartment safely located in the suburbs, outside of the city. Married to Randolph now, part of the academic society at least as a faculty wife, expecting a child, she claims she is "a different person," that she has stepped out of the history of the Wendalls, of "them." Jules, on the other hand, accepting his problematic past, is a man in motion, "light on his feet and full of surprises" (*t*, 478), literally ready for a journey westward. Maureen sullenly refuses to acknowledge either her culpability or her family ties ("I guess I'm not going to see them anymore"). Jules, aware of the depths of her self-delusion, chides her gently but persistently, "honey, aren't you one of them yourself?" (*t*, 478).

The psychologist's "third force" provides a provocative text which shapes this final encounter: theories of the familial double bind, the dual pull of "us" and "them." Laing emphasizes the depravity inherent in the human condition: "We are all murderers and prostitutes—no matter to what culture, society, class, nation we belong, no matter how normal, moral or mature we take ourselves to be."[14] However, he insists that recognition of our propensity for criminality can be the prelude for genuine self-actualization. Thus, having touched bottom, Oates's hero Jules is embarked on a voyage of discovery as the novel ends. He has transcended the brutal demands of society which, Oates seems to say, are misread as fate. Maureen continues to perpetuate an old scenario of romance and betrayal; Jules eludes it.

Thus in many ways, and with intriguing implications, Oates breaks through the deterministic patterns of naturalism. The two novels, *Expensive People* and *them,* are in fact more than doubles. Oates suggests they are intended to make up a trilogy with *A Garden of Earthly Delights.* Rural, suburban, urban; realistic, existentialistic, naturalistic—in each environment, through each novelistic strategy and form, Oates dramatizes alternative modes of resistance, ways of living *in* the public sphere while maintaining the spark of life, the "spirit of the Lord," the core of the creative self.

The trilogy also suggests the self-critical and revisionary quality of Oates's work. Together, the three novels offer a shifting view of cultural history and personality theory, seen through a succession of literary and psychological foci. The classical Freudian picture of traumatic disfiguration and Oedipal malevolence moves from foreground to background in the face of Laing's view of the soul's subterranean and fecund recesses. The garden of Bosch, the artificially manicured suburban vistas, the urban jungle, serve as images of the maimed expectations of the spirit; inverted Edens which suit the blatant travesty of heroism. Oates acknowledges American myths; she also begins to explore new possibilities for both the self and art.

In all three novels, she also takes stock of the academic community which is her patron, her own mine of reference, and her residence. Thus, Swan Walpole fears his bookish fate; Richard Everett, an intellectual prodigy, tutored by expensive people, displays both the wittiness and the deathliness of fabulation. Maureen Wendall turns angrily from literary fictions, instead acting out her perverse version of academic achievement. Ultimately, the character and author, "Joyce Carol Oates," seems to bow to Maureen's contemptuous estimate of the university curriculum and the false promise inherent in its seductive texts.

In *them,* indeed, the writer in residence ultimately seems to relinquish her own control, setting Jules Wendall free to voyage outward, on his way west to remake himself. She resists the academician's urge to label and classify: for the time being, "I'm not anything," Jules declares. "I'm just trying to get along" (*t,* 477). Yet Jules is not, like Richard Everett, a self-erasing cartoon figure. His departure is underscored by a new note of tolerance, acceptance, and love.

The true ending of this extended exploration paradoxically comes in the introduction of *them*. Oates's first words to the reader predict Jules's future as an artist in his own right:

> We have all left Detroit—Maureen is now a housewife in Dearborn, Michigan; I am teaching in another university; and Jules Wendall, that strange young man, is probably still in California. One day he will probably be writing his own version of this novel, to which he will not give the rather disdainful and timorous title *them*. (*t,* author's note)

Richard Everett is an Icarus with clipped wings. Jules Wendall enacts the myth of Proteus, demonstrating an uncanny resilience, an ability to grapple with reality despite its shocks and shifts. Seized by a pursuer capable of multiple transformations himself, the old deceiving god may issue new prophecies and reveal new alternatives for the aspiring self.

Returned to life but still carrying the baggage of the past, Jules Wendall thus is Oates's first tentative representation of a new artistic personality. If Clara and Swan and Richard and even Maureen revert to old types and adopt anachronistic and destructive stances, Jules is an artist reaching beyond a temporary residence toward a creative future promise. Read in this context, *them* can indeed be called optimistic—reaffirming the artist's mediating role, revising the naturalist's traditional conceptions of psychological determinism, suggesting possibilities of restoration and reentry.

In her next novel, *Wonderland,* Oates continues to draw upon traditional literary strategies as she explores the pressing concerns of contemporary American life. But the stakes have changed. The academy of the late sixties, a *Wonderland* setting, has itself become a realm of threatening hallucination. Central to this novel is an evolving, protean personality, seeking both refuge and authority. After an impressive literary apprenticeship, Oates begins to develop and test a new novelistic form, incorporating and adapting a variety of styles and texts; attempting to match the motions of this modern shape-shifter and to advance her own vision of cultural and personal transformation.

4 Personality in Flight
Wonderland

In the dedication to *Wonderland* (1971), Joyce Carol Oates underscores her continuing fascination with the voyaging self, both hunter and quarry. "This book," she declares, "is for all of us who pursue the phantasmagoria of personality." The very word "phantasmagoria"—a shifting spectacle, a magic lantern show, a series of illusions created by the imagination—indicates her intentions. Oates, by the time of her fifth novel, views personality as a fluid and transformable process, rather than a Freudian "product." Her unconventional conception of character disturbs some critics:

> If personality is a phantasmagoria, then what is character, or more to the immediate point, characterization? . . . In Oates's novels the characters simply change. Personality does become a true phantasmagoria, not an organic development from stage to stage, but a random shifting from one manifestation of character and being to the next.[1]

Other readers welcome Oates's extraordinary dramatization of the riddle of the self in the novel, the bold exploration of what Joan Didion calls "the question we all founder on, whether personality has any meaning."[2] Friedman is not alone in finding *Wonderland* the most "ambitious" of the author's first novels;[3] the author herself suggests it represents both an artistic and psychological turning point in her career. Indeed, although it bears many similarities to Oates's earlier fiction, this novel seems to demand more critical attention both as a study of character and as a larger reflection of cultural crisis.

At one level, *Wonderland* is a work of social criticism: Oates's vision of the mounting disturbance of public life and the reverberations within her academic residence; her sense of the challenges to timeless American ideals posed by the time bomb of Vietnam. But her response is ambiguous. In the face of violence in the streets and disorder on the campus, Oates attempts to voice an almost perverse optimism. An unresolved tension between her realistic and visionary impulses marks the novel.

It is also visible in essays written during the same period. In "New Heaven and Earth," for example, Oates offers a counterweight to the pervasive rhetoric of crisis. She imagines a new personality coming into view, a stage of organic human development matching the "fluid, psychic social reality" of the times, a man or woman embarked on a self-actualizing journey rather than a power trip. She exhorts her readers to follow suit in the accents of an evangelist:

> We can transform ourselves, overleap ourselves beyond even our most flamboyant estimations. A conversion is always imminent . . . the "conversion" of the I-centered personality into a higher, or transcendental personality cannot be an artifically, externally enforced event. It is surely as natural as the growth of a plant.[4]

Oates has dramatized "the death throes of the old values" in her first four novels. As a writer in residence, she now evidently feels it her particular responsibility to move her readership beyond these deathly fictions of the ego's rule. In the same essay, she puts her challenge into artistic terms:

> Those more advanced must work to transform the rest . . . those of us who will probably not share personally in a transformed world can, in a way, anticipate it now, almost as if experiencing it now. If we are reasonably certain of the conclusion of a novel (especially the one we have ourselves imagined), we can endure and even enjoy the intermediary chapters that move us toward our conclusion. (*NH*, 54)

Oates may sound like a campus radical; like the self-styled revolutionaries who serve as models for some of her *Wonderland* characters, she valorizes mystics and shamans, and explores oriental and occult texts. Nevertheless, she insists that her project is profoundly conservative: an art of reclamation rather than repudiation. Alive to the protesting spirit, she seeks confirmation of this orphic vision in past and present literature: the prophecies of Blake, Lawrence, and Whitman; the theories of Maslow, Levi-Strauss, Laing. Yet at the end of this remarkable essay, she draws back. Despite her rhetoric of assent, Oates regretfully concludes that the conversion all these men of genius describe is a happy ending that awaits the artist of the future.

Wonderland, Oates's own "intermediary chapter," is an imaginative presentation of this dilemma. Mirroring the agony of the American campus intellectual in the late sixties, the novel takes shape in a world of grotesques, leaders of mesmeric cults, figures intent upon engineering dramatic conversions. The central figure—beginning as tremulous schoolboy, becoming a scholarly authority—is a perennial fugitive in a world of terrorists. Whether we read it as a novel of personality or a vehicle of social comment, *Wonderland* is foreshortened, ambiguous, inconclusive.

Oates's journey to this moment in her own career reflects a somewhat torturous intellectual odyssey. Experimenting with traditional forms and literary models, she has come to believe, like her "demonic" inspiration, D.

H. Lawrence, that "the old stable ego of the character" is "dull, old, dead."[5] The newly freed self, however, might venture into a world of vertigo and nightmare. Oates sees compelling images of that terror in the novels, parables, and diaries of Franz Kafka: a sense that inner and outer clocks are not in unison; the aphasia that strikes the self at the boundaries of consciousness. (Kafka's warning is an epigraph for her collection of essays with the Lawrentian title, *New Heaven, New Earth*: "Once in another world, you must hold your tongue.")

A student of psychology, she also finds new models of the self in process in the work of Carl Jung. Uncomfortable with the Freudian theory which decreed a merciless check on irrational impulses, Jung described a process of individuation: the self's subterranean descent and eventual integration of conscious and unconscious, mythic energies. Jung claimed that modern man, once embarked on such a voyage, could surpass all known limits. Yet he, too, underscored the risks: "the influx of the unconscious into the realm of consciousness, the dissolution of the personal . . . bring with them a state of psychic imbalance."[6]

Oates acknowledges the influence of Jung on her conception of the phantasmagoria of selfhood, the predicament of Jesse, her *Wonderland* hero.[7] Able to absorb multiple shocks and regain his footing, Jesse also seems an uncannily faithful representation of "Protean Man," the contemporary survivor described by psychiatrist Robert Jay Lifton.[8] Of course, his type also exists in Oates's earlier work; for example, the elusive, light-footed Jules Wendall as he evolves in *them*. And as this novel's title suggests, Jesse inhabits Lewis Carroll's terrain, altering his shape to adapt to different circumstances, making his way through the "tremulous packed streets of this life" (*W*, 236).

Wonderland, a work of metamorphosis and transformation, thus represents the shifting philosophical, psychological, and artistic vision of the author and the era. As it unfolds, Oates herself seems to modulate between patterns of positivism and causality and alternative conceptions of reality— the intuitive, the irrational, the transcendent—trying until the final pages to discover a way to accommodate such apparently antithetical views. Tracing the final protean evasions of a hero afoot in a landscape of violence, the conclusion of *Wonderland* is especially problematic. Multiply-revised, Oates's "intermediary" novel remains essentially unfinished.

Yet in the preamble, Oates introduces her wonderland adventure with considerable assurance. A group of literary references and a poem of her own give explicit clues to her complex intentions. There is a sly variation on the traditional novelistic disclaimer—instead of acquitting the writer, it takes the reader's side: "Any resemblance to reality is accidental and should be resisted." A quotation from Yeats suggests how the rational intellect is doomed to frustration in a world of contingency and change: "knowledge increases unreality." A third epigraph from Borges blurs the distinction between fact and illusion, a different sort of phantasmagoria which is part of the magic lantern show of fabulation:

> We . . . have dreamt the world, We have dreamt it as firm, mysterious, visible, ubiquitous in space and durable in time; but in its architecture we have allowed tenuous and eternal crevices of unreason which tell us it is false.

Tellingly, the quotation is from *Labyrinths*. Oates's own poetic epigraph, "Wonderland" (first published with a punster's title, "Iris Into Eye," in 1970), offers an image of the primordial coil—life's original helix, and the spiraling emergence into consciousness. As Friedman suggests, the poem sets the pattern for the novel's movement.[9] In *Wonderland,* there are many labyrinths, both symbolic and literal. Again and again, the hero is trapped in a monstrous design and sent spinning. Jesse's own quest for identity leads him into a medical career where he actually probes the "moist, shadowed, labyrinthine secrecy of [the] brain" (*W,* 351). He becomes both hero and minotaur as patients are led through his "clean, expensive maze." of offices (*W,* 348). In *Expensive People,* Oates created a perverse fabulator whose greatest artifice is apparently her own murder: Nada's Icarian heir is left to thrash about pathetically in a sea of words. But in *Wonderland,* the fall of Icarus is transmuted into the fall of Alice: the opening plunge of a child into a dark, fearful labyrinth peopled by menacing authorities and mutants; a trip through intricate passageways where even ordinary activities—drinking, eating—can be perilous, and where the fugitive is vulnerable to surprising transformations. These all too real equivalents of mythic and literary imagery, these uncanny recapitulations of phylogeny, shape Oates's wonderland narrative.[10]

As the dedication suggests, *Wonderland* is a chronicle of pursuit. In the opening scenes, with meticulous care, Oates describes a contest of hunter and prey which will be echoed throughout the novel. Jesse, born Jesse Harte, is soon sent speeding like his fleet animal namesake from his family home. Initially, he is sickened by the contingency of the everyday world—his father's business failure, his mother's unwanted pregnancy. His literal nausea pervades the early chapters, an ironic counterpoint to the Christmas rituals and festivities in his high school. Filled with childish dread, he imagines he is being shadowed by some mysterious assailant. Soon, his worst dreams (and obviously Freud's worst case) are realized when the imaginary pursuer takes the shape of his own father driving him toward their blood-spattered house. Willard Harte, maddened by the frustration of all his hopes, has killed the rest of the Harte family; he intends to finish the job by killing Jesse before turning his gun on himself. Horrified, fleeing, seeking shelter, Jesse is critically wounded in more than one sense. But he survives.

Like a character from Lifton's psychohistory, he begins his desperate journey. Weaving and feinting, he continues to function in a world of public and private assailants, displaying an amazing polymorphous versatility. To appease and to emulate a succession of father-surrogates, he modifies his manners and appearance; he changes his name not once but several times (from Harte to Vogel to Pederson and to Vogel once again, as if to underscore his propensity for flight).

Grandfather Vogel, sullen and inarticulate, grudgingly provides the orphan his first shelter. Not even an ironic "Eden," the very landscape seems inhuman, primordial and menacing: "Why did everything look so uncreated, so mean?" the boy wonders; it was like "the underworld . . . the bottom part of the real world" (*W,* 51). Healing, however, he senses "everything was coming back to life!" and imagines himself "transformed entirely" (*W,* 57). Jesse gropes his way back toward his old self, asking at last to see his family's possessions stacked in the Vogel barn. But he is betrayed. As his grandfather breaks the protective silence to lash out at Jesse's dead parents viciously and bitterly, spitting out his disgust, Jesse is sent into a giddy descent.

The Pedersen household—Jesse's next refuge—is quite a different evocation of the underground vision, a terrible fantasy come to life. The Pedersens offer Jesse both name and nurturance, but no end to his vertigo. The incredible and monstrous egomaniac, Dr. Pedersen, tells the reeling, confused Jesse "there is a small statue of yourself in your body, and it is that statue you must observe. Stability. Certainty. You will have the patience and faith of concrete" (*W,* 93). Pedersen is a powerful physician, and thus the modern secular Christ: a priest curing supplicants by the laying on of hands, he is "straining to be God" (*W,* 109). Pedersen preaches a pseudo-salvific message; Jesse, listening to his "sacred words," feels "transformed, transfigured" (*W,* 114). Jesse "eats" those words. Soon he becomes the doctor's alter ego, "echoing his rhythmic pauses, emphasizing certain words. . . . It was uncanny, how he drew himself up into a boy who was so precise and articulate, who spoke almost in the voice of an older man" (*W,* 126).

Pedersen has become Jesse's author, a fabulator of terrifying proportions. Jesse is not unaware of the attendant dangers but is unwilling to resist. He is a helpless witness and almost an accomplice to Mrs. Pedersen's pathetic, frantic distress; he hears his stepsister (an obese, grotesque, mathematical prodigy) hiss at him in Carroll-talk, "*Father wants to kill me. Eat me*" (*W,* 140). He actually welcomes Pedersen's imposing rule—being far more terrified of "being excluded from the family of men, jostled about on the streets by people in a hurry, people in crowds, with their own families back home, private lives that excluded his permanently" (*W,* 173). Presiding over the dinner table, the authoritarian Pedersen offers Jesse a reprieve from his own protean history; mealtimes expecially seem a magic time of communion to one so hungry for security. In actuality, Jesse is a participant in an orgy of gluttony and manic ingestion, like Richard Everett and Maureen Wendall attempting to fill his inner space before the panic rises:

> There was something desperate in his throat that urged the food down and demanded more. . . . His stomach was an enormous open hole, a wound . . . there was a shrill hunger in him that rose like a scream. (*W,* 181-82)

Over and over, Oates shows that Jesse's greatest terror is not death, but loneliness and radical isolation. Even when he is awarded the "precious responsibility" of driving an automobile alone—one of Oates's characteristic symbols of self-determination and control—he eagerly and willingly surrenders his privacy to an invisible *Doppelgänger:*

> He was conscious of Dr. Pedersen with him, in the car with him, guiding him, warning him of oncoming speeders and tricky intersections; he carried the presence and the power of Dr. Pedersen with him all the way to Buffalo, Dr. Pedersen's being extended in Jesse's no matter how far he might drive. (*W,* 150)

The psychologist A. H. Maslow is one of Oates's "Third Force" sources and teachers. In one of his last essays, he discusses and characterizes just such a bipolar modern self as Jesse: seeking "autonomy . . . self-sufficiency . . . autochthonous laws of the psyche"; but drawn by a less-recognized counterforce which Maslow labels "homonomy," the "equally-strong tendency, seemingly contradictory, toward submerging ourselves in the not-self, toward giving up will, freedom, self-sufficiency, self-control."[11] In *Wonderland,* Oates dramatizes the disturbing and dizzying swings of the self between these poles, and the desperate, concomitant search for equilibrium.

Paradoxically, it is the obviously unbalanced Dr. Pedersen who introduces Jesse to the principle of balance—"homeostasis," the body's equipoise in the face of colossal and adverse environmental forces. Participating in the Pedersen dinner table quiz-program catechism, Jesse dutifully repeats a paragraph from a text by Walter Cannon, *The Wisdom of the Body* (*W,* 107-8). Interestingly, on the page which precedes that reference, Cannon describes the body's dynamic equilibrium in terms quite suggestive of Oates's own view of the wonder and phantasmagoria of personality:

> When we consider the extreme instability of our bodily structure, its readiness for disturbance by the slightest application of external forces and the rapid onset of its decomposition as soon as favoring circumstances are withdrawn, its persistence through many decades seems almost miraculous. The wonder increases when we realize that the system is open, engaging in free exchange with the outer world, and that the structure itself is not permanent but is being continuously broken down by the wear and tear of action, and as continuously built up again by processes of repair.[12]

Cannon's vision accentuates a kind of messianic mechanism. As she goes on to explore the series of familial configurations in *Wonderland,* Oates illustrates a darker view of homeostasis. To R. D. Laing, whose theories also influenced this novel, it signifies a balance of terror. In *The Politics of Experience,* homeostatic counterpoise is a covert life-denying truce negotiated within the family circle:

> The "protection" that such a family offers its members seems to be based on several preconditions: (i) a fantasy of the external world as extraordinarily dangerous; (ii) the generation of terror inside the nexus at this external danger. The "work" of the nexus is the generation of this terror. This work is violence.
>
> The stability of the nexus is the product of terror generated by its members. . . . *Such family "homeostasis" is the product of reciprocities mediated under the statues of violence and terror.* (Italics mine.)[13]

In *Wonderland,* Oates similarly revises and rejects Cannon's older ideal of homeostasis, on philosophical and even psychosexual grounds. As she declares in *New Heaven, New Earth*:

> Whenever one encounters the Aristotelian-Freudian ideal of homeostasis, in opposition to the Oriental or Jungian ideal of integration of opposites, one is likely to encounter a secret detestation of the feminine. (*NHNE,* 73)

The term thus has negative connotations in *Wonderland,* masking a deadly combat between male and female, parent and child, still far from a Jungian integration of opposites. In Oates's "intermediary chapter," such an uneasy balance offers the only promise of a temporary cease-fire.

In this novel, the university is once again a problematic source of value. Once inside the academic labyrinth, Jesse encounters and begins to model himself after the research scientist as culture hero. Oates claims she is "dazzled" by the marvels of medical science, and "optimistic about the future of medicine";[14] yet in essays she also suggests that the physician's "impulse to 'make well' may be the most sinister of Western civilization's goals" (*NHNE,* 73). In *Wonderland,* the physician is both a self-styled "divinity" and an arch-villain: amoral, egomaniacal, manipulative. One of the novel's most horrifying scenes takes place on a university's pathology research farm, where animals are victimized by inhumane and infernal experimentation and where students participate in cannibalistic rites (*W,* 236–46). *Wonderland* thus is another Oatesian *Frankenstein.*

Jesse is barely able to resist his own destruction at the hands of the novel's perverse "healers." Pedersen is only the first of a succession of imposing self-styled shamans with omnivorous appetites for power and authority from whom Jesse runs for his life. Jesse's deliverance from the freakish Dr. Peder-

sen is clearly unwished for: he defies the doctor's authority out of an awakened sense of compassion, in order to aid his anguished, alcoholic
stepmother's attempted escape from the doctor's orders. His action seems fu-
tile: Mrs. Pedersen is forcibly returned to her redolent kitchen and Jesse is, in
a stroke, disinherited. He leaves in anguish, an "invisible man" bearing Pedersen's grim death warrants (the ultimate fabulator's gesture, a verbal annihilation): "You have no existence. You are nothing . . . now you are
eradicated. . . . You are dead. You do not exist" (*W*, 184).

Ironically, making a version of Pedersen's plan his own, he regains his
poise and sense of destiny (though not, fortunately, his appetite; his Pederson
poundage melts away). Lacking the volition to write his own narrative, he almost passively finds himself going to medical school and thus perpetuating
his imposing mentor's attitudes and beliefs. At the same time, he searches for
another potential father. One attractive candidate is Dr. Cady, a former colleague of Walter Cannon (*W*, 222), who echoes the old millennialist high-
minded rhetoric. The substance of his remarks, delivered in a modern
university lecture hall, is profoundly disturbing. Cady describes the human
isolation, self-enclosure and dissociation which Jesse most dreads:

> The world is our construction, peopled by us; it is a mystery. All we know of the
> world, even our most precise laboratory findings, rests on the perception of the
> senses, but this very knowledge cannot reveal the relation of the senses to the
> outside world. (*W*, 194)

To mask his terror, Jesse responds with incredulous amusement; he wants
to challenge Cady's point of view—infinitely perspectival and solipsistic—a
grave threat to Jesse's own precarious, homeostatic balance. "Isn't the great
lesson of science *control?*" he thinks. "The lessons of homeostasis and cyber-
netics: *control?* What else mattered?" He finally dismisses the professorial
message and temporarily quells his rising panic: "If he had control of himself,
Jesse Vogel, then nothing else mattered in the universe" (*W*, 195). Yet self-
direction seems the last thing Jesse really desires: he is terrified of the Jungian
shadow-self that waits within, a "monstrous . . . secret face" (*W*, 300). He
longs for another counterfeit identity. Even when he sits uneasily in the lecture hall, he tries to project himself into Cady's being: "How to become that
man without debasing himself?" he wonders (*W*, 228). Eventually, he literally becomes Cady's son by marrying the oddly passive, intellectual Helene
Cady. Jesse wills his own submission, in an attempt to arrest the dark and
pulsing energies of his secret self.

Yet he is soon thrown almost fatally off-balance by the oddest character in
this subterranean world crowded with grotesques. Cady's assistant, Dr. T. W.
"Trick" Monk, lives up to his name: apparently committed to the ministry of
medicine, he is a clown, a trickster, a betrayer, another archetypal figure, "the

son of a god . . . failing at his inheritance" (*W,* 227). Manic and manipulative, he is thus a perverse artist, a fabulator spinning mad stories to inflame Jesse's imagination, feeding him with letters and poems which maximize the local disturbance. On the very eve of the Vogel-Cady marriage, Monk attempts to engineer his own death at Jesse's hands, as if to transform the fugitive into an assassin.

Oates clearly relishes the multiple ironies that surround this freakish academic. A death-dealer, Monk's poem of ontogeny and birth is one of the novel's several epigraphs. Although he seems to drop out of Jesse's life and out of medicine, he later reappears as the parody of a father figure, ministering (and pandering) to the counterculture. The poems he had once written in his university days ("Poems Without People") serve—retitled, but not revised—as Vietnam protest literature read at "the Tupperware Corner." A charlatan, an imperial self, a florid and obese "Humpty Dumpty," he can obviously make words mean whatever he chooses them to mean. Monk is an aging, drug-ridden version of Richard Everett. Like the narrator of *Expensive People,* he is concerned about his reviews; he seeks the purity of poetry; he is a gross and gluttonous consumer of Milky Way candy bars (*W,* 483–85). He is also one of Oates's fraudulent academics who prey on young collegians, figures whom she will satirize even more savagely in her short story collection, *The Hungry Ghosts* (1974).

Jesse's ultimate surrogate father is not Monk or Cady, but another physician; the calculating, loveless surgeon, Dr. Perrault (ironically, bearing the name of the great teller of fairytales). For the behaviorist Perrault, transcendence is a lingering romantic delusion; personality is no more than a self-indulgent fiction, "just a tradition that dies hard" (*W,* 335). Jesse yearns to reach out to Perrault ("What if their fingers touched, like that? Innocently and frankly, like that?" [*W,* 321]); Perrault regards Jesse not as a separate being but as his alter ego, his "six-foot self" (*W,* 313). Again, Jesse eagerly surrenders his autonomy: "His mind filled up with Perrault's words, Perrault's grimaces, Perrault's soul" (*W,* 396):

> Jesse had inherited all Perrault's likes and dislikes. He slipped into them as he slipped into his hospital clothes, into his gloves and mask, leaving the trembling Jesse outside in the corridor . . . no one would take Jesse's place with Perrault. He was safe, absolutely safe. (*W,* 358)

Yet such security is costly: its price is arrested development. Jesse winces when he overhears a scientific colleague call him "a copy of a human being" (*W,* 313). And his own feelings continue to surface, even in the face of his mentor's icy disdain for sentimental human relationships: Jesse "could not erase in himself a sense of absolute, utter, sweetish dependence, a helplessness in the presence of the old man that grew out of love" (*W,* 394). Perrault is another academic caricature; he seems a wacky combination of B. F. Skinner and Jung's archetypal "Wise Old Man." Instead of guiding Jesse through the ambiguous delights of the curriculum, he preaches messages of reductive mechanism; instead of offering collegial inspiration, he only admires his own reflection in his mirror-protégé. "He has part of my brain right now," he tells Cady, "memorized in his fingertips" (*W,* 338). Even after Perrault's death, Jesse acts as his surrogate, editing and completing his scientific work. Oates again dramatizes the imposing authority of the intellectual egoist.

Perrault's most outrageous performance comes during one of the novel's ritualistic mealtimes: a dinner party held at his home for Cady, Jesse, and the now pregnant Helene. The physical atmosphere is oppressive. The subliminal commands during this grotesque mock communion are "Eat Me, Drink Me." Once again, food dominates the scene: coarse, peasant-like Mrs. Perrault dishes out plate after plate of food, heavy slabs of "roast beef, oozing watery blood," bowls brimming with creamed vegetables and mashed potatoes, insisting to the assemblage of "wonderland" guests, *"Eat, Eat. Don't listen to them talking, just eat"* (*W,* 333–34). But, ironically, emphasizing the radical detachment of Jesse's professors, the intellectual thrust of their dinner table discussion is a denial of physicality itself. Both Cady and Perrault are enamoured of brains: "The brain would be better off without a body," Perrault declares (*W,* 338). Here the two part company. When Cady, a persistent Cannon vitalist, hypothesizes that there is an "invisible mind" in the brain, an "unconscious layer of personality," Perrault, the complete mechanist, disputes the existence of anything invisible: the self, for him, *is* the brain, no more and no less; nothing spiritual lies either within or beyond the body:

> When you talk about *brains,* and not old-fashioned *personalities,* now you are speaking a language I can understand. . . . I would imagine brains will enthusiastically will themselves to science just as people today will their organs or their entire bodies . . . but first we must educate people out of the vicious sentimentality of loving the body, loving the personality, the personal self, the soul, that old illusion. . . . What is the old self, after all? Only the promise of disease. . . . (*W,* 338–40)

Oates clearly intends to satirize the excesses of behaviorism, and its imposition of diabolical mind-control: her professor-scientist-manipulator is immune to human sentiment and inflated by self-love. Indeed, if he could, Perrault would invest science with the power for *all* human choice. "Only a panel of scientists is equipped to decide when a superior brain must be taken from its old body," Perrault concludes. Even Cady is startled: "When it *must* be taken?" he asks (*W,* 340). Jesse, not willing to discuss the frightening implications of his mentor's theories, clings to his homeostatic poise in frozen silence. Only Helene, overwhelmed with nausea, rises to protest the maniacal projection, defining Perrault as one the novel's murdering fathers: "You're sick . . . you're crazy, you're a killer" (*W,* 340).

This mad dinner party is a grotesque seminar whose topic is the division between body and mind, a verbal encounter of perverse societal and academic attitudes. To these men of science, feelings are a threat to rational control; thus they attempt to reduce the "soul" to an operable mechanical entity, the "brain." The subjugation and detestation of women is also exaggerated in this quintessentially masculine world. Pregnancy, traditionally a benign and hopeful sign, is presented as a life-threatening condition in *Wonderland*: indeed, the pregnancy of Jesse's mother triggered Willard Harte's despair and homicidal fury in the opening scene. Helene's "swollen stomach" looks both "ripe" and "fragile" to Jesse, and he is "afraid something terrible would happen to her" (*W,* 340). His mentors are less sympathetic. As they attempt to suppress their own sentimental impulses, these doctors similarly seek to deny the reality of feminine identity:

> Perrault continued to smile toward Helene. Jesse realized slowly that the old man did not believe in women, in their existence. They did not matter. They could not understand, it was hopeless to talk to them; and yet one had to talk to them out of politeness. . . . And perhaps Jesse himself did not believe in women the way he believed in men. (*W,* 335)

To Jesse, women are not subhuman; nevertheless, they seem mysterious and frightening, represented not by literary heroines but by the curious and monstrous graffiti which draw his wondering stare even as a boy. He imagines a terrifying disproportion between women's minds ("the head at the far end of the body small as a pea" [*W,* 301]) and their bodies, a foreshortened perspective that results from the superimposition of sexual fascination and disgust, desire and dread:

> Someone has added to the drawing with another, blunter pencil, making the body boxlike, the space between the legs shaded in to a hard black rectangle like a door. The arms have also been changed to walls and even the suggestion of brick added to them. . . . It is a mysterious drawing, two mysterious drawings, one on top of the other like a dream that fades into another dream, a nightmare conquered by another! . . . It is something you could walk into and lose yourself in, all that empty blackness. (*W,* 30–31)

Later this boyhood nightmare is confirmed by the actual sight of the drunken, nude, obese Mrs. Pederson sprawled on the bathroom floor:

> The head at the far end of the body seemed too small for it, as if it were an afterthought. So blank, so mottled and curdled a face, it could have been any face at all—it was the body that was important, exaggerated, swollen to the shape of

a large oblong box, a rectangle like a barn. . . . The body was so large that Jesse felt it pull at him. . . . He could not run away. (*W*, 157–58)

When, in the latter part of *Wonderland*, Oates expands the narrative point of view to incorporate the feminine perspective, giving voice to Jesse's wife and then his daughter, the women cannot overcome this hideous vision of their own sexuality. Imprisoned by the culture's misogynistic fiction, they also cannot create a viable identity or support others groping for a sense of self. Jesse vainly seeks a loving ghost writer to complete his story, a Jungian "anima" to offset his animus, to end his loveless and lonely flight:

Somewhere there were words for him, for Jesse, the exact words that would explain his life. But he did not know them. . . . It remained for someone else—a woman, perhaps—to draw these sacred words out of him, to justify him, redeem him as Jesse—he could not create himself. Not alone. (*W*, 349)

But if Oates regards *Wonderland's* doctor-fabulators as perverse versions of "Wise Old Men," the women in the novel are even more radically inverted Jungian types: not earth-mothers, but vampires, narcissistic rather than self-sacrificing, attempting to frustrate rather than realize their "sacred" biological destiny. They are also dangerous wantons, successors to Karen Herz, Clara Walpole, Nada Everett, Nadine. There is the beautiful Reva Denk, who drives the men who love her into self-castrating frenzies. Reva agrees to meet with the infatuated Jesse, but instead of returning his passion, she leads him into an art gallery to see the work of her current lover. Knowing that she has teasingly eluded his embrace, Jesse stands bewildered before the canvases. Reva draws no "sacred words" from his dreaming mind, but rather presents him with images of his darkest fears:

All this mess was a mockery of life, of the natural forms of life. Deterioration of vision. Unbalance, collapse. Spasms. Brain damage. Cancer. A crowding of the natural forms of life, a crowding of the form of the canvases itself—the madness of colors and shapes without human sense. (*W*, 353)

In a further irony, it soon appears that Reva has only agreed to the tryst because she envisions Jesse as a potential abortionist. Infatuated with her own cover girl allure, she offers Jesse not redemptive union but sterility, madness, and deathliness.

Helene Cady's cool intelligence had promised Jesse a refuge from his own fearful sexual desires. But their marriage is predictably flawed. She, too, is deformed, frigid, and fatally divided: "Always she had feared her body," she thinks; detached, she wonders, "Did she inhabit her body like a tenant?" While Jesse, however insecure, is in pursuit of life, discarding old selves, adapting and changing, Helene describes woman's life as a process of burial by accretion, static and cumulative:

> Layer by layer the years formed her: Helene was now a married woman, the same age as her husband, and she was also nineteen years old, she was twelve years old again, she was a child. All of the layers were intense, quivering, conscious of existing. Conscious of being female, a little ashamed of being female. (*W*, 267–68)

Like many of her fictive sisters in Oates's other work, Helene's female identity, defined by male authorities, is a humiliating cosmic trap. Her dilemma is symbolized by the gynecologist's examining table: "All women are equal on that table, their heels caught in those stirrups. All women are the same woman," she thinks (*W*, 275). The vision is self-alienating; Helene literally becomes that monstrous graffiti-self which the boy Jesse viewed with horror:

> And suddenly she saw a young woman lying on a table. Herself, contorted like that: a woman on a table, on her back, her face twisted and demented. She had fallen from a great height and her face was twisted permanently. . . . What was the raw reddened gap between her legs? So vivid it sucked all the air into it—the entire white sky might be drawn into it and lost. (*W*, 278)

During her prenatal examination, she explodes in fury; her body fights off the speculum's mechanical penetration as if the gynecologist were a rapist. Yet she is ultimately vulnerable to a more relentless biological fate. Turning from abortion, she submits to the monster within—a fetus, her living "minotaur": "Small, soft, gentle cells, coils of absolute power" (*W*, 279). In childbirth she feels victimized by external male domination; she is an even farther "distance from herself, from her own body. . . . She was being destroyed by her husband" (*W*, 412).

Helene as everywoman lives in a world of enemies: her unborn children, her husband, a world of gapers and directors who have turned her into a self-hating creature trapped inside a delusively attractive shell. In an inversion of one of Lewis Carroll's metaphors, Helene fights the looking glass. "She hated that moment just before the mirror self is recognized and acknowledged. All her life she had been posing, moving, speaking in front of other people who watched her closely, and so she did not need mirrors" (*W*, 408).

In her final scenes, Helene retreats from life's demands. Grudgingly agreeing to meet a would-be lover in Wonderland East, a suburban shopping mall, she is flooded by long-supressed anarchic energies: her own frustrated sexual longings seem derided and mocked by a violent demonstration of student-war protestors who threaten her, like her own children: "They were young and they hated her" (*W*, 424). Turning away from her suitor, she discharges her passion by viciously slapping the face of a young girl—declaring her divorce from society and self: "It was over: the tyranny of her body, the yearning for other bodies, for talking and touching and dreaming and loving. She had freed herself. It was over" (*W*, 424). But the freedom Helene thus achieves is a sterile escape, the freedom of a catatonic.

As the novel moves into its most problematic last episodes, Jesse's daughter Michele—Shell, Shelley—assumes central importance, playing out old dramas and exploring new roles. She is, as her name suggests, fragile, hollow, vulnerable. More than any other character, however, she offers Jesse the language to complete his own story: giving him a guardian's name, a mentor's part. Ironically, Shelley is cast in Jesse's own fugitive image as a teenage runaway, and Jesse is forced to become that self he had dreaded since boyhood, a pursuing father.

The father-daughter story is the final segment of *Wonderland*'s flight pattern. Initially, Jesse convinces himself he is *not* a menacing, authoritarian, professorial father-figure, imposing assignments of terror: "he only wanted to protect their lives" (*W*, 399). But his means of protection is questionable, a goad to future violence. Shaken by both political violence and private threats—the Kennedy assassination, Shelley's subsequent hysteria—Jesse buys a gun, carrying a concealed weapon from that point on. Adopting not only the props, but Willard Harte's very attitudes, Jesse finds himself obsessed by familial concerns:

> It was so hard to keep a family, Jesse thought suddenly, that maybe it was better to give up. Better to give up, erase them all, destroy them, obliterate them and the memory of them, wipe everything out. A father could wipe out everything he had ever done and be free. A clean, pure, empty being, a void. . . . (*W*, 444)

It is no wonder that Shelley cries in terror, "You want to kill me" (*W*, 445); or that she describes a lifelong fear that her father "would eat us up" (*W*, 461). Thus, she plots her own escape.

In Oates's *Wonderland,* Shelley is Alice; hers is the darkest, deepest plunge. The author once more makes her didactic intentions explicit, identifying the subtext in Shelley's narrative, and even providing a brief reading. In one of her letters to Jesse, sent while she is in flight, Shelley describes her initiation into Carroll's fictive universe:

> When I was nine years old Grandfather Cady gave me a large illustrated copy of *Alice in Wonderland* and *Alice's Adventures Through the Looking-Glass.* I sat with it up on the table before me, a big heavy book, reading the paragraphs one by one and trying not to fall into them and lose myself, trying not to feel terror, *it's only a book;* the neck and the straggly hair and the wild, enlarged eyes, the girl reduced to the size of a mouse, sailing through the air dragged by the red queen's hand, sitting at the end of a banquet table while legs of mutton waddled down toward her to eat her. (*W*, 401)

Elsewhere, Oates mentions these books as part of the imaginative legacy of her own schoolgirl days; she herself reads Alice's adventures more as nightmare than childish fantasy.[15] In Shelley's world, they are uncanny representations of the hallucinations of the drug culture, the brutal handling of jail matrons, transformations brought about by disease and malnutrition. When Jesse finds her lying emaciated and near death in a sordid tenement, Shelley lacks the resources to bring herself back to the surface: "I am not here. There's nobody here," she whispers to her horrified father, "I don't exist and you can't get me" (*W,* 475). It is the ultimate fabulator's act: flagrant, wanton self-erasure. The novel's last scenes rerun the scenario of aggression and submission, pursuit and escape. Shelley has run from her father's control to the arms of lawless exploiters and panderers, who pass themselves off as guides through the world's labyrinths but reduce her to a symbolic object, a "Fetish," a pitiable victim. Calling for help, longing for heroic rescue, she sends her father letters filled with clues to her whereabouts.

Oates has brought her characters to the point where a conversion seems required—but the routes toward transcendence are barricaded by antithetical forces. Thus, as Oates nears the end of her *Wonderland* journey, she wrestles with the problem she introduced in the essay "New Heaven and Earth": how to transform "intermediary chapters" into new visionary conclusions. Shelley's story seems the most promising candidate for literal as well as metaphoric conversion. Even as a child, she fumbles with ordinary language, lost for "the right words." Her father uneasily commands her "to speak only in complete sentences." For Shelley, however, the only complete sentence found beyond the world of books is death. The very finish of art terrifies her: "To be a complete thought," she thinks, "you have to come to the end of yourself" (*W,* 431).

Running for her life, Shelley moves out of the range of conventional literary beginnings and endings: her history emerges out of cinematic flashbacks and curious postal fragments. In contrast, Jesse is woefully weary of living in a world of incessant change; Shelley's flight is another threat to his fragile balance. Unlike his daughter, he avidly seeks completion of his life sentence, filled with "despair that nothing was ever finished, nothing was ever clear to him" (*W,* 288).

Clearly, Jesse is cheated of a happy ending, the promise of coming of age. An early Oates reader, Ralph Berets, comments on the resulting frustration for both the hero and reader of *Wonderland.* Noting that it "does not follow a traditional 'Bildungsroman' pattern," he suggests Oates may be testing new models of Jungian "individuation." Nevertheless, he finds that Jesse's trip reaches a dead end:

> Jesse's quest throughout the novel has been to discover, through ritualistic means, a way to return to his origins or transcend his personal limitations. . . . Instead of accomplishing this task, as we would have expected from earlier traditions that incorporated this quest motif, in the modern setting the hero comes up empty handed every time and ends up with death and not resurrection leaning on him. (Berets, 12)

To Berets, such an inverted rite of passage represents a critique of contemporary American life. Yet Oates's failure to resolve her hero's desperate quest may signify a deeper level of artistic disturbance: a loss of faith in fictional narrative itself.

Oates had raised this issue before the publication of *Wonderland*. Characters in her earlier work express contempt for literature; they find themselves more attuned to cinematic representation. Thus, Jesse seems to share Swan Walpole's view of reality when he imagines that human events come "out of the darkness of a movie house—flashing out of the confused splotches of color and light that [make] up the screen's images, like the underside of a dream forcing its way to the surface of the mind" (*W*, 228). But Swan is fearfully certain his life is part of a master plot, with a prearranged finale. In *Wonderland*, Jesse observes his life as something only experienced in parts. Betrayed by a succession of possible scenarios, sickened by what Laing calls "ontological insecurity," he is "absurdly, abruptly grateful for the movies ... for their progress in patches and spurts, not as a coherent story but as the jagged bits of a story that never quite added itself up to anything believable" (*W*, 228).

As she has done in earlier novels, but here with more devastating effect, Oates uses academic metaphor to expose the disjunction between literature's story and life. Like her student in *them*, Jesse has a curious reading disability. But while Maureen is a resistant reader, Jesse is helpless in the face of shapely and imposing fiction:

> Years ago, his freshman English instructor at the university had told him there was something odd about his understanding of literature—he was unable to follow a plot. . . . The necessary pattern, the rhythm that demanded completion, the internal heat, the gravity that forced everything to a suitable conclusion. (*W*, 228–29)

Literature is, for Jesse, as it is for Maureen, for Swan, and for Richard, a lie. But while these characters stridently affirm their own reality, Jesse seems in danger of losing his identity when he uneasily confesses "he did not know what a 'story' was" (*W*, 229). No form—literary, cinematic, familial, academic—can give ultimate significance to his shattered and unfinished life.

Perhaps it is not suprising that the quest for an ending is also Oates's chief artistic problem in *Wonderland*. Struggling to move beyond "intermediary chapters," she designed not one but several scenarios of completion for the novel, forced into the role of fabulator as she tried those endings on for size. And although Friedman believes that the final edition brought Oates's quest to a satisfactory conclusion, the alternative endings of *Wonderland* continue to raise questions for readers of the novel.

Each suggests a different direction for both the author and her fugitive hero. The first takes the form of a dramatic allegory: a play (actually performed off-Broadway) which appeared in 1970, the year before the publication of *Wonderland,* in *Partisan Review.* Significantly, it is called "Ontological Proof of My Existence"; it is a parable of the divided self. Its heroine, Shelley, is a hapless young woman held captive in a sordid tenement apartment. She is also a character in search of an author, uncertain of her physical and psychic identity, lacking a mirror to confirm her existence or at least provide a shape for her terror. Oates suggests she is a jigsaw puzzle waiting to be put together by the men in her life. One by one, they come on stage. Peter is first, her pimp and the self-styled pure ego of the drama, contemptuous and abusive, claiming that Shelley can only exist by his choice. The Jesse-figure, Father, arrives next, bearing a slide projector to remind his daughter of her biological and familial past. Peter sarcastically calls him an "old god! Old mythology" (*OP,* 495); in the youth and drug culture, Father—the superego—is prematurely enfeebled and impotent.

Father's weakness goads the others into violence. Shelley and Peter knock his projector over, muddling and scattering his images of history and identity and sending him away distraught and confused—just as the last man, Shelley's husband Martin, enters. To complete this odd pyschodrama, Martin seems to represent the id or sexual drive; but he, too, is crippled, bound by Oedipal urges: "My mother is suspicious . . . she worries about me. I'm only thirty-two" (*OP,* 497). At Peter's urging, he wrestles the limp, exhausted Shelley to the floor. The play ends with her muffled cries. Peter stands in the spotlight, a mockery of his Dostoevskian forebears, the isolated and arrogant survivor: "I prize my existence personally. I am a young man standing at a sink in a condemned building, in a condemned city." Yet his egoistic triumph offers him no reprieve from his own ontological doubts; as the curtain falls, he plaintively asks, "Will we all die, then? Will we all come to an end? Will our existences be questioned so cruelly?" (*OP,* 497).

The play ends with the general collapse of Freudian and literary ideologies. Oates dramatizes the surrender of authority—perhaps the prelude to new visions of the self, but at this point in human history, premature and even dangerous. Working with the same ideas in the concluding scenes of her novel, she also warns that the self surrenders its authority only at the greatest risk. The objectivity which her mad scientists advocate paves the way for a fascist's hegemony. Paternal control—as Oates shows from the novel's earliest pages—simultaneously protects and threatens the dependent self.

Shelley's friends from the counterculture in *Wonderland* are like Peter in the dramatic version: exploiters with even more ruthless designs on her body and spirit. Dropouts, they turn against the very curriculum which has created the context for protest: "History is dead," they claim; "Passion is the only destiny. . . . Books are dead . . . the hell with books and reading" (*W,* 429). Shelley's lover Noel debases her in the name of revolution, leading her, painted and naked, a "Fetish" rather than a woman, on a leash along a public beach. Without the desire or instinct for self-preservation, she almost dies in a fall, encouraged by Noel and his group: "I saw the street coming & gave in to it, I let myself go, there is no resistance between matter and spirit if you can dominate" (*W*, 461). When her father appears, Noel sadistically orders her to jump from the window again. Indeed, in *Wonderland*, Joyce Carol Oates exposes the "mystic awareness" of the radical youth movement as a fraudulent mask hiding a face full of hatred. When Jesse moves among these young activists on the city streets, he is conscious only of a perverse and nihilistic "communion of noise":

> They were children's faces in the street, rising and blossoming and on the verge of detonation. Their faces strained to explode. Mouths and eyes out of shape, distorted, a lovely sleeping yearning to them as they pressed forward into the back of other kids. (*W*, 449)

Instead of love Jesse feels a rising, self-confirming rage:

> Jesse hated this formlessness. He was seized with a sudden hatred for it, almost a nausea . . . hated that merging, that mobbing. . . . Better to destroy them all, Jesse thought. Better to die than to descend into this frenzy, to be lost in this anonymous garbage. This strange mass consciousness revolted him. (*W*, 449)

In "New Heaven and Earth," Oates speaks in revolutionary accents. But in *Wonderland*, the "mass consciousness" born on the campuses of the sixties is finally a counterfeit rather than a true conversion of spirit, perhaps more dangerous than the old mythologies. Unmoved by the "greening of America," perhaps disappointed in her own quest for transformation, Oates voices a compelling conservative critique. Her protean hero Jesse turns away from the slogans of communal peace and love: "He would return to the world in which he was a single human being, a single consciousness with a destiny he must fulfill" (*W*, 449). Even if that destiny makes him a killer-father, it may be preferable to the destruction of moral and cultural value set in motion by these lawless children.

In Oates's novel, Jesse does not suffer the fate of the grieving but impotent Father in "Ontological Proof of My Existence," but his route nevertheless seems uncertain. In the hardcover first edition of *Wonderland*, Oates sounds a tentative note of optimism. Jesse threatens and bribes Shelley's lover, and prepares to bathe her, to heal her, to bring her home—only to be met by her terrified resistance, and to see her again run from his arms. Breathless, he pursues her to the borders of the city, to the chain-link freeway fences, and finally to the edge of a body of water where a boat mysteriously waits. He helps her into it; all at once they are "bobbing free . . . in the rough current." Jesse has relaxed his own quest for control: "he did not know the name of this water or where it might lead him. . . . 'Don't be afraid, Shelley,' he whispered. He threw . . . the pistol in the water." Drifting down the stream in the moonlight, he anguishes over human fate, and mourns the passing of the others he has tried to love, all inexplicably scattered in a limitless cosmos:

> Where were they all going, abandoning him? Was there a universe of broken people, flung out of their orbits but still living, was there perhaps a Jesse there already in that void, the true, pure undefiled Jesse, who watched this struggling Jesse with pity? . . . The boat drifted most of the night. Near dawn it was picked up by a large handsome cruiser, a Royal Mounted Police boat, a dazzling sight with its polished wood and metal and its trim of gold and blue.[16]

Shedding the trappings of his old personality, Jesse awaits his soul's deliverance and a possible resolution of life's contradictions. Oates seems to envision him free of crippling mentors and father figures, on the opening leg of a journey toward self-realization, toward individuation, with the wraith of his daughter at his side.

Although this ending offers a glimpse of remedial and even visionary possibility, Oates seemed troubled by it, obsessed by a nagging sense of its inappropriateness which she described in interviews, personal correspondence, and essays. In 1972, she wrote,

> It has been months since I've finished *Wonderland,* but I can't seem to get free of it. I keep reliving parts of it. . . . It's like a bad dream that never came to a completion. It's the first novel I have written that doesn't end in violence, that doesn't liberate the hero through violence, and therefore there is still a sickish, despairing, confusing atmosphere about it.[17]

By the middle of 1973, she had moved to revise and "correct" her fiction, to align the ending with what she believed were the true alternatives of her characters, rather than the outcome she herself might have preferred:

> My sense that the original ending of *Wonderland* was an ego-imposed ending and not the true ending came to me in a kind of dream, a very powerful *intellectual* dream without visual images of any kind; I got up immediately and wrote the second ending, without hesitating, and without revision . . . it seemed to me that my entire life was to be channelled through this re-routing (or my life might possibly have come to an end!—it was almost that dramatic).[18]

In another essay, Oates comments as a practicing critic on her own process of revision, using *Wonderland*'s endings to exemplify her personal recognition of the demands imposed by art and the necessary submission of the artist to the characters, the texture of reality, and to the story demanding to be told. As she describes the novel's history, she also acknowledges the perennial tension between her academic and creative impulses:

> Only once in my entire life did I very consciously—very intellectually—resist my intuition regarding something I wrote (the conclusion of one of my novels, *Wonderland*): with the result that, in deepest humility, I had to revise it after its publication in the United States—causing the kind of confusion and inconvenience I dread.[19]

Having moved toward visionary possibility in the first hardcover edition of *Wonderland,* Oates in the definitive edition retreats from a view of transformation. The novel thus is a kind of palimpsest. Her re-edited ending is briefer, more violent, and foreshortened. The first lines of the original hardcover text—a nightmare of pursuit—have been eliminated entirely. Having discarded his marks of identification, but now keeping his gun, Jesse locates the wasted, half-conscious Shelley in a sordid Yonge Street loft. Accepting his paternal legacy, he waves his pistol, seemingly more to rescue than to kill: "*No dying tonight. Not on my hands*" (*W,* 478). Terrified, Noel flees, and Jesse is filled with Faustian glee and a sense of his own potency: "the power to hold her here and to keep her from dying . . . how he loved this control, this certainty!" (*W,* 478). The father and child move toward the threshold, not toward a mystical dream or a mysterious stream, but back into the reality of the urban environment. The enfeebled Shelley continues to protest that her father is a murderer and "a devil," to which Jesse can only reply, "Am I?" (*W,* 479).

To Friedman, the second ending is formally satisfying, bringing the story full circle. For Oates, this is a victory, but on terms which mark our time and her novel as intermediary and perhaps untransformable. Jesse has consciously chosen to impose his will in the face of Shelley's continuing resistance, to write a finish to his own history of protean evasion by assuming a starkly conventional role, restoring an uneasy, homeostatic balance appropriate in a world of homicidal and psychic threat. The route of Jungian individuation is closed to all of these characters. Modern society is still trapped in a combative scheme; the radical campus insurgents are compromised and corrupt. Jesse's final stance might once have seemed heroic; he is, after all, a rescuer and healer. But even in this second version of *Wonderland* it is clearly problematic. Oates leaves no doubt of his predicament as we hear him exult in surging hatred, even after his own lifelong experience as the prey of terrifying hunters: "What joy, to shoot him in the face!" (*W,* 477). His saving act seems as loveless as Helene's vicious slap in Wonderland East.

This may explain why Oates has called *Wonderland* an "immoral novel," an experience "behind me now," a book "which I won't ever reread, myself."[20] In a sense it is a self-erasing and certainly a disturbing text. Yet while she settles for less than she had initially hoped, she has begun to clear some space in our littered and ravaged psychic territory, dramatizing the struggles of a new sort of character—fluid, fugitive, protean—who may some day be the agent of cultural transformation. At this point, however, Oates tells us in her revised *Wonderland,* recognition of the phantasmagoria of personality only provides a vision of selfhood which little in our traditional literature or intellectual history equips us to accommodate or understand.

5 Beyond the Looking-Glass
Do with Me What You Will,
The Assassins, and *Childwold*

Late in her seventh novel, *Do with Me What You Will* (1973), Joyce Carol Oates interrupts her narrative to present a piece of news footage—the report of a maddened father's homicidal pursuit of his runaway child:

> The father kicked the door in and began screaming at them. . . . The girl and the others stared at him and saw a man of middle age, in a windbreaker, weeping, holding a Springfield in his hands. A few seconds later three people were dead, including the daughter, and a fourth—a young man in his twenties . . . was dying, part of his face blown away. (*DWM,* 420)

By now, readers can recognize a familiar Oatesian device: a variation on a theme previously introduced and reworked in other fictions. In this case, she presents yet another version of the problematic finale of *Wonderland.* Interestingly enough, however, this is no fiction but a true story: the factual event that served as the germ and inspiration of Oates's earlier novel. Oates suggests that there is no line between reality and fiction in the contemporary combat zone; the combatants themselves move through a world without safe categories, forced to take the law into their own hands. A curious reminder of the unresolved tensions of *Wonderland,* the scene stands in an interesting relation to *Do with Me What You Will*—her next novel, which also begins in a realm of uncertainty, betrayal, and multiple pursuit—but this time ends in love.

Oates reopens the questions left unanswered after *Wonderland's* deathward plunge in order to seek new alternatives, both formal and thematic, for the self in process, the phantasmagoria of personality. Like so many of her novels, *Do with Me What You Will* is a family drama, describing the relationships of a series of parent-victimizers and terrorized children desperate to arrest the slippage. But the two novels resolve the struggle in radically different ways. While Jesse Vogel dedicates his life to achieving homeostasis, adapting his personality and even his body to suit a succession of father-surrogates, the heroine of this novel, Elena Howe, fights for her life *against* the stasis imposed on her by a society of parents, gapers, and worshipful admirers. Jesse becomes judge and jury in *Wonderland's* brutally foreshortened second ending, willfully resisting his impulse to gun down the young nonconformists who have abducted his daughter. Elena, surrendering her will, throws herself on the mercy of the court and a new life begins to take shape before her dazzled eyes. Acting as her own ideal critical reader, Oates thus deliberately takes up her own images, themes and models of character with revisionary intent.

Both novels set the stage for abduction and betrayal in familiar territory, again exposing the schoolroom's false security. In the first scenes of *Wonderland,* Oates ironically juxtaposes familial conflict and high school holiday rituals which offer the hero no protection against the homicidal intentions of his father. In the opening of *Do with Me What You Will,* another menacing father, Leo Ross, lurks on the periphery of school property, where his enchantingly beautiful daughter, Elena, unaware of her danger, plays on the other side of an "ordinary chain-link fence . . . the universe condemned to a few acres of real estate" (*DWM,* 16). Divorced from his wife, Ardis, and denied visitation rights to his daughter by court decree, Ross has plotted Elena's abduction with absurd care. In clownish disguise—wig, false glasses, stiff grey hat and oversized topcoat—he waits tensely for her appearance with the anxiety of a lunatic lover.

Elena represents, even at the age of seven, a goddess to Ross: the sight of her is heartbreaking; her face is "a miracle, yet terrible; that face. It did exist. Because it existed, the universe was not at peace. . . . It was a face to be dreamed over, cherished. . . . You would have to snap your fingers, shout, shake something to make a commotion before those eyes would come into focus" (*DWM,* 18). He harbors no homicidal intentions; indeed, he thinks "she's worth dying for" (*DWM,* 33, 34). But such possessive and fanatic adoration, as Oates shows from the start, is also monstrous and grotesque: Ross nearly kills himself to reach his daughter, as, with a burst of preternatural strength, he lifts up the fence. The child, naively compliant, the good school girl who puts herself unwittingly in peril, crawls under it, out of the safe and bounded playground and into her father's punishing custody.

Yearning for escape, Ross bears the signs of fatal rupture both psychologically and physically: driving, doubled over in pain, his car veers toward near-accident. He is falsely comforted by the trappings of power and order and plan: maps, freeways, the gun he carries (as inadequate to ward off the world's threats as the gun Jesse buys after the Kennedy assassination). Father and daughter move, in a parody of westering, toward the pure streams of Yellowstone Park, but once there, they are pelted by the cold rain of an indifferent universe. Opening the cabin door, they meet a horrifying sight of nature in the raw:

> There was a wolf—or maybe a fox or a coyote. It was dragging a long snake. The animal only glanced at Leo and his daughter and then whipped the snake up into the air, cracking it. Then it began to eat the snake. "Hey! Get the hell out of here!" Leo yelled. . . . "I didn't know they were such cannibals," he said. He closed the door and looked at Elena, who was terrified. He hoped this wouldn't poison her against Yellowstone Park. He said, "This trip of ours is an educational adventure" (*DWM*, 36–37)

In her study of "individuation" in Oates's fiction, Rose Marie Burwell sees this scene as a Jungian vision; the snake is "both a collective and universal principle of evil and a personal symbol of male sexuality."[1] But Jungian images only suggest Oates's wider textual range: an array of mythic, poetic, and even clinical reference. She is also reimagining the Miltonic parody of her first novel, *With Shuddering Fall* as she describes "Eve's" initiation into the combative and bestial world, and mocking the lingering romantic concept of nature as peaceable kingdom. Oates's allusive composite vision may seem hallucinogenic, but—as she signals in the Jamesian epigraph—it is all too real: "the world as it stands is no illusion, no phantasm, no evil dream of a night; we wake up to it again for ever and ever; we can neither forget it nor deny it nor dispense with it." The epigraph prepares the reader for a multi-leveled narrative. In *Do with Me What You Will,* Oates exposes the false but pervasive mythologies (Jungian archetypes among them) whose effect is to deny reality and thus cripple the human personality.

One target is the pseudo-science of popular psychology. "Children can survive anything," Leo Ross thinks, denying his culpability and driving desperately onward (*DWM*, 40). This is a dangerous fiction. On their harrowing journey, Elena regresses to the infantile, barely able to swallow milk, losing the power of speech. She takes on a fetal look: her eyes swell shut, her scalp is encrusted with the residue of hair-dye Ross has used to disguise her radiant beauty. Finally, through his own pain and insane visions, Ross realizes the child is dying. His fantasy disrupted by this reminder of mortality, he writes out a legal confession and abandons Elena to the police, the psychiatrists, and her mother Ardis. Ironically, when Elena is located, Ardis seems more concerned with Elena's appearance than with her health ("Imagine, dyeing a child's hair black! *Black!* A child with that light a complexion" [*DWM*, 53]). Yet the autistic, anorexic and paralyzed child is aroused by the sound of her mother's jarring voice. "I love you," she murmurs to Ardis—breaking her comatose silence, but also surrendering her enfeebled will to another questionable and powerful authority (*DWM*, 56).

Jesse's life had been determined by his father's appetite for death. The pattern of Elena's existence (and the structure of *Do with Me What You Will*) is also shaped by this initial episode of perilous abduction, manipulative tutelage, and paralyzed compliance; yet in her case it is a prelude to a series of providential awakenings. Oates thus sketches out a far more hopeful vision of male-female dissonance in this fallen world, where love and cannibalism are dangerously close.

The novel is also her first extended feminist critique, justifying its dedication to the president of N.O.W. Medical science and the obsession to "make well" provided the ethical framework of *Wonderland*. "Law"—the authority of the masculine intellectual—is the realm of value invoked in this novel, a system of regulation and argumentation which Oates suggests may do violence to the feminine self. Ross seems only half-mad when he tells Elena she should be ruled by magic rather than by lawyers and courts. "What has the law to do with love?" he asks (*DWM,* 24). When Ardis appears on the scene, prattling of lawsuits and indictments, she is crassly if skillfully exploiting male conventions, reserving her pose of feminity as a fall-back position. Having manipulated the authorities through legalistic maneuvers, Ardis slyly throws herself on their mercy, declaring "Oh, hell, the law is too much for a woman to figure out" (*DWM,* 550). Her own display of approved "feminine" qualities of affection and nurturance is also fraudulent, vastly different from the reality of her ugly, selfish relationships with daughter and husband. It is perhaps understandable that Elena opts for inaction, the strategy of the somnambulist.

Oates's feminine model contrasts with the masculine mode of action in *Wonderland*. Jesse (like Jules before him in *them*) attempts to withstand life's assaults by continuous flight; Elena finds the best protection is Maslowian "homonomy"—in her case, acquiescence carried to an almost pathological extreme. She is not the enthralled, enchanted heroine we have met in fairytales, but the feminine type aptly described by feminist critic Nina Auerbach: "Imagine a Sleeping Beauty who only seems asleep, for her powers are secretly superior to those of the wicked witch who subdued her and the handsome prince who aroused her."[2]

In *Do with Me What You Will,* Lewis Carroll is again the cocreator if not presiding genius. Oates's reference is explicit for any reader who might otherwise miss her didactic intentions. Men and women meet in group encounters where "a game might be in session, involving parquet squares like squares on a chess board, people like players who had come bravely out onto the board to risk themselves" (*DWM,* 136). This looking-glass world is above ground, even more terrifying than the subterranean labyrinths of *Wonderland*. Indeed, the mirror image serves as a mocking reference point for Oates's heroine, enforcing societal expectations and masculine desires, concealing rather than revealing Elena's true nature. To Oates, this is Eve's predicament—the tragically divided feminine self she has imagined since her earliest fiction. At first sight, the mirror frames the compliant mask of the beautiful heroine; but as Oates explores the mysteries of the feminine interior, it becomes a terrifyingly permeable boundary, "like a trick mirror," through which "someone is watching" (*DWM*, 389–90). It is the emblem of a new Narcissus, a reflection of the ontological doubt and paranoia of the claustrophobic modern self.

Jesse creates himself as a surrogate for a series of "fathers." The traumatized Elena serves as an image rather than an original; a prefabricated text rather than a poet or genuine muse. Thinking back to her childhood terrors, Elena remembers how intensely she desired to placate her father-abductor: "*I was smiling like a mirror with his smile*" (*DWM*, 34). Similarly, she tries to live her adult life as the face in the mirror which everyone admires, sternly suppressing every rebellious, personal, errant impulse. When her mother— Ardis, "Bonita," "Marya," a comic mistress of disguises glimpsed in teasing mirrored reflections—assumes the custody of Elena's life, Elena becomes the quintessential feminine mirror image, the fashion model:

> Men propped her up onto stools, tilted her face, shaped a smile with their fingers, left the smile, came back to it in a few minutes and reworked it, bringing their serious, frowning faces close to hers and yet not close at all. She felt them but she did not really feel them. There was a distance between them; she was not threatened. . . . *A little doll.* (*DWM*, 62)

The relationship of photographer to model, in which each considers the other an object rather than a sensate being, becomes in turn the model for Elena's erotic experience, requiring her to be distant, plastic, and dependent. *In Do with Me What You Will,* Oates demonstrates with horrifying clarity that such acquiescence puts the heroine at mortal risk. Elena must rely upon her directors to turn her face from blinding lights, to move her out of the path of danger. Under their sway, she becomes a sleeping beauty indeed: "the most important thing in life is sleep. . . . Absolute unconsciousness," Ardis ironically advises (*DWM*, 59), and Elena obviously takes her at her word. As her inner life petrifies, she becomes more and more dependent upon outward reflections to believe that she exists at all. Thus, even at one of the crucial junctures in her life, the meeting her mother arranges with her future husband, Marvin Howe, Elena must look beyond them both to confirm her own presence:

> Elena could see herself faintly, or someone who looked like her, in a frosted mirror not far away: the head held high, stiffly, the head of blond hair like a wire cloud around her head. She checked the image every few minutes to make sure it was still there. (*DWM*, 91)

Ardis also influences Elena's view of sexuality by promoting her own contemptuous view of men: "They're like automatic washers that must go through certain cycles, one after the other, it's all so predictable and boring."

Marriage can only be good "for women who have no imagination, who can't think of anything better to do with their lives" (*DWM*, 77). Since Elena obviously is relegated to that category, her mother negotiates a marriage contract on her behalf, insuring Elena's financial security but deepening her ontological insecurity. During the "pretrial" bargaining process, she even programs her pliant daughter to attempt suicide if more reasonable methods fail; and she readily agrees to Howe's final terms, which exclude her permanently from Elena's life. The conversion of a living bond to a legal arrangement represents the ultimate perversion of human relationships for Oates, even worse than the devious and life-denying maneuvers of Clara Walpole in *A Garden of Earthly Delights.*

On the other hand, it seems an ideal arrangement for the mysterious and prominent lawyer, Marvin Howe. Howe is a composite figure: a modern egoist created by prevailing models in law, literature, philosophy, and psychology. Coming from obscure origins, recognizing Elena as a beauty worthy of idolatry, he is another of Oates's Gatsby imitators, hoping to defeat time by wedding himself to something incorruptible—and thus inhuman. His view of Elena is also akin to the blind masculine madness which possessed her father, Leo Ross. With forensic flourish, Howe sets forth a deposition of worshipful love; actually, it is a hymn of self-infatuation which denies her physical and spiritual reality. Howe plays Pygmalion in reverse, turning a real woman into a lifeless icon:

> To me you're someone in a vacuum, you're from the outside of everything that's physical and degrading. . . . Isn't it? I am a convert to whatever you represent and all my strength has gone into it, into you; I can't stop my love for you, my belief in you. . . . Because it really is my salvation . . . you (are) like a woman in a dream to me, a woman who is dreaming but who is being dreamed as well. (*DWM*, 532–34)

Clearly, despite the misreadings of this novel by some feminists, Oates shares the outrage which lies at the heart of the contemporary feminist critique. Her picture of Elena Howe as mirror is a striking recreation of Virginia Woolf's portrait of a lady in *A Room of One's Own*: "Women have served all these centuries as looking-glasses, possessing the magic and delicious power of reflecting the figure of man at twice its natural size."[3] When Howe wins possession of Elena, it is her looking-glass self which promises him the realization of his most monstrous imaginings, a radical fusion of the American Dream and myth of the *Ubermensch*:

> From the time I was a child I felt the world wasn't large enough for me. Even those vast spaces, the scrubland of Oklahoma! No, I wanted somehow to make it expand into other dimensions, to *force* it into expansion. . . . I want to stretch the boundaries . . . push the world out into another dimension, distort it, change it; I'm like anyone who takes chances and isn't afraid: let's say great conquerors, religious leaders, madmen. (*DWM*, 127)

Woolf had described such a universal masculine need with characteristic irony: "How is he to go on giving judgment, civilising natives, making laws, writing books . . . unless he can see himself at breakfast and at dinner at least twice the size he really is? . . . The looking-glass vision is of supreme importance because it charges the vitality; it stimulates the nervous system."[4] Howe is not representative but extreme: the narcissistic masculine type, renaissance man in caricature. "I love myself. . . . I love hearing my own voice" (*DWM,* 129), he intones shamelessly. Claiming he loves Elena, claiming he loves the law ("the law is what's left of divinity" [*DWM,* 129]) Howe in fact is sincere only when he is hymning a song of himself.

Under Howe's "sheltering" influence, Elena's flickering and fragile personal energy progressively winds down, a repetition of the entropic fall into deathly silence that marked her childhood abduction. Ironically, Elena attains the state which seemed ideal to the *Wonderland* hero: statuary, aphasia, catatonia, stone. Conditioned to mirror the outside world, it is all too easy for her to become the victim of a dark Medusa.

Thus, Oates evokes the order and structure of myth and legend, fantasy, treatise, and fairytale. She also enlarges the conception of the disordered self she has investigated in earlier novels, hypothesized by Jung, Lifton, Maslow, and Laing. "To turn oneself into a stone becomes a way of not being turned into a stone by someone else," Laing suggests in *The Divided Self,* describing the very condition of petrification which Oates's heroine exhibits.[5] Indeed, with no other way to elude Howe's imposing control, Elena again goes "into stone" (*DWM,* 304) in the novel's central and crucial scene.

Oates stakes out new imaginative territory as she experiments with form as well as literary reference. The cinema has been a source of metaphor in earlier novels; in this novel Oates refines her cinematic technique even further. Through a brilliant series of fragments that come into her field of vision like successive movie frames, Oates represents the disintegration of Elena's sleeping-beauty-goddess self. Propelled in a round of empty activities, Elena's nausea rises. In a gesture of last resort, like the desperate child she is, she telephones Ardis (now the star of a television talk show!) but is literally and symbolically put on hold. The clock ticks off minutes, her own watch stops. Reduced to a Kafkaesque initial "E," Elena finds herself in the center of the city, in front of a mammoth statue. The Alger Monument, "The Spirit of Detroit," a male figure holding a prayerful family group in one hand, ironically bears a message of freedom, spirituality, and communion:

> E. comes closer so that she can read the inscription. II Corinthians 3:17: "Now the Lord is that spirit and where the spirit of the Lord is, there is liberty." The inscription continues, explaining, "*God, through the Spirit of Man, is manifested in the family, the noblest human relationship.* (*DWM,* 164)

Yearning upward toward the stone apparition, an idealized view of the family she has never had, she surrenders to a vision of an inhuman state—perfected—but emotionally and psychically dead.[6]

At this moment, however, in one of the collisions, coincidences and juxtapositions that define the novel's narrative rhythm, Elena's life intersects with that of her future lover, Jack Morrissey. Her deathward spiral is arrested; a journey toward recovery, the real subject of this novel, begins. Jack's own story is also introduced at this point. Like the operator of a stop-action camera, Oates reviews the footage of Jack's biography; his father was a murderer, defended by Marvin Howe, who in effect has served as Jack's ghost writer and ventriloquist. He once prepared the young Jack to be his father's star witness in the courtroom; thanks to Howe's brilliant defense, the elder Morrissey was acquitted. With heavy irony, Oates emphasizes the plasticity of law and the Satanic powers of a master practitioner, for the jury's verdict in effect rendered the *victim* guilty (*DWM,* 211).

The effect on Jack is twofold: it fills him with moral confusion and it gives direction to his otherwise shapeless life. Like Jesse, he eagerly makes himself over to please Howe, his surrogate father. But unlike Howe, who accumulates great material holdings, Jack becomes a lawyer committed to liberal causes. One of the fine set-pieces in this novel dramatizes Morrissey's role in the civil rights movement, a scenario of frustration in which he unwittingly puts his southern black clients into jeopardy. Married to another self-styled activist, Jack continues to search for ways to fulfill his desire for justice.

As if to mark the difference between masculine and feminine quests for selfhood, Jack never becomes a true clone of his mentor. Howe is cool and impecably dressed; Jack is emotional, disheveled, pushing through a court perennially in session, bedeviled by growing self-doubt and human concern, more and more disillusioned with Howe and with the legal system. Fearful of Howe's influence but even more moved by a sense of compassion, he cannot turn from Elena's distress when he comes upon her, frozen catatonically in midcity and midjourney. His bullying and prodding rouse her from her spirit's sleep at the last minute: Elena comes back to life again, remembering "her mother had talked to her like that." Like a child, she allows Jack to lead her away from the statue and toward his waiting car (*DWM,* 304–5).

Jack at first serves as another authority figure to whom Elena gratefully submits in order to receive further sentence or instruction. She willingly becomes his passive passenger, "always relaxed when she was being driven somewhere; she had never learned to drive herself" (*DWM,* 307). As she rides home with Jack, she is stimulated by the violent race for supremacy fueling the rhythms of the city. Adding another dimension to the feminist critique in *Do with Me What You Will,* the freeway journey becomes a masculine agon:

> An exciting contest was taking place, in fact dozens of contests . . . men jockeying for position, men who couldn't see one another but sensed the presence, the

power of the other men . . . like a river gone mad and carrying debris furiously
along, snatching at its banks, yet rushing forward without hesitation, with im-
mense power and majesty. (*DWM,* 308)

Oates is again picking up old themes and threads, but with a difference.
Here, the race car world of her first novel, *With Shuddering Fall,* is reimagined with both wit and relish, now vulnerable to an artist's—and a woman's
—angle of vision. Staring not at a mirror but out of Jack's window, sheltered
by his genuine human concern, Elena moves beyond her initial timidity:

There was a peculiar grace everywhere, even in the bulkiest of trucks; it must
have been the grace of the driver, his clever calculating soul. You would imagine that soul of each driver, inside each car: a kind of miracle. (*DWM,* 308)

At this moment Jack and Elena join forces. Oates announces it with a new
narrative stream of consciousness. Running along with the more conventional plot is a curious "sound track," an evolving discourse which Oates presents in an italicized dialogue between two lovers. Telling the tale, reviewing
and arguing over the accumulated evidence, sifting through the memory of
their difficult and problematic passage, they also attest to their union and survival. Oates explores the creative possibilities of the speech-act; she also
weds her twin themes of law and love. Glimpsed through the diffracted and
fragmented narrative, the adulterous relationship of Elena and Jack emerges
as the central focus of the novel, both criminal and loving, open to conflicting
and confirming judgments.

While the relationship is remedial for Elena, rescuing her from madness
and possible suicide, it radically upsets the balance of Jack Morrissey's existence. In his search for rational solutions, Jack has thus far found a way to
quell his fear of a malevolent universe. That very fear of chaos and primal,
undifferentiated energy had once inspired Jesse Vogel's *Wonderland* flight.
Before he meets Elena, Morrissey both worships and dreads the "divinity" of
the law (his legacy from Marvin Howe). More tellingly, Jack has been terrified by language—the magic of art and of law. He has felt the power of rhetoric, the "word-making machine" grinding out the fictions which society
desires. In his daydreams, he envisions a cosmic "control panel" impervious
to human manipulation:

He believed in human control and direction, in his own control, his own powerful will. . . . In his imagination he could see a kind of control board, with
small light bulbs that flashed occasionally to indicate catastrophes, accidents of
annihilation that would be catalogued and assessed as history . . . in fact, made
into history and immortality. One of the lights flashes: another inch of the globe
gone.
  Was anyone working the control board?
  No. (*DWM,* 272)

The image suggests Kubrick; the vision comes from Kafka. As in Kafka's work, law is a central metaphor for the paradoxical human condition in *Do with Me What You Will*. Again, the novel is enriched by this intertextual resonance. Oates's chapter headings correspond to a process closer to *The Trial* than to an actual legal case. Only after the background testimony, "admissible" and "inadmissible" evidence, is there presentation of the "crime" and the rhetorical "summing up." Again, Oates explicitly identifies her literary sources: Jack himself has "skimmed through" Kafka's work. Allowing himself "no time for fiction," Jack sees an unsatisfactory version of his own life story in the pages of *The Castle* and finds no good legal models in *The Trial*. An activist, he *is* impressed by Kafka's persistent demand for justice and his protagonist's stubborn resistance: "one thing stayed with me, the fact that the man kept fighting and didn't walk away . . . and I admired him for this" (*DWM,* 424).

As a counterweight to Kafka, the novel bears traces of another favorite Oatesian influence, D. H. Lawrence. In a long essay, "The Hostile Sun," Oates, working as writer, critic, and student, discusses Lawrence's double vision of human possibility: his conception of the transformation of the self through erotic encounters as well as his "egoistic fantasy" of savage rites, "new-primitive" images of ancient Aztec rituals.[7] Oates echoes these images in *Do with Me What You Will*. Driven by his passion for Elena, Jack imagines himself sardonically as a "human sacrifice": the pagan king who is the victim of a thirsty goddess:

> These Aztec youths were evidently allowed to become gods for a short period . . . or maybe they were selected, I don't know . . . on the understanding that they would eventually have their hearts cut out at the altar in some kind of religious ceremony. They agreed to be gods, and then they agreed to have their hearts cut out. I wonder if the godliness is worth it? What comes at the end, the public ceremony. . . . (*DWM,* 427)

In an even clearer Lawrentian parallel, Jack becomes Elena's erotic agent: Elena awakens from her spiritual torpor through sexual orgasm. The dazzling embrace—tellingly, in Morrissey's car as well as his arms—unexpected, intense, a moment of grace stills her childhood terrors and warms her frigid body into life (*DWM,* 369–70). No longer in thrall to Howe or Morrissey, she takes up her own quest, flooded for the first time with desire.

When she revised the ending of *Wonderland,* Oates drew back from mystical alternatives to reenter and represent a world of violence and human betrayal. In this novel, the possibility of mystical communion—again, no panacea—is envisioned in the half-lunatic testament of a contemporary prophet, Mered Dawe. Unlike the hate-filled flower children of *Wonderland,* Dawe is a genuine seeker, preaching of "simultaneous" rather than "chronological" existence, the "free life," the "lightness" and "weight" of love, imagining a "cyclical scheme" (Miltonic echoes, but he is no Satan) in opposition to "selfish wholes" (*DWM*, 403–6). Yet he is fatally out of tune with the modern world: Oates takes pains to show him caught between generations and categories. His sermon of love provokes disorder and riot, and he ends his career beaten, in prison, a pathetic and absurd martyr, at least legally indistinguishable from the criminal delinquents, hedonists and anarchists who had flocked to hear him. "Mered had come too soon," Elena thinks sadly as she moves through this novel's corrosive intermediary chapters (*DWM*, 514).

Once more, Elena is close to breakdown. Walking on a remote beach, she becomes prey to self-loathing vagrant thoughts. But this time, Elena is rescued by her own will to survive, awakened by the threat of real attack and criminal violation. Out of the corner of her eye, Elena sees a battered, "rat-colored" car (an O'Connor echo), bearing anonymous predators; she almost feels "a kind of ecstasy," as she undergoes imagined assault. All at once, Elena is shocked into recognition of her own power to incite violence, and moves out of the rapist's range (*DWM*, 514–15).

For lawyers, including those figured in this novel, the "not guilty" verdict is the greatest victory. For lovers, Oates insists, admission of guilt and the recognition of their human complicity frees them from life imprisonment. Out of a new sense of personal responsibility, Elena has the courage to ask Howe for her legal and personal freedom. Her plea is not self-gratification but self-defense: "I might be careless of myself . . . I might make someone hurt me . . . I don't want to make someone into a killer" (*DWM*, 516).

The novel's final scene, like the ending of *Wonderland,* is an attempt to resolve conflicting and life-threatening human desires. It is also a curious act of revision: a replay of the opening seduction scene. Elena moves uneasily toward Morrissey, aware she is stalking him, hunting him down, yet pleading "she did not want to be a criminal, like everyone else" (*DWM,* 523). Oates has reintroduced the language of Nietzsche to describe this battle of wills. Such "criminality" seems, in the present circumstances, the only route to love:

> Everything seemed to come to a standstill. Never in her life had she conquered any territory, achieved any victories. Never. Never had she been selfish, never evil or adult. And now if she wanted Morrissey she would cross over into adulthood to get him, into the excitement of evil. Extending her freedom, as men do, making a claim . . . almost against his will, forcing him. It saddened her, it was degrading. Spiritually, she loathed it. As a woman she loathed it. Yet there was an excitement in the risk she would run, the possibility of getting him, even the possibility of not getting him. If she wanted love, she must have him. (*DWM,* 525)

Standing outside of his apartment building, she awaits Jack: "a man hurrying, with the dark abrupt impatience . . . that seemed always to be propelling him forward against his will." His appearance somehow solves the riddle of her own existence: "Elena understood: she had felt it herself, years ago . . . scrambling beneath a fence someone held up for her, not knowing why she was doing this but knowing only that she would do it, that she must" (*DWM,* 541).

Those who object to this novel see the ending as part of a masculine fantasy: a seeming capitulation to an erotic romantic ideal. Certainly, the scene is ambiguous, although far less so than the original or revised scenes of *Wonderland.* Elena has damaged innocent bystanders: Jack's wife, his newly-adopted child. In personal correspondence, Oates suggests her ending is bound by reality's limits: Elena is necessarily caught up in the violent patterns of contemporary life. Oates's comment characteristically evokes her literary, academic influences and artistic mentors—Milton, Nietszche:

> Elena surrenders to the necessities of ironic love, and of living in time; a combative world in which the paradise of innocence is forever lost. She will not have an easy life with Jack, nor should one hope for an "easy" life in which one's passivity causes others to behave in criminal ways. Better to be a criminal oneself, than to provoke criminality in others.[8]

Oates insists that the recognition of complicity is the first step toward a better life—no paradise, but a world far from *Wonderland.*

In *Do with Me What You Will,* the very word "transgression" thus recovers its roots: the act of passing through ordinary limits opens new territory for the self. Mystical flights are unavailable; prophets are premature; would-be reformers and zealots often endanger their supposed beneficiaries. After her first abortive flight in *Wonderland,* Oates accepts the problematic present: the old "western religion" of romantic love:

> If what is available to an individual is romantic love, then it must be—it will be —this kind of love that liberates. . . . Ours is still a time of romantic love; the time of a more communal, transcendental love is not yet come. *Do with Me What You Will* suggests such transformation.[9]

It is important to note that the novel does not end with the kidnaping. Instead, it is played out in the italicized realm of dialectic, the teasing and questioning speech of the now-married lovers, Elena and Jack. Oates has moved past the radically foreshortened conclusion of *Wonderland;* the ending of *Do with Me What You Will* is instead an "intermediary" passage. Even the title of the novel—literally, the legal plea *nolo contendere*—can better be translated as the prelude to religious conversion, St. Augustine's prayer to "love . . . and do what you will."[10] *Do with Me What You Will* is a multileveled intertextual experiment: an anti-romance, an inverted fairytale in which the princess or goddess comes off the pedestal, assuming human burdens and revealing human frailties.

In her next two novels, Oates continues to track the alternative routes of protean survivors, at the same time playing with other novelistic conventions. She has specifically identified one, *The Assassins* (1975), as a "political" novel.[11] It is indeed political in theme and treatment, an absorbing meditation on contemporary American political history. Plot and paranoia become virtually synonymous, as if we were in the realm of fabulators like Coover and Pynchon—or the front page of the *Washington Post*. The blurring of fact and fiction, her technique in *them* and *Wonderland*, is even more disturbing here—and more effective. *The Assassins*, Oates's portrait of a slain American political leader, is pieced together from a gallery of contemporary figures: he is a misanthropic man who gains political victory and public adulation; a man whose death imperils the exercise of democratic freedom; a man whose charisma seems to grow in his absence. To create her own political narrative, Oates draws freely upon American history from Lincoln to the Kennedys.

Yet at the same time she shows how history is shot through with elements of the uncanny, providing an array of confusing clues to the assassination plot in this novel. Filtered by the perspectives of multiple narrators, certainties are shaken and undermined, and tentative explanations are subverted by the wildest and most improbable counterpoint. The three voices of this novel —artist, lover, and prophet, two brothers and the widow of the assassinated political leader—articulate their claustrophic anguish. Searching for renewal, Oates's characters instead experience their limitations; nightmare and history provide mutually confirming patterns of reality. Even when the real assassin is unmasked, the storytellers seem unable to suspend their profound disbelief.

In *Do with Me What You Will*, Oates describes a heroine who derives the energy for growth and transformation from negative capability. In *The Assassins*, Oates takes up the same theme with a vengeance. While the heroine, Yvonne, understands that "the essence of life is ambiguity, complexity. . . . The essence of paranoia is the inability to tolerate ambiguity—even for brief periods of time" (*A*, 224), she is nonetheless driven to find "a reason for everything. Nothing without its reason. Causality: sanity. Chaos: insanity" (*A*, 230). Exercising her analytic powers, suppressing her passions, she is loveless and exultant: "She was in control then, always in control" (*A*, 288). Ironically, Oates again shows that such control is a perverse form of bondage, submission to the devious designs of the novel's monstrous missing person.

That character, the central figure of *The Assassins*, is Andrew Petrie— former senator, the elder son in one of the nation's first families ("older than the country itself"), a brilliant and merciless political conservative. His name

itself testifies to his univocal force. He is a "petrified" man, deified in the popular imagination after his assassination, when he is literally and metaphorically "trapped in stone" (*A,* 4). He is an artist-manqué: his work, a
body of philosophical commentary hailed as a masterpiece of the rational intellect, is better seen as an obsession with "transforming the consciousness of
America." The entire novel, Oates suggests in an interview, should be read as
an anatomy of "megalomania and its inevitable consequences"; it also describes "the peculiar conditions of our era."[12]

Three separate but tragically related personae attempt to sort out real plots
from imagined threats. The novel is again punctuated by documents: fragments of hate mail, echoes of obscene calls. Yet even when they are able to
distinguish invention from fact, the central characters cannot come to terms
with their own assassin-impulses. Their prayers and pleadings rebound aim-
lessly in a cluttered and disorderly world, crowded with objects that have no
meaning beyond sheer physical presence. However different they are, Oates's
three narrators are frustrated by life's asymmetry and incoherence, seeming
to share the fear of the "labyrinthian risks" (*A,* 159) of public and private life.

The novel's first narrator is Hugh Petrie, Andrew's brother, an artist-figure
of a peculiar sort, a master of flagrant and often bawdy caricature. Indeed,
Hugh is himself a caricature, a manic egoist whose nagging voice almost
overwhelms the story. Oates herself half-playfully muses about Hugh's sinister autonomy:

> Had I my own way the first section of *The Assassins* would be much abbrevi-
> ated. But it was impossible to shut Hugh Petrie up once he got going. . . . Hugh
> did not want to die, and so his section went on and on, and it isn't an exagger-
> ation to say that I felt real dismay in dealing with him.[13]

Ingenious and crafty, locked in a prison house of self as well as language,
decorating its walls with obscene graffiti, Hugh is one of Oates's "expensive
people," an *enfant terrible* grown old, worn thin. In his cartoons, he attempts
to "grasp the perfect deformity . . . the essence of personality" (A, 75). Grotesque though it may be, Hugh's vision of humanity is no more contemptuous than the superman's-eye-view of Andrew Petrie. When his own gangling
person and his bizarre art suffer repeated rejections, the humiliated Hugh designs his own end: it becomes an unwitting caricature of his brother's death.
Even his attempt to blast his brains out is a fiasco. His body is permanently
disabled: his brain survives in an iron lung with a mass of feeding tubes, denied the power of speech. He attempts to forge a profound critique of liberal
values; yet the effect is less like Nietzsche than Woody Allen:

> The individual is all, the individual is the end of everything . . . and so we are,
> so indeed we are, we princely ones! . . . But that doesn't quite solve the over-

whelming problem of our era: how to get through the long weekends. (*A*, 538–39)

Hugh is an outlaw-self, a lonely and isolated joker (*A*, 438). Blinded by his own deformities, he cannot read Andrew's far more perverse and sinister story:

> *As if he spoke the truths they must not speak. As if he spoke the forbidden, outlawed, unspeakable truths in order that they might please the crowd by refuting him.* . . . . Forcing them . . . into the agony of hatred that preceded and accompanied the desire to kill. (*A*, 264)

Hugh is doomed to hover, disembodied, on the margins of suffering. The novel's second narrator, Yvonne, is Andrew's fleshly medium: in his lifetime, his mistress, nurse, and comforter; after his death, his legate, editor, and curator. Her body itself becomes the meeting place for Andrew's political protégés and enemies, a provocation for the as-yet-undiscovered assassin. It is in her narrative that Andrew Petrie assumes tangible form and shape. Yet surrogate authorship is risky: as the events of Andrew's political career, his triumphs and betrayals, his public and private existence become clear, Yvonne's own identity fades. The horrors of her childhood, her abandonment and loss of love, are pushed to the periphery of Andrew Petrie's life, replaced by lies and other forms of fiction. Oates finds intriguing analogies between the critic and the consummate political wife, serving as surrogate and thus assuring her subject his desired reputation and a kind of fabricated immortality. After his assassination, Andrew exerts a ventriloquist's influence over her work, language, and thought so powerful that it is she who seems the victim.

One of the novel's most interesting scenes is Yvonne's visit to a national academic "think tank," the Yaeger Institute. Crowded in its galleries, written across scrolls and commemorative plaques, are the words of great and near-great political figures of the twentieth century, with a modest photograph of Andrew Petrie displayed among portraits of diplomats, presidents, ambassadors, and industrialists:

> Members of the Institute or guests like Yvonne could sit and discuss the issues of the day's seminars—peaceful uses of atomic energy, new concepts of genetic control, the philosophy of activism vs. the philosophy of detachment, violence in popular entertainment, man's place in a post-modern age. (*A*, 397)

Representing her "martyred" husband in the halls of the powerful, where "the individual is the highest reality," Yvonne perpetuates Andrew Petrie's conservative, paternalistic, anti-democratic vision, playing the role she has learned far better than her own. Yet she also harbors rebellious impulses:

Liberalism is a mask, Andrew had written somewhere, a phase of personality like any other, a phase of expediency: Adlai Stevenson at the United Nations, for instance, lying beautifully and intelligently about the Bay of Pigs, *on our side for once.* Conservatism is a mask: a phase of personality, a phase of expediency . . . one must determine which attitude was most required by history . . . one *must* jump into the arena.

"To the conservative all life is holy," Yvonne said. "The individual is the highest reality. . . . We must believe that," she said, "or . . . just the opposite." (*A,* 410)

Yvonne's final words, which display the moral bankruptcy of her absent author, are drowned in the animated exchange of presidential aides, former Kennedy associates, ethicists, and even an Apollo astronaut. All at once Yvonne herself is drowning in this sea of words, unable to endure the political "carnival." Her monologue, unheard by the others, suggests the absurdists's language:

We do these things because we are the people doing these things because these things are to be done, at this particular time, and we are the people who are doing them. . . . Our enemies are everywhere, they steal our words from us . . . steal them and turn them upside down . . . and we steal their words from them . . . we change them, the words are always the same words but changed, turned upside down . . . and we are mirror images of one another. (*A,* 412–13)

Yvonne fights her way out of her surrogate's role, only to become a helpless victim. Robbed of a sense of purpose, her own life willfully stunted, she endures an imaginary assassination, envisioning her dismemberment at the hands of strangely familiar but nameless assailants. She is the spiritual sister of Elena Howe, lacking the lover who might save her from the dark vortex of hallucination.

Stephen Petrie, the third voice of the novel, is the only member of the Petrie clan not literally or figuratively defaced and/or decapitated by the end of the narrative. He is another sort of artist, programmed by transhuman voices. But his mystical act of self-effacement infuriates Andrew, inspiring a hymn of monstrous self-love:

Do you know, Stephen, that there are people who believe passionately in me? . . . When I give a lecture or a speech they are there and the mere sight of me drives them into a frenzy . . . they interrupt my speeches with bursts of applause, I have to beg them to stop. . . . Even those who threaten my life seem, in a way, to be addicted to me. They too love me—in their way. They need me. Can't do without me. . . . (*A,* 528)

Clearly, Andrew is threatened by Stephen's priestly posture. "No," he cries, denying the value of Stephen's vow of "poverty, chastity, that pose of constant humility . . . those big brown doggy eyes; I'd go mad. I'd slash my throat" (*A,* 529). On his part, Stephen hears his brother's perverse wish for "self-murder" (*A,* 542), but seems bound by conventions of the confessional to preserve Andrew's ugly secrets. His own narrative becomes an act of penance, a prayer for the soul of his slain brother (recoiling from an early blow, he continues in his imagination to turn the other cheek). It is also meant to fill a larger void, the region of his absent God. Like other figures in Oates's gallery of premature mystics (Mered Dawe in *Do with Me What You Will,* Nathanael Vickery, who will follow in *Son of the Morning*) Stephen lives to see his prophetic dreams mocked in the derision and disbelief of a cynical and secular society.

In *The Assassins,* Oates seems more comfortable in the role of a fabulator and jester, working with the clownish texture of American public life. Even in her portrait of Stephen, there are unmistakable notes of mockery: Stephen's early trances seem more like *petit mal* episodes than religious visions. Yet she is also moved by the mysterious empathy which sets the religious mystic apart in a world of egoists. Hugh invents suffering; Yvonne allows her terrors to engulf her; Andrew, the absolute solipsist, hires his own assassin. Stephen, in contrast, survives in order to bear the real pain of society: "Is it meant to be this bad, or did things go wrong?" he cries. "Is it supposed to hurt so much?" (*A,* 524).

Thus, it is through Stephen that Oates attempts in *The Assassins* to remedy the loss of love and value. Again, she locates remedial texts on many shelves. As a boy, Stephen had been fascinated by the primordial landscape of America figured on stained and crumbling pages of an old atlas in the Petrie library:

> There was no *United States.* . . . Where the *State of New York* now reigned there was only the notation *Iroquois* and subordinate to that word, *Senecas, Cayugas, Onondaga, Oenidas, Mohawks.* The Adirondack Mountains were indicated; the Catskills; the St. Lawrence River. . . . But everything that belonged to a specific moment in history . . . expressed in peculiar enchanting human language, was unrecognizable. . . . The world had been a different world. (*A,* 49)

Staring at the map, Stephen sees modern states fade into ghostly "premonitions." The "new world" lies undiscovered once again. Grasping the unclaimed territory, Stephen makes his own inky "X" upon the page "as if to locate himself" (*A,* 491). It can be no more than a temporary claim for Stephen; as, in the rising terrors of a Beckett drama, it is quickly obscured:

> *I am here,* Stephen said . . . *I was here.* Afterward, leafing through the book again and pausing at the map, the thought would come to him: *Someone was here.*
>
> And yet no one was there. Repeatedly, no one was there. (*A,* 491)

By the novel's end, Stephen's God is also not there. He is left to wander through charted territory—carrying terrible secrets (he knows the identity of the assassin, he has been privy to the ugly vision of Andrew's perverse complicity, Hugh's pederasty, and Yvonne's mindless and loveless adultery). He seems fated to serve humankind in a world of permanent dislocation and to minister only to those with a depressed capacity for intelligence and wonder.

Yet in private communication and public interviews, Oates suggests that because of Stephen's presence, her political fable is not uncompromisingly pessimistic. While Stephen loses his way on that ancient map, it turns up in quirky and curious form as a gift from Hugh to Yvonne, not only bearing a new and cruel "X" (the spot where Andrew died) but the trace of Stephen's original claim, never really obscured. Stephen himself remains a genuine seeker, attentive to the fissure and fracture which characterizes contemporary life. And while *The Assassins* is in many ways a chronicle of dismemberment, showing the stunted body politic, it engages another subtext. Oates subtitles it "A Book Of Hours," suggesting the presence of a liturgy which Oates at once deconstructs and reifies. Sacrifice is self-serving or cannibalistic; celebrants are drugged or maddened; trust is betrayed; work is mocked or trivialized. Oates's critique extends even to the art and act of fiction: *"Plots, plots!"* cries Hugh Petrie. *"The world is a network of plots and all of them cruel, sinister, subterranean. Innocents . . . haven't a chance for survival in such a world (A, 538).*

She has gone far beyond the images of communion which form an ironic pattern in *With Shuddering Fall.* In fact, the innocent, Stephen Petrie, *does* survive in the assassin's universe; his life itself is a refutation of Andrew Petrie's cynical view of the average human being as "a cripple, a wreck, a parody" (*A,* 471). In the power of imagination's "X," individual discovery and claims are perennially renewable; in the amazing (if at times laughable) multiplicity of artistic practice there are prospects for connection and solution. For Stephen Petrie, no matter what the evidence, life seems a miracle. At the end of this drama of assassins, Stephen joins other Oatesian protean heroes: a hopeful pilgrim, he can "accommodate [himself] to anything" (*A,* 568).

Characteristically, the novel which follows *The Assassins* takes up many of its agonizing visions and revisions to offer a complementary reading of the world. But *Childwold* (1976) is more than an ingenious reordering. It is a celebration of life's capacity for renewal and the resources of the human imagination.

Childwold is, by Oates's account, "in a kind of diffracted way, a complete world made of memory and imagination." She also suggests the complexity of its formal structure, a self-conscious experimental fiction embodying her concerns with physical and metaphorical homeostasis:

I had wanted to create a prose poem in the form of a novel, or a novel in the form of a prose poem: the exciting thing for me was to deal with the tension that arose between the image-centered structure of poetry and the narrative-centered and linear structure of the interplay of persons that constitutes a novel. . . . The one impulse is toward stasis, the other toward movement. Between the two impulses there arose a certain tension that made the writing of the novel quite challenging.[14]

Again, as in *The Assassins,* Oates uses strategies of diffraction, motion, and intertextuality in both form and theme. The novel is a collage of narrative voices, drawn from memory or the vivid present, ranging from the refined to the vulgar. Conscious of the terror of the assassin's realm, Oates explores a world of fluidity and abundance—once glimpsed by young Stephen Petrie on the crumbling family map. *Childwold* reanimates that primordial landscape, providing renewal for the awakening artistic self.

"So much, such a profusion!" cries one of a chorus of narrators, dazzled by Childwold's buzzing space, a "universe of trash, of beauty" (*C,* 64). Like a master ventriloquist, Oates projects her story in different accents, through a wide range of perspectives: a virtuoso performance, although one critic suggests with some justification that "it may overwhelm the struggling reader."[15] Oates offers no chapter headings nor does she explicitly identify her storytellers. Rather, she treats *Childwold* as if it were indeed a prose poem, with each major character emerging unannounced to speak in a distinct—and eventually recognizable—voice.

Significantly, in *Childwold,* Oates returns to Eden Valley, that rural backwood region which served as the setting for her earliest fiction. It is the residence of her fourteen-year-old heroine, Laney Bartlett. Laney's second-person narrative, apparently addressed to herself, describes her peculiar relationship with an extravagant grotesque, a childless, orphaned, fortyish writer and recluse, Fitz-John Kasch, who is the novel's putative hero, and, appropriately, a first-person speaker. Laney lives amidst a child's souvenirs in a chaotic but vibrant household at the edge of town. Kasch lives alone amidst the debris of lost hope in a dusty apartment, the last of his line, a failed husband, longing for bookish self-gratification and a "voyeur's pleasure" (*C,* 111). Instead, Kasch is drawn unwillingly from a quasi-academic perch into the violent and sordid world below, lured by the combination of innocence and wantonness that he sees in Laney and by the fraudulent allure of her mother's perfume. He "saves" the child, acting out a defunct storybook romance. Indeed, he defends all of the Bartletts, and even kills their murderous assailant. Yet Kasch ultimately appears to be a tragicomic rather than heroic figure—wacky, confused, schizoid, in solitary confinement.

Woven into the pages of this anti-romance are interior monologues and third-person accounts of the other members of Laney's family. Her mother Arlene, lazy and promiscuous, requires someone else to narrate her story whether it be Kasch, or the man he kills (her former lover) or the policeman who comes to investigate the crime. Unreflective, earthy, and tenacious, a latter-day Molly Bloom, Arlene is the only character to survive the rush of events fundamentally unchanged.

Laney's grandfather, Joseph, is one of the novel's solo voices. He lives in a vivid world of memory peopled by ghosts of old friends and lost lovers. He has championed life, preserving the family line, literally saving Arlene when his wife once sought an abortion. He also harbors the secret of an illicit love. Throughout *Childwold,* the old man is pursued by menacing spectres of guilt; finally, he surrenders his spirit and body to black-winged death. A fifth narrator is Laney's brother Vale, a mutilated Vietnam casualty and a brutal rapist. Too disfigured to return to Childwold, he expresses his frustrated love and longing by anonymously shipping his family a truckload of Christmas gifts purchased with stolen money. Vale is another Oatesian figure who cannot read a story. His violent experience in the agony of Southeast Asia has radically reordered his perception: he has lost his capacity to see "chronological sequence" (*C,* 117) in the chaos of modern events. In his criminal consciousness voices blur and overlap and clash.

In contrast, Kasch attempts to impose metafictive order on existence: "If you doubt me," he cries defiantly to his off-stage love, "you will cease to exist." Mockingly, he inverts the imagist's credo, changing it into a fabulator's motto: "There are no things but in words" (*C,* 109). Language *is* reality to Kasch, the only glue that holds human personality together; life is a tissue of linguistic deception and cinematic mirage:

> How real the world strikes us, the world of the present moment, the world of daylight! Tactile, it is; palpable. Demonstrable. . . . Yet once the world slips into the past tense, once it shifts into "history," it is revealed to have been insubstantial, illusory; descriptive. And we, caught in it, are not insubstantial as images in a film . . . ? A certain force, perhaps no more than linguistic habit, connects me with the Fitz John of those years, a boy in his mid-teens, but I have no true memory of him. (*C,* 128)

Like many Oatesian heroes, Kasch is desperate to slow the film, to stop the menacing slippage, to correct the fatal "error of the body" by denying his physical nature (*C,* 225), to become both more and less than human. When he *does* retreat from the world of the streets, he becomes the vehicle of mysterious thought-waves:

> The interior life constitutes the authentic life, and actions performed in the exterior world are peripheral. Reality is what I am thinking, what is thinking through me, using me as a means, a vessel, a reed, even, streaming through me with or without my consent; the interior life is continuous, unhurried, almost undirected, unheralded. (*C,* 138)

Oates is fascinated and repelled by self-reflexive, self-centered artists: characters like Max, Trick Monk, Hugh Petrie, and now Fitz-John Kasch, all of whom seem to go mad. "Enchanted, enchained, inchanting" (*C,* 265), Kasch attempts to convert the Bartletts, to transform them into fiction, to deny time and change. But like Hugh Petrie, he becomes "fictional" himself, caught in a monstrous double bind: a character in a family scenario which others have set into motion. Recognizing the absurdity of his existence, he muses near the novel's end, "If only we had had the grace to break into laughter" (*C,* 290). But he is unable to emerge from his self-enclosure. Indeed, occasions for outright laughter are rare in Oates's novels. On the other hand, *Childwold* does offer the occasion for Oates to demonstrate her own metafictive wit: wordplay, the weaving of narrative voices, allusions and other references.

In fact, *Childwold* is Oates's most intricate fabulator's game since the publication of *Expensive People* in 1968. Vladimir Nabokov is the "father," and *Lolita* is the obvious intertextual bridge to Oates's characters and themes. Oates has elsewhere praised Nabokov's novel for its "wedding of Swiftian satirical vigor with the kind of minute, loving patience that belongs to a man infatuated with the visual mysteries of the world."[16] The eccentric Fitz-John Kasch perhaps can be understood best as her version of his grotesque voyeur, Humbert Humbert. Both are aging intellectuals, zany professors, whose only issue is their esoteric, unread manuscripts; both have unslakable sensual appetites: both long for incestuous union, pursuing both mothers and daughters. Both are arch-fabulators themselves. Yet for Oates, such a stance has unacceptable human costs. Kasch is caught up short by life's demands, seduced and betrayed by art. His use of language—puns, allusions, portmanteau words, typographical manipulation—is ultimately the sign of his mental breakdown rather than imaginative authority.[17]

Oates thus functions as a resisting as well as attentive reader. As is the case with her other allusive experiments, Oates's novel is not meant to be a virtuoso's trick or a worshipful copy of Nabokov's work. While Oates ranks *Lolita* as "one of our finest American novels," she also warns that Nabokov's "purposes" are "to deceive, to conceal, to mock, to reduce Nature to an egoistic and mechanical arrangement of words"; she sharply criticizes his academic detachment, his genius for "dehumanizing" character; "obsessively conscious," he denies the divinity of the world in favor of the divinity of his own personality.[18]

Oates thus sets herself an ambitious task in *Childwold*: Nabokov's novel is both her target and her inspiration. Humbert Humbert's nymphet is an artifice, created in his hero's perpetually lustful imagination. In contrast, Oates creates Laney from many points of view. In this novel, she also suggests in an interview, her mad academic must be disciplined, and handled with considerable authorial care:

> The problem with creating such highly conscious and intuitive characters is
> that they tend to perceive the contours of the literary landscape in which they
> dwell, and, like Kasch of *Childwold,* try to guide or even to take over the direc-
> tion of the narrative.[19]

She does not allow Kasch the liberties she allowed Hugh Petrie. When he
holds sway in *Childwold,* Kasch displays the linguistic bravado of a Nabokovian wordsmith and delivers a self-aggrandizing performance. But Oates is
bent on revising Nabokov's fable: she intentionally shifts the primary focus
of her novel from the decadent masculine fabulator to the youthful object of
his designs and desire. *Childwold* is finally not an ingenious solipsistic display, but a critical act of reauthorization.

Oates also uses the novel to broaden her academic critique, taking up
themes from earlier novels. Like Humbert, but also like Marvin Howe, Andrew Petrie, and other teacher figures, Kasch initiates his beloved pupil to
the world of art: orderly, "deliberately . . . created" in contrast to Childwold's antic and natural mess and sprawl. Laney is stunned by the symmetry
and order of the museum exhibits Kasch shows her. Yet almost immediately
she is thrown back into the stream of life, awakening into womanhood, feeling nature's irresistible urgency in the "fascinating, frightening" menstrual
flow, "secret and aching as if it were angry." Far from the cool galleries, the
academic kingdom of Kasch, Laney enters another privileged "residence,"
where her spiritual and physical being converge:

> The air rings with life . . . your vision goes out of focus. You are not dizzy, you
> are not lightheaded, you see the coin-sized splashes of sunlight, you hear them,
> you feel them burst in your blood. . . . It's lovely, it won't hurt, nothing will
> hurt for long, it's what you must accept, it's normal, it's beautiful, it's alive, it's
> living, you don't own your body, you don't own the creek, you can't control it,
> you mustn't try, you must float with the current, the plunge of the rapids, you
> must close your eyes and move with it. (*C,* 197)

Laney must close her dazzled eyes in order to fully experience this visionary
moment: "everything is spilling toward you, around you, inside you, through
you, your blood flows with it, you are rivers and streams and creeks, there is
a heartbeat inside you, around you" (*C,* 197). Half child, half woman, she surrenders herself in order to discover the secret springs of life, the *élan vital* hidden from the prurient eye of her crafty and crazed instructor.

Oates brings her heroine through and past this mystical initiation. Significantly, Laney's coming of age also involves an intellectual awakening. Her
private tutor Kasch has indeed changed her life, although he will never receive or understand her course evaluation:

> You read and reread, you underline passages, you make notations in the mar-

gins; sometimes you try to decipher Kasch's notes, but his handwriting is too small. . . . Life is a flow, a powerful directed flow, not to be stopped, not to be stopped for long. You read, absorbed, shivering with excitement. You forget everything else. (*C,* 238–39)

Childwold helps us understand how and why Oates has accepted the terms of her academic residence. There are many marginal texts in this narrative: notes from James, Pascal, Santayana, McCullers, Steinbeck, Hemingway, Wharton, St. John of The Cross, as Oates draws freely from her own library to suggest the exciting passages open to the artist.

Clearly, Laney Bartlett outpaces her mad professor and would-be author. Kasch cries out in despair: "Where are you, why have you gone so far? The books you read are not my books, the language you use is not my language. You are no longer recognizable! You are no longer mine!" (*C,* 290). Unlike Kasch, Laney has made peace with the body's "errors"; she will not lose touch with the child in herself. Empowered by a sense of art as vibrant as her sense of physical being, it seems evident that Laney, Oates's youthful alter ego, will write her own story. Unlike Jules Wendall of *them,* Laney can draw directly on the resources of the literary past; she is already working to transform them in her own hands and heart.

Kasch, the eccentric artist, lover, and killer, has uncannily predicted Laney's form of fiction, even classifying it—"paedomorphic"—and suggesting wryly that it could promise renewal of the race itself through exploitation and cultivation of the infantile. For him, it is a mad joke, one of his portmanteau words. For the reader of this novel, it should be taken more seriously. *Childwold* itself is paedomorphic, embracing primary data and sense impressions, an imaginative embodiment of the process of "dreaming back," the portrait of a young artist. Raising her voice above that of the perverse lover, the promiscuous mother, the autocratic and loveless English teacher (*C,* 119, 142), the twisted criminal, and the maddened fierce old man, Laney Bartlett begins to test her own creative shaping powers as she moves toward a world of adult responsibility herself.

The last words of *Childwold,* appropriately enough, are not the words of the fabulator, Kasch, or any of the novel's allusive literary voices, but a child's words. After he slays Arlene's drunken assailant and former lover, Kasch is institutionalized. Released from one prison, he promptly entombs himself in the enclosure of his own choice: the ruined Bartlett house, a collapsing, ramshackle house of fiction. At the end of the novel, Laney Bartlett stands outside in a field of "insect-ridden blossoms," watching his shadow moving behind the windowpane, calling up at him: "Kasch? It is really you? Here? After so long? But why? Am I here, calling to you? Waiting for you? Kasch? My love?" (*C,* 295). Attuned to the throbbing landscape, she senses her own power to restore Kasch to life through the artistic imagination. Presumably, she will do so in *Childwold*. For now, with renewed love and hope, she waits breathlessly for "a sign, a sign."

In her formally inventive eighth novel, Oates weaves a complex verbal tapestry. It is a difficult work, no child's play for the reader, who must have a good ear to follow the polyphonic narrative. *Childwold* can be seen as a lyrical memoir of adolescence, a long poem. It should also be read as an ambitious literary critique. Oates finally resists the seductions of *Lolita* in her own seductive text. Turning Nabokov's plot back upon itself, reimagining the nymphet first as a bewildered child, then as a sensitive, wondering, even triumphant herione, Oates offers an optimistic counterstatement to *Lolita*'s final dark grimace.

A tribute to art, intellectual exercise, a stylistic *tour de force,* and a poetic autobiography, *Childwold* displays the full range of Joyce Carol Oates's skills and strategies. Something of a metafictionist herself as she plays on "paedomorphic" themes, Joyce Carol Oates has moved through the academic house of mirrors and past menacing reflections of predators, false counselors, and assassins into a scene which almost beggars the imagination—profuse, unhurried, continuous, sensual, teeming with felt life, offering the promise of radiance, regeneration, and metamorphosis.

6 Sacred and Profane Visions
Son of the Morning and *Unholy Loves*

Early in Joyce Carol Oates's ninth novel, *Son of the Morning* (1978), a sad and broken father stumbles upon a tiny grave:

> He had happened to walk through an abandoned cemetery in Childwold, a tiny settlement some miles to the west of Marsena, and came across an aged, weathered gravestone that had nearly broken his heart with its crude naivete: BYE BYE MAMMA FROM BABY WILLY. . . . The grief of his own son's early death had swept upon him and he found himself weeping for several minutes, bitterly and helplessly. (*SM*, 49)

Oates reenters her own familiar mythic space; but Childwold is no longer a world teeming with life and promise. It has become another blighted Eden, corrupted by the death of innocence. It is also the setting for one of Oates's most interesting narratives, a daring plunge into the mindscape of a "god-infatuated, god-mad" religious fanatic.

Victoria Glendinning describes *Son of the Morning* as a "hugely ambitious novel," but questions Oates's double intentions, the psychological dialectic between scholar and passionate observer which again keeps critics off balance:

> There is a hungriness in the writing of Joyce Carol Oates . . . an appetite for huge themes and violent emotions, in seeming tension with her analytical academic side. It makes for great vitality; it also breeds a . . . resistance in the reader. . . .

Overcoming her own resistance, Glendinning reads *Son of the Morning* as academic, "the basis for a sociological study . . . of Pentecostal religion."[1] Oates agrees that the novel is rooted in social history, coming out of "an era of intense religious upheaval"; yet she claims it is as much "prayer" as social document, a work of fiction both sacred and profane.[2]

As is obvious by now, Oates is fascinated with the American evangelical figure, a character who feels himself in the mysterious grip of "god trance" and thus open to the truth of miracle. Stephen Petrie in *The Assassins*, Mered Dawe in *Do with Me What You Will*, and the many characters who display a self-appointed sense of divinity (such as Max in *With Shuddering Fall* and Dr. Pedersen of *Wonderland*) live on the periphery of her earlier fiction, all in some sense alienated and eccentric figures. But in *Son of the Morning,* Oates embraces the prophet, Nathanael Vickery, probes his imagination, shares his vision, and draws him into the center of her world. She moves into the terrain of Jim Jones and Elmer Gantry, demonstrating the power of this American type and the range of her own fictive imagination.

Unlike the setting of *Childwold,* the rural landscape of *Son of the Morning* is clearly remote from human desire. Looking about, the narrator is conscious of "the texture of poverty, of futility; a pity. Strange, that it should be surrounded by such physical beauty—such blatant, indifferent physical beauty" (*SM,* 93). Similarly, the coltish grace of adolescence and the pulsing sense of awakening Oates pictures in *Childwold* is given a brutal turn in *Son of the Morning.* In this novel, children grope and stumble, graceless intruders in an adult universe; any lingering visions of romance are cruelly blasted in the savage violence of the opening episodes.

Oates insists that each of her novels is "a world unto itself."[3] In this spirit, *Son of the Morning* virtually demands to be taken on its own terms. The allusion to Milton's Satan in the title is disturbing and highly ambiguous throughout. From the earliest pages, the author retires behind an anguished fictive persona. Even in the epigraph, this peculiar narrative voice demands a supernatural hearing: "For One Whose absence is palpable as any presence —." It is the first of the many attempts in this novel to shatter the silence of an absent God.

When God departs from Stephen Petrie in the last pages of *The Assassins,* the young man asks himself silently, "Why has God forsaken me?" (*A,* 533). Immediately, he changes the "me" to "us," suppressing his own private brooding, relaxing his demands to hear, to know, to understand:

> Stephen knew there was no choice any longer—you accepted the miracle and that was that. You opened your lungs and it flooded you. That was that. Simple. Useless to brood upon it or philosophize or mourn or make jokes. The street was crowded with miracles, the nursing home was crowded with miracles, that was that. The miracle is the most irresistible form of necessity. (*A,* 562)

Similarly, Stephen's conversion had come without warning, "like a dam that had burst . . . I brought myself to the Church filled to the brim with God, on the brink . . . of catastrophe" (*A,* 507), the edge of madness. His final stance is one of humility and resignation; his last words, and the novel's, are signs of acquiescence: *"Thank you . . . I can accommodate myself to anything"* (*A,* 568).

The tone in *Son of the Morning* is radically different from Stephen's puritan narrative in *The Assassins,* although Oates describes it too as "a novel that begins with wide ambitions and ends very, very humbly." The novel attempts from the start to break the boundaries of ordinary fiction: "a first-person narration by a man who is addressing himself throughout to God." With only a hint of irony, Oates explained to a curious interviewer that "the ideal reader is, then, God. Everyone else, myself included, is secondary." Not only in the opening pages, but in the historical flashbacks, the hallucinations, and the realistic, even satiric narrative of cult activity and conversion, *Son of the Morning* seems "saturated with what Jung calls the God-experience."[4] Drawing on a range of available novelistic strategies, Oates attempts to render that experience as it exists in modern America, fusing the technique of confessional poet and social realist in a work which again eludes easy categoriation.

The narrator is the key to her intentions. He keeps his actual identity secret for most of the novel, yet he seems starved for revelation. He raises complaints to God, desperate to hear his voice, asking that ultimate reader for pity: there is "no loneliness . . . like that of a man whom You have once loved—and then abandoned" (*SM,* 141). But as he begins to assemble the shards of poignant and bitter memory and yield to the menacing phantoms of the imagination, his own art seems to undermine his penitential and prayerful impulses: "Is this a revelation, I ask myself. Or an aspect of my punishment" (*SM,* 4). Much of his revelation is history, rather than self-exposure: he describes events erupting in the brutal world of "sheer rapacious nature" (*SM,* 132).

The novel's first episode, an imaginative reconstruction filtered through this brooding narrative presence, thus dramatizes the savage massacre of a pack of wild dogs: a debasement of the classic hunt. The hunter is the first representation of the infernal agency suggested by the novel's title; but Ashton Vickery is both bestial and satanic. Bringing home a bloodstained bag to win his promised bounty, he is conscious only of his thirst ("Jesus God, Mamma . . . you got some lemonade or something fixed?—my mouth tastes like a buzzard's crotch" [*SM,* 21]) and his sense of almost sexual consummation. He leers avidly at the textual evidence of his exploits in the local newspaper. This violent and disturbing scene is a shocking prelude to the even more vicious rape of Ashton's teenage sister Elsa, the next event which in turn leads to the "virgin" birth of the novel's hero, Nathanael.

Nathanael Vickery, a Pentecostal prophet and highly successful preacher and evangelist, is a familiar American figure. In preparation for this story, Oates immersed herself in scholarly research: "I spoke with people involved in intense religious experience and spent innumerable hours rereading the Bible. It was quite a disturbing year, I must say."[5] The finished novel reflects

Oates's academic perspective, not only in the Miltonic title, but in the character of Thaddeus Vickery, Nathanael's reclusive and bookish grandfather (and the tearful witness in Childwold's cemetery). Dr. Vickery, the novel's first articulate character, has turned his face from the spectacle of Tennysonian nature, red in tooth and claw, to bury himself in the mechanistic world of medicine and the consolations of Stoic philosophy:

> In Lucretius he read with great interest that there is no hell (except earth itself), and there are no gods, no intrusion from another sphere into the lives of men. What is heaven? What is hell? Chimeras. Wisps of fancy. There is no spiritual world, only a materialist world in which soul and mind are evolved with the body, grow with the body, ail with the body, and finally die with the body's death. There is nothing permanent: the universe consists of atoms: the law of laws is that of evolution and dissolution everywhere. Wiping at his eyes, Thaddeus Vickery discovered in these ancient, placid words a kind of beauty, a grave and noble simplicity he had not hoped to encounter in his lifetime. (*SM,* 54)

Yet even as he lectures to himself and underscores the classic text "with a shaky pencil like an ancient scholar," his victimized daughter screams in the agonies of childbirth elsewhere in the doctor's house. By the time the crazed Elsa leaves home, abandoning her child, Dr. Vickery has retired from the physical world of Yewville, seeking refuge in a bloodless realm of literary and philosophical ideas.

Nathanael, then, is raised by his grandmother as a kind of miracle: was he, the narrator wonders, divine "compensation for the earlier outrage?" (*SM,* 41). Presumably, his story will provide an answer. Under the care of his fundamentalist Christian guardian, young Nathan finds himself in a god-struck universe, taught through both work and terrifying symbology of the immanence and literal presence of Jesus. Nathan's identity is forged in conversion: the voice of his own imagination seems to the child the promptings of Christ. Born again, reimagining his gestation, he "remembers" the actual sensations of warmth and light and is equally convinced that God at that very moment pronounced his "sacred name" (*SM,* 56–57). His grandfather can only shrink in skeptical dismay from the child's "fantasies about Jesus" (*SM,* 84).

In contrast, his grandmother is convinced by the child's absolute faith, and awed by his visions of a punishing God demonstrated in spirit-writing and glossalalia. When she witnesses the literal embodiment of the biblical serpent in the evangelical prayer service, she makes no move to protect her five-year-old grandchild. She faints when Nathan is elevated above the crowd of snake handlers, apparently bitten by a copperhead, although the narrator hints at a more visionary possibility. Nathan is nursed back to life by the addled Dr. Vickery. Resurrected and traumatized, literally and physiologically transformed by the experience, he goes on to bear witness to seven more revelations when God, like the evangelist's snake, "seized him in the flesh."

At this point, Dr. Vickery is shocked out of his stoic silence to raise one last outraged skeptic's protest: Jesus, he cries, is "hateful"; his evangelistic miracles were Hellenic "commonplaces"; He was, in fact, a "maniac," insisting upon his own divinity (*SM,* 135). But the "heart of the reason" proves no match for "knowledge that transcended mere facts" (*SM,* 168). The doctor's flagging energies are given ironic shape in the image of his hourglass, which, blocked by aggultinated lumps of sand, can no longer perform a timekeeping function. When he dies of a stroke, his grandson assumes fearful credit for having an evil eye; and the doctor's possessions, including his well-stocked library, are burned by his pietistic and vengeful wife. Free now of even the vestiges of academic influence, Nathan is ready to take on the problematic role of savior, to initiate the fallen world into a "time of signs and wonders" (*SM,* 166).

At the same time, the narrator becomes more conscious of his own authority and the grandeur of his conception. He takes on a wry and witty air when he describes the crowd of charlatans and confidence men (and women) who collect around the charismatic Nathan and make him a cult figure. Characters who might be equally at home among the "wild-blood" grotesques of Flannery O'Connor begin to appear in this novel: the blowsy and seductive Esther Leonie Beloff, who tempts Nathan to fulfill his sinful desires; her preacher-father, Marion Miles Beloff, leader of the flock at the Church of Jesus Christ Risen, who has learned to indulge his own profane and fleshy appetites in preference to a more sacred calling: "As a young man he had tried anger and righteousness but found it extraordinarily hard work—like reeling in a thirty-pound catfish with no help" (*SM,* 215).

But the parodic tone shifts when Nathan's own vision fills the screen. In a remarkable scene at the center of *Son of the Morning,* Preacher Beloff and the self-proclaimed prophet conduct a debate which pits "honest" charlatan and biblical literalist against freakish visionary. "I'm not flesh," Nathan tells Beloff; then raises the rhetorical stakes when Beloff objects. "We are more than flesh," Nathan insists. "We're proverbs" (*SM,* 222). In his imagination, then, God becomes word! It is the first of a series of stunning inversions, and more than mere wordplay. The prophet wins the final round, simultaneously silencing the baffled religious entrepreneur and reinvoking the novel's early and terrifying feral imagery:

> You *know* . . . that our souls are always with God and never *not* with God. Even in hell it's God hiding behind the flames and the big black snakes and the jaws that snap at one another and the howls of the damned. . . . Even in hell it's God, it's Christ, it's a form of *us* behind the visions—as if we were hunters sighting our prey through a scope but the prey was *us*—looking through what we thought was a telescopic lens when it was only a mirror!
>
> Beloff rose with a shriek. "No more! Stop!" He could bear it no longer. . . . "My God, stop. Do you hear! Do you hear!" (*SM,* 226)

It is one of many modes of conversion in the novel, an artful juxtaposition of the sobering and the comic, an example of what Oates claims to have learned from Franz Kafka: "to make a jest of the horror."[6] The effect in this narrative is to blur the categories, to present a universe of incessant slippage, in which both believer and skeptic play the fool, and Nathan the prophet moves into Satan's role.

Conversely, tragic violence is transformed by bald and outrageous burlesque. Thus, when Nathan, maddened by his mortal sinfulness, literally plucks out one of his eyes, it is viewed simultaneously by "live" worshippers and a national television audience as a kind of grotesque entertainment, making him the most popular prophet in American history. When his shaken and deranged mother comes to his bedside, the half-blind Nathan rouses himself to the work of redemption, begging and then commanding her to pray with him. Her refusal is an ironic allusion to the *non serviam* rebellion of Joyce's Stephen Dedalus as well as that of Milton's Satan. Yet the intertextual network dissolves as poor Elsa Vickery explains her resistance: "But I—I don't want to ruin my stockings!" (*SM*, 262–63).

As Glendinning suggests, the strategy of reversal characterizes this curious novel. Yet Oates uses it to emphasize the radical disjunctions of modern American life. It allows the narrator to break into his history, whether in self-abasing or self-pitying prayer, or in accents of celebration and wonder: "I am continually astonished by the varied nature of the world; of even the human world, which no one can chart" (*SM*, 266), he reflects. Like thousands of his less articulate but equally obsessed American contemporaries, he turns on the late-night radio gospel programs, searching for God in the ringing accents of Brother Reed, the baroque inflections of a harpsichord, and the final blast of furious and accusatory static (*SM*, 266–67). Oates continues to use her fiction as the occasion for social satire.

As part of her critique, midway through the narrative, a new character appears who is one of Oates's academics—or a caricature of one—Japheth. His role seems to be to satirize the position of Oates herself! Like Hugh Petrie of *The Assassins,* and the politicized student activists in *them, Wonderland* and *Do with Me What You Will,* Japheth describes a "revolution of consciousness" in the air. He, too, is a preacher of sorts, mockingly echoing Oates's own "New Heaven and Earth" prophecy, the "end of old cultural ideals . . . combat, of strife, and competition and endless contests—the worship of masculine virtue—virility" (*SM*, 321–22).[7] He elects to join Nathan's cult, the Seekers for Christ, infatuated with the man and the legend. In the process, he articulates his own unresolved inner debate with academe:

> "My mind veers off into two wholly distinct directions," Japheth said."The earthly, the mundane, the practical; and the ethereal, the spiritual, the . . . ut-

terly outrageous. I can't bring the two directions together. . . . I had intended to get a Ph.D. along the way while forcing the two together, but it simply didn't work. So I've given up. The earthly must go its own way while I cast my life with the other. . . . The earthly, the mundane, the practical . . . the *sane* . . . Can't be taken seriously once one has tasted the other world. (*SM,* 301)

Again, the narrator's perpective swings with almost bewildering rapidity here between parody and genuine inquiry. Japheth brings Nathan to an academic reception in an attempt to cure the assembled intelligentsia through the force of healing ministry; the scene becomes another occasion for ironic juxtaposition, as Nathan extends an exorcists's promise and his healer's hand to a sinful sociologist (*SM,* 331–43). But Oates's comedic intentions are succeeded by her sense of tragedy in the scene that follows. Nathan shifts from a playful role as God's holy fool to serve as terrorized witness to a world gone mad: "When the floodwaters recede there is a jumble of things," the narrator intones, also shaken by apocalyptic visions, "broken parts, fragments, coils and loops and shreds" (*SM,* 344).

Many of Oates's heroes literally reenact reigning American myths defined by our literary past; as when Jules sets out for California in *them.* In this spirit, the prophet Nathan takes his ministry to the American West, only to suffer his last and most devastating "crucifixion." Instead of a vision of perfect wholeness, Nathan is confronted with the horror of the physical world, a "chaos of molecules," a Dantesque horror, a "seething mass of life," and a "shapeless, twisting and undulating and coiling and writhing and leaping . . . ravenous" mouth of God (*SM,* 361–62). On the banks of Oates's own mythic locale, the Eden River, the shaken Nathan baptizes himself in the name of that lost infant buried long ago in Childwold. "William" Vickery is reborn to tell this story in the face of God's "jesting spirit" (*SM,* 375). We finally know the narrator's name: it has been this prophet-turned-poet, yearning to believe his lost vision, who has lived through seizure, stroke, assault, and the madness of a Christ-complex, in order to tell the tale:

> You who read this—you cannot guess at my dread, or my self-contempt because of that dread. I am sick with apprehension. I am a gargoyle crouched atop human shoulders, boar's head, dog's head, swollen beastly lips wet with saliva (*SM,* 355)

Feral images resurface as the narrator embraces his ambiguous human condition, attempting a curious and characteristically Oatesian *un*balancing act:

> The phenomenon of language draws us together as sisters and brothers not in Christ but in the Word; yet the phenomenon of language falsifies my experience as it is transmitted to you, for you cannot know, you cannot guess, at the meaning of the spaces between words, the blank white emptiness of silence. . . . Into

which I might plunge myself yet, for perhaps only so desperate an act would return the Lord to me. (*SM,* 355)

The narrative epilogue seems, in light of this last revelation, not the hum-
ble resolution Oates herself describes to interviewers but an uneasy act of
deferral. William, born of a "speech act," returns to Yewville, in search of
those revelations which might prove and restore his own divinity. He rejects
the sensualist's escape, feeling that "man's hunger for God . . . cannot be satisfied by earthly food" (*SM,* 378); he rejects the profane world. Yet, without
prophetic "insanity," his hope to work with the Word as an artist may also be
foredoomed: "My vision cannot be double, I have not the anodyne of madness" (*SM,* 380), the narrator declares in self-mocking despair.

Again, the Oatesian hero is trapped between categories, neither Satan nor
angel. But Oates herself has one more subversive detail to represent: scan-
ning the news, the narrator is visited by old photographs of himself—for he
reads the bogus story of Nathan, a prophet in seclusion who still commands
the faith of thousands of pilgrims and aspirants. It is a ludicrous joke; do
what he will, William/Nathan has become the king of religious confidence
men. "I tried to put Your playfulness out of my mind," (*SM,* 381) he complains, vanquished and at the same time comically resurrected, simultaneously cut off from the sacred and cheered by the irrepressible, risible,
profane dimensions of contemporary life. Oates leaves the novel deliberately
unbalanced.

Finishing *Son of the Morning,* Oates declared herself "quite drained, quite
depleted. And as baffled as ever."[8] Her next novel displays a dramatic change
of voice and an apparently radical shift of scene. In another sense, however,
Unholy Loves (1979) also revisits familiar Oatesian territory, making once-
peripheral concerns central. The academic metaworld, breeding ground of
assassins and fanatics, refuge of enfeebled idealists and pedantic anatomists
in *The Assassins* and *Son of the Morning,* is the stage for Oates's first true
"college novel." She has already entered that parodic space—Japheth, the
graduate student-turned-mystic of the earlier novel is obviously an academic
at home in a city of words:

> As long as he could articulate his condition and express it in concise, witty lan-
> guage [Japheth] believed he was safe. So he took notes on his own dilemma.
> Fancifully, he imagined a film—it would have to be a short, rather amateurish,
> but *artful* film—that dealt with the comic predicaments of an accident-prone
> individual whose accidents became increasingly comic and increasingly dan-
> gerous. (*SM,* 283)

Regarding himself in the third person, moving into cinematic attitudes, Japheth is the most immediate precursor of Oates's academic portraits in
Unholy Loves.

Nonetheless, it seems a dizzying dive from the rhetoric of apocalypse to the wounding but trivial gossip of university receptions, cocktail parties, poetry readings, and more decorous teas. Oates herself, in an interview, describes the capacity of fiction to absorb such radical shifts: "What isn't tragic belongs to the comic spirit. The novel is nourished by both and swallows both up greedily."[9] Indeed, at closer inspection, *Unholy Loves* is an academic novel which defies the conventional expectations of any single genre. Exploiting her own privileged view of the academy, offering an insider's satiric critique of its failures and its promise, Oates enlarges the boundaries until her college novel also transcends its traditional limits.

Oates is not alone among contemporary artists who, finding themselves in residence, have reexamined academic territory with serious artistic intent. Bernard Malamud's *A New Life* underplays the level of brittle satire, underscoring the hero's bumbling teaching efforts and awkward attempts at amour; S. Levin escapes from Cascadia with a sense of honor and a promise of renewal. Saul Bellow's *The Dean's December* is more unabashedly academic, a novel of ideas: Albert Corde, the fictive Dean, resigns his post to affirm his conscience and meet his social contract. His learned astronomer-wife remains absorbed in her calculations at Mt. Palomar; when the ex-Dean joins her, he prove himself capable of the freer ascent of the liberal and liberated imagination. More recently, John Gardner's *Mickelsson's Ghosts* presents a powerful and compassionate account of young and vulnerable college idealists and beleaguered former activists. For Gardner, as for Oates, the academy is not only the realm of disinterested intellectual sport; it is a complex human environment where moral commitments must be taken seriously. It is from that perspective that many modern authors in residence launch their social critique; it is from that source that some hope to draw a rich and allusive picture of the aspiring self.[10]

Just as the university has come to serve as the artist's special modern patron, the academic novel has undergone significant change as a genre. Carolyn Heilbrun, scholar, teacher, and writer of academic mystery novels (under a pseudonym), has commented upon "the peculiar shaping power" of the realm in which she teaches and of which she writes, "the moral universe" of the college novel.[11] Similarly, critic Geoffrey Hartmann insists that "the academy is, despite everything, a good place"; like Oates, he valorizes the protean self, defining the ideal academic as "amphibious," able to see clearly and act responsibly in both the ordered world of the university and the more fluid and chaotic social milieu.[12]

Oates confirms Hartmann's taxonomy when she focuses on the university setting where she herself lives and writes. In her short fiction it has frequently served as an arena of intellectual discourse and human passion, simultaneously a citadel of ideas and a place of disillusionment. She imagines it as the residence of "hungry ghosts": an ironic allusion to Eastern mystical tradition and the title of her collection of satirical short pieces, set in a fictive North American university. She retranslates it as a description of the furies and follies which preoccupy academicians and pervert their original (and presumably loftier) ambitions. The university in Oates's longer fiction is often envisioned as a conservative place, a refuge and repository for the elite and cultural past, a vast collection of art and literature which the more savage society—the fanatics and barbarians of Yewville and Eden Valley—would otherwise fearfully and vengefully assign to the flames.

Indeed, Oates has shown a curious ambivalence about academe in her fiction leading up to *Unholy Loves*. She sympathizes with the desperate strategies of the outsider to gain admission. Richard Everett is the victim of entrance exams. Jules Wendall is exploited almost as a plaything by the college youth culture in Detroit; as a scholarship boy, Jesse remains an outsider in a *Wonderland* medical school. The university accepts the mountebanks, like Trick Monk, but barely tolerates the genuine activists like Jack Morrissey, of *Do with Me What You Will*.

Oates has also subjected herself—an insider at the institution—to the outsider's critique, through satiric allusions to English teachers and, most notably, in the angry correspondence addressed to "Dear Miss Oates" by Maureen Wendall, in *them*:

> I used to get dizzy in your class a lot. Why did you think that that book about Madame Bovary was so important? All those books? Why did you tell us they were more important than life? They are not more important than my life. . . . You always talked too fast in class. . . . We would sit trying to make sense of it, your words, and faster and faster you would talk, getting away from us. . . . You left us behind. (*t,* 312–13)

Maureen's voice rises to an agonized crescendo:

> I listened to you, I lay awake nights thinking of how I must not fail. . . . But I did fail anyway, you failed me. . . . You said, "Literature gives form to life," I remember you saying that very clearly. What is form? Why is it better than the way life happens, by itself? I hate all that, all those lies, so many words in all those books. (*t,* 317–18)

This course evaluation becomes an anthem of hatred and rejection:

> I hate you and that is the only certain thing in me. . . . You write books. What do you know? . . . Oh, we women know things you don't know, you teachers, you readers and writers of books, we are the ones who wait around libraries when it's time to leave . . . we are always wondering . . . what terrible things will come next. (*t,* 320)

Maureen goes on to marry an English teacher, gaining her own residency in a curiously vengeful act.

Seen in context, the letters to the English teacher from her student should be read as part of Oates's ongoing academic critique. In a sense, she is flagellating herself on behalf of all artists in residence for their detachment from the hungers of the real world. The university figures literally and metaphorically as one of the forces that divide American society, sorting men and women into categories of "us" and "them."

The academy is also a central focus and setting in two of her best known shorter works, "In The Region of Ice" and "The Dead." In the first story, a nun (again, an English professor) fails her best student in more than one way, paying a high price for her ivory tower retreat.[13] That story is her most sobering critique; Oates will return to it with revisionary intentions, obsessed by a sense of academic failure. "The Dead," part of Oates's collection of *Marriages and Infidelities,* may be the best example of her academic satire. Oates evokes one of her "demons," James Joyce, in the title; his decadent Dublin is transformed into the debased environment of her own former residence, a midwestern Catholic university.

In Oates's tale, a writer—no longer in residence—returns to her former campus to be honored for her work. Hypocritical and fawning colleagues (including her former lover) crowd around her; she gasps for air and longs for narcotic palliatives. With a wry inner grimace, she also recalls her earlier involvement as an academic insider, sitting in on a master's oral examination which demonstrated only the candidate's total *lack* of mastery of discpline, subject, and idea:

> The candidate was a monk, Brother Ronald. . . . Mr. Honig asked nervously, "Will you describe tragedy and give us an example please?" Brother Ronald frowned. After a moment he said, "there is Hamlet . . . and Macbeth . . . " He seemed to panic then. He could think of nothing more to say . . . could only stammer, "Tragedy has a plot . . . a climax and a conclusion. . . . It has a moment of revelation . . . and comic relief. . . . " (*MI,* 468–69)

Ilena, the heroine, is astonished; she thinks, "Was it possible that this candidate was considered good enough for an advanced degree, was it possible that anyone would allow him to teach English anywhere?" she asks Brother Ronald to define "Gothicism," and the heroic couplet; he declines to do so. She asks if he can describe or even remember any of Shakespeare's sonnets. Finally, growing desperate, she asks for the title of *any* poem, but is still greeted by the monk's perspiring silence. As the panel waits, the time set for the examination runs out, and the student, whining that it had been his order's idea and not his own that he gain a master's degree, is dismissed. Without even glancing at Ilena, the chairman of the examining committee decides Brother Ronald's fate: "We will give him a B." Ilena soon resigns from the faculty (*MI*, 470).

Such scenes, interesting in themselves, are also significant as preparatory exercises for the seriocomic *Unholy Loves*. At first glance, it appears to be one more satiric novel of university manners. Its chapters unfold as a series of Woodslee rituals, receptions and dinners and luncheons, witty and restrained compared with Oates's more monstrous fables of ingestion: table talk, rather than the alimentary orgy, takes precedence. Pedants mouth the latest critical *chic*, or flirt with shopworn and trendy intellectual "heresies": "Hadn't Joyce realized," drones a professor of English, aping John Barth and other fabulator-critics, "that literature ended with the publication of *Ulysses*, with the publication of—nay, the very conception of—such episodes as Wandering Rocks and Cyclops? . . . Literature is dead. Exhausted. We have now a kind of metaliterature, shrugs and vaudeville routines and grimaces, schoolboy stuff" (*UL*, 42).[14] Academic leadership is equally unimpressive. Woodslee's deans focus on typical administrative issues:

> What is the issue tonight? Parking. Once again, parking. . . . Parking and parking-lot assignment and the shortage of space. And bitter, bitter feeling between the divisions and departments, between the faculty on one side and the administration on the other. . . . There have been fist fights in the parking lot nearest the library. . . . Tickets issued by university police have been ripped to shreds. (*UL*, 279)

But *Unholy Loves* is academic in more than one sense. At the level of satire, it chronicles the daily life at an elitist eastern university; it is also allusive, with echoes of Eliot, Auden, Yeats, Frost, Dickinson, and even Joyce Carol Oates, audible in the conversation and critical in the novel's development. And finally, like the work of the heroine, writer and professor Brigit Stott, Oates's academic novel is obliquely autobiographical.

Oates's satire and self-parody are thus meant to serve a more serious turn. Behind the wry grimace, she is genuinely fearful of the human future, apprehensive of the pervasive American tendency to undervalue the life of the mind, and almost absurdly grateful for the academic propensity to take ideas seriously. Amid her gallery of familiar university types, Oates presents sympathetically rendered studies of artists and visionaries. She also offers a chilling view of the secret life of the victims of departmental plots and the incessant intellectual sniper fire—the stillborn thinker, the handicapped hangers-on, terminal cases betrayed by tenure machinations, and especially the beleagured faculty wife:

> Ah, Sandra's head spins. She wants to laugh aloud. People to her left are quite happily discussing a new book by Joseph Campbell, a couple just behind her are

making plans to go to Montreal to see the Canadian National Ballet—and she is a young woman who once, not long ago, wrote fastidious papers on such subjects as Plato's *Meno* and the art of Donne's religious sonnets and the secret meaning of *Moby Dick,* before taking up the more practical study of library science. (*UL,* 204)

Childwold had celebrated a universe of "trash, of beauty"; but in the pedants' realm, daily life is a despised subject:

She is still herself, still Sandra, but her mind is filled with trash, she can feel it sinking beneath the ugly weight of these thoughts, and even the early . . . the naivete of her aspirations here in the Woodslee community seems . . . pristine and enviable . . . she will never be so innocent again. (*UL,* 204)

Simultaneously nourished and depleted by her several sittings at the table of the omnivorous modern university, Stott, the novel's heroine, launches her own intellectual and emotional quest. Not demoralized, trapped, or intimidated like the uncredentialed Sandra, she finds a constant inspiration for literary and scholarly efforts in the work of the great intellectual masters, her "holy loves." Yet around her, the philosophers' great conversation has dwindled to the lecturer's occasional *bon mot* and the undergraduate's embarrassed stammer. Like Ilena in "The Dead," Brigit Stott imagines she is an anachronism, the priestess of a dead vision.

It is into this campus scene, and into the teeth of a savage winter, that a celebrated but aging British poet, Albert St. Dennis, arrives to serve a term as artist in residence. Half-dotty and frail, the old man introduces an unwitting and unwelcome note of parody to the pretentious discourse; often drunk during his Woodslee days, he rejects the campus obsequies in favor of a more appropriate profane response. He is one of Oates's favorite Yeatsian images, a tattered clown made flesh. Indeed, St. Dennis refers to Yeats directly in his own vision of the inextricable relationship of life and art: "Life is the 'untranslatable speech' the poet confronts," he muses. He anticipates his year at Woodslee as a time to begin "rewriting the book of himself" (*UL,* 10), to relocate his ideal readers; thus, he also agrees to appear in a series of public performances meant to add lustre to his and Woodslee's name.

Instead, his appearances are the last acts of a besotted, ghost-ridden, garrulous old man. Professors who had nursed secret hopes that St. Dennis would memorialize them in his poems or in some future dedicatory prose soon are embarrassed by his antics, uncomfortable with both his presence and his more frequent lapses and absences. Since his Woodslee schedule has apparently been prearranged, he continues to stumble through the academic rituals. Interestingly, as the center of campus activity, St. Dennis also serves as a catalyst, stirring Stott from her physical lassitude and her spirit's sleep. He is responsible for initiating the novel's "unholy" love affair between his younger admirers: he clumsily but effectively joins the hands of Stott and the *Wunderkind* of the Woodslee faculty, music professor Alex Kessler.

Moving through crowded social space and jammed lecture halls, these three characters play out the major scenes of Oates's academic drama. Again, while their actions and much of their language is subject to parody, Oates's concerns over intellectual and personal values are not. Beyond bizarre episodes of the flesh—seductions, drunken plunges, eccentric appetites—the three are joined by their persistent sense of the value of art, the "one contestable good" (*UL*, 54), a source of mystery and magic even in the debased modern university. Earthly and "unholy" acts of love can be reduced to "something technical, a mere skill, at best a kind of talent" (*UL*, 55): art on the other hand is "something impossible to fathom. The one is a diversion, the other is life itself," Kessler thinks. For Stott, too, existence is a verbal enterprise, a matter of artistic creation; she feels she must "imagine herself into being" (*UL*, 301) at every instant. Death, "hideous in any case," can only be imagined in terms of language: "irreparable," Stott shudders, "a breaking off of speech" (*UL*, 302). Around Woodslee's lunch and dinner and coffee tables, mock communicants mouth old riddles and rituals: but their bread remains bread, and their water is converted only to tears of self-pity. In contrast, animated by a grotesque stick of a man, Stott and Kessler circle in a curious and even graceful lover's dance of life, far different from the bestial choreography of Oates's earliest work, drawn beyond the confines of residence.

As the novel moves toward closure, Oates slowly untangles these three unholy lives. St. Dennis falters, and his story flickers to an end; the life of his own poems is only fitfully glimpsed through his overblown theatrics at a campus poetry reading. He finds obsequious students and faculty equally repellent, apart from his two "protégés." The old poet alternates between hallucinatory flashes and "voices" from his earlier life, memories of lost loves, drunken boorishness, and occasional and surprising eloquence. Hoping that his words will take fire and ignite sparks of recognition, he literally sets fire to himself, fatally careless, and dies, breaking off speech without apparent issue.

Kessler's case is even more complex and problematic. He is Oates's satiric incarnation of the academic egoist. A handsome man, spoiled by infatuated and doting mentors and in love with his own talent and the vision of his outlived precocity, Kessler is eventually exposed as a failed teacher and stillborn artist, trapped in the prison of self. Clearly, his arrogance has been encouraged by the academic tradition itself, the product of generations of professorial father-figures. It has cost him both the artist's necessary discipline and the more human gift of sympathy. Only his mind is slovenly; to deflect criticism, he decks himself out with gems and a primadonna's self-perfumery.

The most telling example of Kessler's shallowness comes during one of his rare performances, one he has planned for a faculty cocktail party for St. Dennis. When the old poet's violent attack of nausea, evidence of intoxication and failing physical powers, interrupts Kessler's playing, the self-absorbed younger man can only interpret the gagging and retching as a musical critique! Humiliated and victimized by his injured self-esteem as much as by St. Dennis's behavior, he retreats into petulant silence. Ironically, his most promising and interesting project, a song-cycle based on St. Dennis's sonnets, thus attains a perverse form of immortality: it is invulnerable to critical barbs and time's assaults because it will never be completed or performed. From his passionate and then cooling affair with Stott, Kessler drifts into more compromising homosexual unions, fatally at ease in this academic house of mirrors.

Oates presents quite a different view of the artist in residence in her portrait of Brigit Stott, woman, novelist, alter ego. Again, Oates seems to draw upon images and scenes from her earlier work. Like her version of "The Dead," *Unholy Loves* describes the snow that blankets the campus and muffles its fraudulent conversation. But while Ilena in the short story finally lies swooning in a drug-induced vision (the "snow" of cocaine), Stott forces herself to awaken, to confront her fleshly needs and spiritual aspirations, to acknowledge the urgency of both sacred and profane longings in the dark, germinal recesses of her creative imagination. She has one advantage over Kessler from the start: her woman's life has made her wary of both harassment and dishonest artifice, the real lesson she has learned from lustful colleagues masquerading as her mentors.

Since the university offers the female academic few role models, Brigit's quest is modeled after that of a "holy" love, St. Augustine, whose work gives this novel its name (as it has previously supplied the title for Oates's *Do with Me What You Will*). "To Carthage then I came," wrote the classic penitent, "where a cauldron of unholy loves sang all about mine ears." Jabbing her finger into *The Confessions,* Stott blindly locates this very passage in the library. The act seems a parody of scholarly "research," more akin to literalistic textual "readings" by fundamentalists (like the men and women in her previous novel, *Son of the Morning*). It is certainly a curious habit of mind for an academic acolyte. Yet it seems to echo and expose the peculiar religious quality of Oates's lifelong bookish pursuits:

> Always, when she has been most unhappy, she has wandered into libraries, often into the libraries of unfamiliar cities; she had spent hours like this, rather like a blind woman, drawing her fingers across the shelves, across the books, choosing a book at random to open. (*UL,* 257)

Searching through sacred academic texts, Brigit consciously avoids the shelf where her own novels are stored, fearing to view the anonymous assaults of readers' marginalia. "So many books," she thinks dizzily. "Shelves and shelves, row upon row, floor after floor: a galaxy" (*UL,* 258). Her eyes open now, she deliberately takes down a volume by St. Dennis, *The Explorers,* new to her, and a longed-for miracle occurs: the magnificant voice of the old poet rises from the text and drowns out the world's profane clamor and her memories of his failing powers. Returning to her apartment, she finds the peace of understanding rather than death's "brutal" signature graven in winter's "absolute silence." Instead of rejoining the empty academic routine, she finds herself able to miss dinner, to allow the telephone to ring unanswered. Stott all at once becomes a medium for art, in an act of creation which seems to have a life of its own. Dangerous, it calls her very purpose into question, like a self-mocking cry from Beckett:

> Her work intrigues her and frightens her. She cannot approach it. She *must* approach it . . . but when she does, when she reads through what she has written, the voices rise jeering and impatient. *Who are you to attempt anything! What do you think you are doing!* (*UL,* 259)

Many literary and academic images converge in this episode. Oates echoes and alludes to Emily Dickinson's "Hour of Lead"; she also provides a privileged glimpse of her own personal and private sphere. As a creative force pulses through her heroine, Oates seems to be describing her own process of composition:

> She writes in longhand, slowly and carefully, with an almost morbid fastidiousness, in journals bought at old-fashioned stationers' stores. The journals resemble ledgers. (In fact as a child she began with one of her father's ledger books, he must have given it to her to play with.) She writes in dark ink with an old fashioned fountain pen. (*UL,* 250)

For Stott, as for her creator, "the act of writing is sacramental; it must take time, it must be a little difficult, a little awkward" (*UL,* 250). Soon, if she can wait it out, the process may tranform her groping self:

> Brigit looks through her notes, intimidated by them. She is lost, it is hopeless, she can never handle so much material. But the characters are living people, they demand to be heard in their own voices, they are far more real than the people Brigit sees in Woodslee, they *will* insist upon the mad proliferation of details that constitute their lives. . . . The interior life is rich and deep and strange and inexplicable, and the exterior life—the "social life"—is no more complex than it needs to be. *Brigit Stott* is a character she lavishes little skill on: it is a vessel, a means, a transparency. (*UL,* 260)

Interestingly, Oates here repeats the very words of her mad academic, Fitz-John Kasch of *Childwold,* but with vastly different effect. Working out of both sacramental and demonic love (*UL,* 263), Brigit Stott has a mystical experience, rescuing her from the dark night of the soul. Relaxing her anxious grasp of pen, of ledger, of scattered notes, she surrenders herself to the vast creative "membrane" of art, and in the act of denial, discovers another dimension of the self.

> There is a consciousness . . . that permeates language and is somehow given birth by it, and it is always with us, we are never free. From birth onward we are surrounded by it . . . a cocoon of words . . . a living web of language. The world is filtered through it. There is no world except what is filtered through it. (*UL,* 267)

Oates's heroine survives her hour of lead, conscious now of a new challenge: how to hold on to her own identity in the face of art's imposing power? She has seen the transparent self-assertion and imperialistic designs of Kessler, her demon-lover. Tentatively, somewhat fearfully, she moves from her solitary writing desk into a universe of influential "narrators" that she must admit into her own consciousness.

Although it is generally treated as a minor novel, *Unholy Loves* takes on great importance as a revelation of Oates's larger artistic and critical project. It is also the most vivid and unambigous dramatization in her work of the predicament of the artist in residence. Sensible of the delights of the university, Oates continues here to demonstrate its false pretentions. At the same time, she describes the dilemma of the writer as medium, working in realms traversed by literary ghosts. Her multiply revised texts have already testified to the powerful authority of the creative imagination, influencing a work even after its publication. Equally significant is the statement Oates makes in *Unholy Loves* about the quest for integrity: the central concern of her previous novel, *Son of the Morning,* and in some sense her perennial subject.

Choosing to work in a genre ordinarily associated with parody rather than prophecy, Oates again displays the surprising resiliency of literary conventions. In her experiments with genres, in the very act of breaking traditional rules, she attests to art's inexhaustible vitality. She also seems to delight in paradox. The would-be prophet in *Son of the Morning* is left a mourner, finding his sacred quest a diminished thing. But Brigit Stott, in the secular quest of *Unholy Loves,* is brought to a recognition of the transpersonal force of poetry, a mystical vision all the more miraculous because it is nurtured in what Oates sees here as a profane setting.

After her library experience, Stott finds herself able to work again; she is also able to grieve for the lost St. Dennis, to be inured to faculty gossip, to maintain her perspective in the waning passions of her affair with Kessler. In the academic world that, as her satirist's eye shows all too well, is not always a good place or a moral universe, some prurient publishing scoundrel will no doubt soon take up the task of probing and unmasking the dead poet's scandalous biography. In contrast, Stott's art will extend St. Dennis's influence; her own imaginative work will have the resonance of his genuine poetic voice.

Thus, as the novel ends, Brigit Stott moves beyond the artist's sins of pride and possession and the academic word-games of critics and literary *poseurs* to pursue a genuine vocation. The other characters resume their places in the charmed circle of Woodslee. Death has rescued poor St. Dennis from further indecent exposure. The vain Kessler has returned to his real passion: himself. Reanimated, flushed with the excitement of her new work, Brigit Stott greets her jealous former lover with sympathy and wry amusement; she understands the nature of academic residence on more human terms. "Perhaps it is not serious at all," she muses, "perhaps it is only a kind of luncheon. . . . Nothing tragic about it; nothing heroic . . . merely life itself; ceaseless" (*UL,* 316). She has found a way to protect herself from "unholy loves": when Kessler approaches her again in the final scene, they strike out at one another, but only Stott draws blood.

It is almost irresistible to seek literary sources for a novel so frankly academic. David Kirby suggests that *Unholy Loves* owes its ending to *The Wings of the Dove.* Indeed, Stott refers to that novel, calling it James's "most beautiful work," admiring its complexity, its presentation of "an exquisite, maddening riddle never satisfactorily explained" (*UL,* 37). Kirby claims that Oates's novel "ends exactly as does *The Wings of the Dove,* with two lovers recognizing that they can never be lovers again."[15]

But this unorthodox academic novel is better seen as part of Oates's own quest to represent the god-stuck seeker, the visionary moment, the invasions of passions and power unauthorized but visited on the self, undermining intellectual control. Most importantly, unlike James or Dickinson, the novel's literary forebears, Oates refuses the consolations of renunciation when she ends her work with a blow. For Kessler, it is one more humiliation issuing from a world unworthy of his best academic efforts. But from the point of view of Oates and her heroine, Brigit Stott, it is a remedial gesture, an image of grace, a call to life. It is a sign not of stalemate, but of rebirth: the acceptance and fusion of symbol and act, an outward show of inward passion, another motion toward an as yet unrealized human future.

7 Mythic Residence
Bellefleur, Cybele, and *Angel of Light*

In 1980, writing for the *The New York Times,* Joyce Carol Oates predicted that American fiction of the coming decade would be "outrageous and beautiful and idiosyncratic," characterized by "lyricism and airiness, luxuriant space," all possible within the novel's "elastic confines."[1] Her novel *Bellefleur,* also published in 1980, reflects the author's exuberant mood. It is a work of plenitude, leaping and flowing with the rhythms of a rich and teeming world, an encyclopedic and celebratory text. A house of mirrors, it registers the play of uncanny resemblance—obverse reflections of fantasy and document, a mocking juncture of history and game.

Although Oates intends to explore nineteenth-century literary traditions, her eleventh novel is hardly a traditional text. In *Bellefleur,* Oates seems to enlarge the margins of discourse, pushing against temporal restraints in order to exercise what John Knowles calls our "need to narrate."[2] Elsewhere, Oates has described her work as "a kind of massive, joyful experiment done with words." *Bellefleur,* certainly massive and frequently joyful, is a multileveled experiment in mixed media and blurred genres, as Oates tests the resources of historical and fictive narrative, playing for time.[3]

Bellefleur is not romance, not quite historical fiction; rather, it is a transparency, a fabrication which allows us to see through the pretensions of each genre. Dealing with the substance of the past, it does not privilege documented material over legend, fable, or religious belief; a work of the imagination, it incorporates facts, historical personages, and the realist's critique in its unconventional weave. The mimetic act (at once an act of deception and fidelity, duplicitous at the core) fuels its dazzling display. More like Penelope than Scheherezade, Oates has multiple intentions in *Bellefleur:* to preserve fiction's house from prevaricators, usurpers and the self-advertising graffiti of fabulation; to unravel and deconstruct our conventional but factitious designs, readying the mind's eye for new images of experiential reality. Listening to tales of the family's storied past, the Bellefleur children stand in for us as readers: they demand to know, "did it *really* happen?" The narrator's quizzical answer is also the author's question in this novel: *"Really?*—what do you mean, *really?" (B,* 19).

Introducing the first collection of critical essays on Oates published in

1979, a year before *Bellefleur* appeared, Linda Wagner aptly describes the author's artistic project: "Her intention is less in technical innovation than it is in trying the border between the real and the illusory, in testing the space in which those two seemingly-separate entities converge.[4] In *Bellefleur,* Oates not only tests but occupies that resonant space, resisting contemporary conceptions of minimalist art, aware of earlier claims of American writers: patriarchal surveyors, obsessed with the need to generate real archives, to people the vast unmapped landscape with autochthonous figures, to establish residence; to create a usable past.

In an archly revisionist spirit, she presents an old fashioned American family chronicle. Yet Oates's own post-modern intentions are visible at the outset in her playful prefatory statements. There is her Author's Note, far different from the usual disclaimer, demanding that the work be read on its own terms:

> This is a work of the imagination, and must obey, with both humility and audacity, imagination's laws. That time twists and coils and is, now, obliterated, and then again powerfully present; that "dialogue" is in some cases buried in the narrative and in others presented in a conventional manner; that the implausible is granted an authority and honored with a complexity usually reserved for realistic fiction: the author has intended. *Bellefleur* is a region, a state of the soul, and it does exist; and there, sacrosanct, its laws are utterly logical.

To scale the castle walls and gain entry into the family domain, Oates mockingly offers a ladder with missing rungs: a pedigree stripped of the ordinary useful dates. Masked by layers of ingenious fabulation and filled with passages of credulous testimony, the novel is an assault on the constraints of narrativity itself: the conventions of history and geography, the deathward trajectory of chronological order.

Oates sets her own sense of imaginative time against the historian's linear timetable. Signaling her designs on the reader, she takes the novel's epigraph from Heraclitus, philosopher of incessant change: *"Time is a child playing a game of draughts; The kingship is in the hands of a child."* By the novel's end, the epigraph is refracted and re-presented through the point of view of several family eccentrics, as well as by the sometimes intrusive and sometimes invisible narrator. Heraclitus provides the preface to an 800-page treatise by Bromwell Bellefleur, *A Hypothesis Concerning Anti-Matter,* "hundreds of equations, and graphs, and sketches, and impatient desperate doodles," proclaiming the existence of a "mirror-image universe" beyond our clockwork, impervious to calculation or cartography:

> There is no pathway to that other dimension, whether it is called "future" or "past." Only by way of miraculous, unwilled slits in the fabric of time that link

this dimension with a mirror-image universe of anti-matter can one pass freely into that other world. (*B*, 544)

But episodes from the Bellefleur past have already made a lie of Bromwell's visionary optimism. In one of the chronicle's darker chapters, Samuel Bellefleur has an *un*willed glimpse of his own racist nightmare through the looking-glass. Sequestering himself in the mansion's "Turquoise Room," reappearing with less and less frequency, he echoes the vision of Heraclitus: "Time is clocks, not a clock: you can't do more than try to contain it, like carrying water in a sieve" (*B*, 124). Eventually, fatally out of synchrony, he vanishes into the woodwork, becoming one of the haunting presences in the family house. His outraged father chops away the menacing surface of the mirror in the Turquoise Room, but exposes only a blank and featureless backing.

Oates's anecdotal history is presented like a family album with the pages askew, loosely bound by tantalizing fragments of fact and gossip. The voice of the narrator may fall to a whisper, overwhelmed by the power of language itself. At other times it commands our attention, audible in italicized epic catalogues and lavish descriptions, resonating with an irrepressible appetite for hyperbole. "Bellefleurs always exaggerate" (*B*, 260), one family member muses; it is an almost comical understatement in a novel in which everything seems larger than life. From the very first sentence we witness a dynastic act of story-telling. Beginning at the level of formula ("It was many years ago. . . ."), it twists and turns and expands, catching up event, landscape, weather, and the house of Bellefleur in a breathtaking torrent of words:

It was many years ago in that dark, chaotic, unfathomable pool of time before Germaine's birth (nearly twelve months before her birth) on a night in late September stirred by innumerable frenzied winds, like spirits contending with one another—now plaintively, now angrily, now with a subtle cellolike delicacy capable of making the flesh rise on one's arms and neck—a night so sulfurous, so restless, so swollen with inarticulate longing that Leah and Gideon Bellefleur in their enormous bed quarreled once again, brought to tears by their mere mortal bodies; and their groping, careless, anguished words were like strips of raw silk rubbed violently together (for each was convinced that the other did not, *could* not, be equal to his love—Leah doubted that any man was capable of a love so profound it could lie silent, like a forest pond; Gideon doubted that any woman was capable of comprehending the nature of a man's passion, which might tear through him, rendering him broken and exhausted, as vulnerable as a small child): it was on this tumultuous rain-lashed night that Mahalaleel came to Bellefleur Manor on the western shore of the great Lake Noir, where he was to stay for nearly five years (*B*, 3).

Language thus creates an appropriately elastic vehicle for the characters,

both historical and fictive, who fill the Bellefleur stage: the documentary footage includes glimpses of Abraham Lincoln look-alikes, John Brown and Joseph Bonaparte. Holding up a fun-house looking-glass, the author challenges
our capacity to distinguish reality from illusion in a succession of distortions,
involutions, and hallucinatory images; at times, like the Turquoise Room
mirror, it teasingly comes up blank. Evoking Lewis Carroll, Oates pushes us
toward the mirror's edge, a region of parody, lunacy, and metamorphic dissolves, where matter becomes anti-matter. Nearing the flip-side of history,
braving catastrophe, she wrenches her tale from its chronological moorings,
hopscotching back and forth through the sequential grid, undermining our
expectations of sequence—and with it, our traditional sense of consequence.
Like other Oatesian literary exerpiments, *Bellefleur* demands an experimental *reader.*

Hurled into the sweeping narrative flood, we are immediately introduced
to the fugitives from time's stream: the Bellefleur clan, names reechoing and
generations tangled in knots of inheritance. Some, like Raphael Bellefleur,
will almost drown in the coils and pools of time; some will be carried off in
supernal flight; others resurface, driven by sexual and dynastic lust, to lend
authority to the tale. History drops from the pleats of memory, out of order,
but in imaginative context. Both the writer's and reader's task is one of reassembly.

The Bellefleurs themselves play with multiple "draughts." As everyone remarks, they are almost genetically addicted to games of ratiocination, games
of chance. Winning, they assume unwarranted power to tame and create
their own kingdoms and history; losing, they plot revenge or mutter curses,
unwilling to accept the possibility of an indifferent cosmos. Despite their obsessive desire to control their destiny, they display a peculiar susceptibility to
occult transformation. Characters slip into disguise to live out what they assume is only masquerade, only to find themselves trapped in the phantasmagoria of fairy tale. Samuel Bellefleur moves through a mirror and out of
reach; Raphael Bellefleur is absorbed in his watery reflection. The beauteous
Hepatica Bellefleur falls in love with a crude and shaggy laborer, assuming
the role of a Grimm heroine; instead she is drawn into a perverse erotic fable
in which beauty turns *into* beast. It is more than a jest: "Fateful Mismatches"
(Hepatica's story) could aptly title most of the family couplings, preposterous
transgressions of biological, social, psychological, and temporal boundaries.

In this novel, Oates again exploits her academic residence: a world of texts,
sources, influences, and analogues. But her novel is less allusive than it is ex-
uberantly inclusive. Her strategy is metamorphic: legend shades into history;
in the process, fiction becomes fact. Specific literary conventions are em-
braced and magnified in the adventures of Leah, the Bellefleur matriarch,
whose obsessions seem a blend of *Gone with the Wind* and Yoknapatowpha

guilt. The final destruction of the Bellefleur mansion, the holocaust set off by Gideon Bellefleur's maddened kamikaze plane crash, is more than a little reminiscent of the equally flagrant and fantastic aerial bombardment in Fitzgerald's "The Diamond As Big As the Ritz." In a larger sense, *Bellefleur* resembles the collections of mythographers and ethnologists; it includes philosophical treatises, oral history, and evidence of backwoods chicanery, tall tales, and violent blood-feuds. In this realm of sign language, the house which embodies the family's haunted mind, like Usher's, must inevitably fall.

The fall is often parodic; it also exposes the miscues and false premises of the human intellect. The family poet, Vernon, inhabits a world of metaphor ("A man's life of any worth," Vernon often intoned, "is a continuous allegory" [*B,* 296]); but he is not at home in the realm of mortality. He makes ludicrous and finally fatal miscalculations; giving a poetry reading in the rough and tumble backwoods, Vernon himself falls victim to a savage audience. At the other extreme, the family scientist, Bromwell Bellefleur, searches for empirical evidence in order to make sense of the physical world. Even as a child Bromwell performs autopsies on stillborn puppies; he charts the extrasensory perception of his baby sister, in utero and after her birth. Yet instead of resolving life's ambiguity, his observations lead him into a wonderland of mocking mirror images: "Might there be," he wonders, "exact replicas of everything we have here, and would never *see* here, without the reality of that other universe, the lead backing of our mirror?" (*B,* 229).

In his attempts to bring such questions to closure, Bromwell is trapped (as the narrator seemingly is not) by the limitations of language. He is comically wedded to the lexicon of the scientist, even when he rhapsodizes about life's flamboyant display: to him, it is all "clearly a matter of a metabolic current, unstoppable, a fluid, indefinable energy flowing violently through all things from the sea worm to the stallion to Gideon Bellefleur" (*B,* 226–27). Only rarely will he try his hand at metaphor: "Nature is a river that carries you swiftly along. . . . Soon your world is everywhere, and there's no need to hide, and you can't even remember what you were fleeing" (*B,* 226–27). Taking up the paedomorphic style of *Childwold,* Bromwell registers his prematurely adult bafflement: his stunted body seems to give it physical form. Although he will survive the Bellefleur holocaust, he is an isolate, out of communication in a world of change and slippage, where murderous youth can slip into feral canine and back to loutish boy; where a narcissistic child no longer knows where the drowning pool ends and his gaze begins. Oates moves her text daringly in and out of focus, alternating between acts of prestidigitation and authentication. She challenges the tyrannical rule of beginning, middle, and end, emphasizing other narrative modes which suggest a kind of cosmic misrule: memory, dream, fate, magic, desire. Texts give way to signs, evidence of a different mode of seeing, a more protean habit of mind.

One of the novel's most pervasive images, the "Noir Vulture" (in this world of inversions, a white predator) demonstrates Oates's strategy of playful transgression in *Bellefleur*—the magic realism we might find in a Márquez novel. Gigantic, the bird casts ominous shadows over the family imagination, darkening children's dreamscapes. It also occasionally emerges from the twilight zone: it assails a mountain hermit; once, it actually carries off a helpless infant. Emmanuel Bellefleur, the family cartographer, charts the vulture's domain, unrolling his oddly figured parchment and fingering the bird's habitat with a wickedly curved talon of a fingernail (*B*, 333). When Gideon Bellefleur uses that map to track the vicious predator, he is led across imagination's boundaries, stumbling upon a group of dwarfish bowlers in their Catskill hiding place—once upon a time created by Washington Irving. But Oates draws her characters back into her own chronicle. One dwarf, in turn, steps out of the pages of Irving's historical fable to become Nightshade, a servant at the Bellefleur castle: "a troll, imagine, at Bellefleur, in these modern times!" (*B*, 338).

In this metamorphic novel it is no wonder that the dynastic family ambitions are constantly undermined. Even the relentless (and apparently ageless) mapmaker, Emmanuel, "covering every acre on foot," can never finish his surveyor's task:

> The project he had set himself was a difficult, even a merciless one, and though he'd already covered many thousands of feet of parchment with his mapping and notations, he was really nowhere near finished . . . for one thing, the land was always changing, streams were rerouting themselves, even the mountains were different from year to year . . . a fastidious cartographer could take nothing for granted. (*B*, 332)

A fastidious cartographer herself, Oates presents Emmanuel as an artistic alter ego, whose efforts to fix the contours of reality are by necessity foredoomed. Force seems to breed counterforce: human plans are undone and set awash by nature's unpredictable rampaging energies.

Emmanuel's mission is less reprehensible than the lust of the other Bellefleurs who long to impose their egoistic family plot on the world around them, from the original Jean-Pierre to Leah. They perpetuate the species; they people the mountains. But they cannot, finally, resist nature's inexorable force. The defeat of human effort is nowhere clearer than in the remarkable tale of Great Grandmother Elvira's birthday celebration. Leah's plans for this family centennial are magnificent in their scope and energy; yet the party is best remembered as a symbol of human failure on a grand scale. A catastrophic hurricane scatters the celebrants, provisions, and decorations, canceling all chances to convene the far-flung Bellefleur clan. In the wake of the storm, human efforts seem puny indeed.

As the overweening Bellefleurs test the limits of pride and of possession, deathly struggles rage outside the castle walls: dogs multiply dangerously and run in murderous packs; foxes right the imbalance of over-fertile nature by tearing each other to pieces; thousands of rats invade the Bellefleur's estate in a desperate struggle to survive, requiring the efforts of a latter-day pied piper. Nature's metamorphic energies are not always hideous. As we have seen, *Bellefleur* opens with a storm and the appearance of a vicious beast who slashes Leah when she opens the door of the mansion to admit him. Miraculously transformed, the animal appears the next day as Mahahaleel, an indolent and luxuriously plumed cat, confusing Gideon Bellefleur, whose move to defend his kingdom is not only checked but mated.

Bellefleur thus dramatizes the striking incongruence at the heart of literature and history: the factitiousness of plot, whether self-devised or providential. Life—risky, marginal, unpredictable, unmappable—is kaleidoscopic, generated out of violence, snatched from the literal and figurative jaws of chaos. It eludes Gideon's posturing, Vernon's poetry, Raphael's pantheism, Bromwell's experiments: seen through such angles of vision, it is human history which seems malevolent.

Juxtaposing the horrifying and the comedic, Oates asks us instead to reconsider our cherished mythology of dominion, to acknowledge the grotesquerie of our existence. The novel's heroine, Germaine, is thus primarily an observer, rather than actor, rarely speaking but implicitly present for the recitation of this metamorphic family history. She is first introduced as a fetus with supernal powers over her mother, Leah. She is born, kicking and screaming, as an androgyne, with the vestigial genitalia of a half-formed male twin protruding from her infant abdomen. While the Bellefleur matriarchs stand by, shocked by this ghastly sport, Leah's mother—pragmatic, unromantic, indifferent to society's opinion—puts an end to the horror with "three skillful chops of the knife," giving the baby and the family new birth (*B*, 102). By the novel's end, Germaine's curious powers have been absorbed into the Bellefleur legend. She has become the witness who will survive to tell the tale, and, perhaps, to weave a different sort of narrative.

In *Bellefleur,* Oates sets up an intriguing contrast between the chronological patriarchal saga and the cyclic rhythms of a woman's text. Thus Germaine's life emerges in brief episodes which serve as fictive counterpoint to the history of an earlier survivor, Jedediah Bellefleur. Ahead of his time, one of Oates's god-struck prophets, inept in the world's ways, he quits family life for a hermit's existence in the verminous waste and howling expanse of the unmapped mountains. Curiously, after the family fortunes are gained and lost and the house of fact and fiction set ablaze, the narrative flips back through a chronological loop, resuming with the story of Jedediah's home-coming. Out of sequence, his return nevertheless functions as the novel's "ending": the prophet sheds his penitential rags to take a up a husband's re-sponsibilities, reknotting the broken threads of Bellefleur history. It is almost as if Oates herself has succeeded in her own fabulist's quest to twist the tail of time; to read significant patterns into a world of contingency and change.

Yet the introductory family pedigree, undated after Jedediah's return, teas-ingly suggests that Oates does not intend to settle for the old terms of histor-ical fiction, however they may affirm the human prospect. Rather, she has attempted a new experiment in narrative form to match her own revisionary sense of human history. *Wonderland* represented a tentative "filmic" narra-tive structure. *Bellefleur* is also the work of an auteur, setting a cinema of the imagination into motion with a montage of special effects accompanied by an alternately rising and diminishing soundtrack. Oates rewinds her narra-tive clocks in a whirl of activity, a fluid unreeling of impressions almost too brief for precise identification: images of Einsteinian relativity, snatches of folk song and poetry, the skin drum which chillingly anticipates Buchenwald, tawdry soap-opera romances, amusement park simulations.

The narrative form which replaces the defunct saga is in fact feminist craft.[5] In a letter to the editor of *The Women's Review of Books,* Oates has identified "quilt-making" as one of her recent subjects. It is certainly a refer-ence to *Bellefleur,* a novel shaped from reusable fragments to fit on a new frame.[6] Throughout the story, Aunt Matilde's quilted handiwork fascinates Germaine, the child who survives androgynous joining and will escape her father's final terrorist act:

> The quilts, the enormous wonderful quilts!—which Germaine would remem-ber all her life.
> Serendipity: six feet square, a maze of blue rags, you could stare and stare and stare into it.
> Felicity: interlocking triangles of red, rose-red, and white.
> Wonder-working Providence: a galaxy of opalescent moons. (*B,* 328)

Matilde's work provides a sense of continuity in a world in which "every-thing shifts, changes, grows fluid, transparent" (*B,* 315). It is a different way to chart a pedigree, to mark time:

> The living and the dead. Braided together. Woven together . . . taking in centur-ies. . . . The living and the dead. Centuries. A tapestry. Or was it one of Matil-de's ingenious quilts that looked crazy to the eye but (if you allowed her to explain, to point out the connections) made a kind of dizzying sense? (*B,* 114)

Matilde's favorite quilt in *Bellefleur* is a type known as a crazy quilt, an origi-nal, intricate, asymmetrical piecework, a collage of multiform and particolored oddments shaped to the maker's canny touch. She has named it "Celestial Timepiece":

> Celestial Timepiece was the largest quilt, but Matilde was sewing it for herself
> —it wasn't to be sold: up close it resembled a crazy quilt because it was asym-
> metrical, with squares that contrasted not only in color and design but in tex-
> ture as well. (*B,* 328)

Curiously, but not surprisingly in terms of the artist's subversive designs, it offends the family's arch gamesman, Grandfather Noel:

> Noel complained that Celestial Timepiece made his eye jump. You had to
> stand far back to see its design, and even then it was too complicated—it gave
> him a headache. "Why don't you just sew some nice little satin comforter," he
> said. "Something small, something pretty."
>
> "I do what I am doing," Matilde said curtly. (*B,* 329)

With this quilt, Matilde initiates Germaine not into the timebound world of recorded history but into the timeless world of women's art:

> "Feel this square, now feel this one," Matilde said softly, taking Germaine's
> hand, "and now this one—do you see? Close your eyes." Coarse wool, fine
> wool, satins, laces, burlap, cotton, silk brocade, hemp, tiny pleats. Germaine
> shut her eyes tight and touched the squares, seeing them with her fingertips,
> reading them. "Do you understand?" Matilde asked. (*B,* 328)

Seeing, understanding, Germaine gives rapt and wordless assent. In her hands she holds a story woven of memory and desire, the finery of ritual min- gling with the pleasures of everyday use.

Piecing together a quilted novel is more than a fabulator's witty conceit; only to someone ignorant of the quilting process does a crazy quilt seem a haphazard contruction. Certainly unbound by conventional patterns, taking shape rather than filling in precise and prearranged outlines, it nonetheless represents a deliberate joining of past and present, personality and history, incorporating facts and fragments into an enticing, touching, and often dis- turbing fabrication.

At the close of *Bellefleur,* we hear Jedediah's bewildered cry as he faces the human spectacle and feels his own pulse: "I don't know what to believe" (*B,* 558). In the early chapters of the book but actually at a much later moment in history, Leah reveals the abyss yawning beneath her own deisgns: "I don't believe in anything," she rages (*B,* 70). Leah and Jedediah seem to have much in common; they are figures in a saga enlivened by blood-feuds and the machinations of old gods. Yet, if we stand back far enough from the patched and multitextured surface, Oates offers us the whole cloth ready to be worn again in the problematic modern world. In *Bellefleur,* Oates has begun a series of revisionary experiments with nineteenth-century narrative genres. In the process she raises key questions about both fiction and history: how to give form to prodigality; how to fabricate, with both humilty and audacity; how to represent the miltivarious but sacrosanct laws of the imagination.

Oates calls *Bellefleur* her "postmodernist investigation of the family saga."[7] It is also intended as the first movement of a "quintet," a series of novels which are also re-drafts of nineteenth-century genres: the saga, the romance, the detective story, varieties of gothic narrative. Exposing the designs of each genre through ironic imitation, Oates perhaps inadvertently brings down the house of traditional fiction. Her explicit intentions, as she suggests in essays and interviews, are honorable: she is staking her own claim to the literary heritage.

Curiously, however, her next work seems out of sequence. *Angel of Light* (1981) is a twentieth-century novel, dealing with young terrorists who find themselves unwittingly caught up in primordial dramas of betrayal and revenge. In an interview after the publication of *Bellefleur,* Oates remarked, "the young people, one by one, leave the castle . . . and some of the pretensions of 19th century imperialist America." In the strident accents of *Realpolitik,* Oates suggests she herself has stepped out of the castle and into the modern political scene because of a "particular empathy with adolescents."[8]

We know we will not see the last of the Bellefleurs; even in this time scramble, there are always children to take up the game of draughts and imaginative re-drafts. But for children of the twentieth century, political games lead to the edge of madness. As Cara Chell observes, *Angel of Light* is a fable of modern apocalypse.[9] It is also another act of artistic trespass, crossing the boundaries of literature and history, dramatizing adolescence as a border state.

Indeed, adolescents figure centrally in much of Oates's fiction. They are literally between the categories, in perilous passage. We have seen them in her earlier novels: grotesque prodigies (Bromwell Bellefleur and Richard Everett) future artists (Jules Wendall, Laney Bartlett), unworldly prophets (Nathan Vickery, Stephen Petrie), victims who seem to invite assault (Swan Revere, Karen Herz, Maureen Wendall, Shelley Vogel). Protean, sensitive, on the margins of adulthood, they are striking representatives of the "lost" post-Vietnam generation. Oates's youthful characters mirror the contradictory aspirations of our culture and our time.

In *Angel of Light,* the adolescents—Owen and Kirsten Halleck—bear an even weightier symbolic burden. They are children of privilege (Harvard, and Eyre preparatory academy); they have grown up in the shadow of the Capitol and the Pentagon, privy to its gossip and its cabals. They are also heirs of the American "angel of light," a term coined by Thoreau for John

Brown in his famous "Defense." Oates's deliberate allusive design casts her political novel in larger type. *Angel of Light* is a modern version of an imposing cultural myth, the tragic legend of the house of Atreus, with Owen and Kirsten playing out classic roles of child-avengers, vehicles of justice.

Although the novel seems a product of the late sixties and Watergate, it has an older genesis. Curiously enough, *Angel of Light* was one of Oates's first novels: she told an interviewer that she began writing it in 1959, but put it aside.[10] By 1981, she was ready to take up its themes again, hoping to relate the deepest concerns of contemporary academic and public life to more timeless mythic configurations.

To come to terms with this multivalent novel, it is interesting to consider its relationship to Oates's other work, and its own imaginative genealogy. Oates continues to explore the possibilities of myth; her *Bellefleur* expands to fill a mythic territory not only of her own making, but drawing upon American archives. An earlier novella *Cybele* (1979), provides a particularly fascinating gloss on *Angel of Light*. Again, it is myth in modern dress. Adolescence is the lure and dream of *Cybele;* its "hero" is a voyeur, a man struggling in the tragicomic crisis of middle life. Locke, the hero, one of the Edwins to whom the volume is dedicated, is the prisoner of his own vanity and desire. Oates makes ironic use of the popular romance: her story is structured as a series of infidelities and assignations. Indeed, this novella flirts with the conventional requirements of several genres. Its plot is stylized, moving with deliberate speed toward a preannounced tragic conclusion. Yet it also is sophisticated satire, exposing the sexual peccadillos of the affluent suburbanite, a figure perhaps more at home in the fiction of John Updike (his chronicle of infidelity, *Couples,* was published a year earlier).

Oates seems interested more in myth than in manners. Edwin Locke reflects on his predicament in terms already part of the Oatesian repertoire: literature itself is no solace but a terrifying mirror of his paranoia. Thus, pathetically seeking love in a sordid massage parlor, he cries out to the stolid masseuse,

> "I want to live. I have a right, don't I, to *live.* I don't want to die without . . . without having lived. For most of my life I was playing a game but I didn't quite know it. . . . The game of Edwin. . . . It's like being back-stage during a play . . . once you *see* the play from that angle it no longer works. And you can't help what you see. Stage make-up and phony histrionic gestures and blinking lights. . . . Chalk on the floor to indicate where they should stand. . . . I said, let the goddam play continue without me. . . . I want to live, is that so evil? Is that so crazy? You wouldn't understand, you're too young yourself . . . it's the oldest story in the world and you have every right to laugh at me." (*Cy,* 146)

Like many an Oatesian hero, Edwin sees a literary plot in his own madness.

The novella is sprinkled with more pointed literary allusions. Edwin must deal with lawyers as part of his complex marital and extramarital predicament, including the firm of "Bushy and Bagot"; his mock-romances are staged at the Round Table. But the most telling structure of reference is announced in the title and expressed in the framing device of the story, the chillingly oracular narrative voice. Drawn from the pre-Olympian pagan past, "Cybele" is a creature of implacable and mysterious force, who must be propitiated by ecstatic self-castration; she is as deadly as a queen bee to her male pursuer.

Robert Graves, in his study of *The Greek Myths,* describes Cybele as the remnant of an ancient orgiastic matrilinear cult, a goddess later transformed into the Venus of the patriarchal Attic culture.[11] Sexual hegomony hangs in the balance in this process of re-mythologizing; Cybele's issue is androgynous. Oates's reference to this myth is further evidence of her growing concern with gender. Here, it represents a scholar's allusion; she gives it artistic form in the grotesque neonate, Germaine Bellefleur. (Oates's philosophy of androgyny, articulated in critical essays on Woolf, Bazin, and Heilbrun and in an address to colleagues at the Modern Language Association, also involved her in a feminist critical debate during the turbulent seventies.[12])

In *Cybele,* Oates is fascinated by androgynous grotesques in the unisex sixties: Cybele thus becomes an appropriate narrator for Oates's contemporary myth. She is cruel and selfish: "There was once a lover of mine who worshipped me, and became reckless with his life, which was soon taken from him" (*Cy,* 11), she begins, parading her own narrative technique in the opening chapter. She is jealous of her powers; she rejects Edwin contemptuously in the last episodes for his attempt to cast life into the shape of fiction:

> I can't credit him with any insight, any depth. The final belief, it has been said (but not by one of *my* lovers), is to believe in a fiction, a metaphor, which you know to be a fiction, there being nothing else; you must love it as if it were . . . something more, and less, than a fiction. In that way you are transformed, made (for a time) immortal.
>
> My lovers, however, are mortal. (*Cy,* 194)

With obvious satiric intention, Oates attempts to fit a modern love story into a deathly if classic matrix, choosing the only locale where such a hybrid might seem natural: the university environment. Edwin Locke takes his pathetic goatish quest (in the "sweet" month of mock-Chaucerian April) to campus haunts. Inflamed by lust, he reads the signs around him as the material for an epic catalogue:

Steppenwolf Coffee Shop; Victor Brink for Mayor Headquarters; Les Images

Gallery; University Arms Apartments; University Drugs; Giles Prosthetics; Shawnee Chicken Take-out; Legal Aid Center; Women's Caucus for a United Front. . . . young people everywhere. (*Cy,* 154)

Aroused by the youth culture and their young bodies, he imagines himself the hero of a romantic interlude set in an off-campus bookstore:

On the peeling walls, high above the bookshelves, tattered yellowing posters of Allen Ginsberg, Ché Guevera, Marlon Brando as the Godfather, Marx, Lenin, Walt Whitman, Castro, Lee Harvey Oswald, Anaïs Nin, Pogo, Gary Gilmore, Richard M. Nixon, Groucho Marx . . . Jane Fonda in a Spacewoman's outfit, Mick Jagger, Beethoven, Charles Manson, Fritz Perls, Linda Lovelace, Scrooge McDuck, Malcolm X., Janice Joplin . . . Edwin feels unaccountably excited, cannot say why, peers through a corner of the metal shelves at a girl sitting cross-legged in the next aisle. (*Cy,* 157)

The girl, insouciant and self-possessed, bears a mythic name, Iris; Edwin joins her narcissistic drama already in progress, and rescues her from the shopkeeper's invective in one of the novel's many word-duels. But she is immune to the strategies of her aging would-be lover. She barely tolerates his adoration, interrupting his passionate love-making to review an old assignment. Again, Oates unambiguously alerts the reader to her own academic intentions:

Sooner strangle a child . . . a babe . . . in its crib, than, how does it go, suppress your desires, oh shit, how does it go?
How does what go?
The saying, you asshole! The poetry!
What poetry?
Blake. Something about strangling a baby. (*Cy,* 152)

Oates (and her sybilline narrative persona) is merciless in her critique of both members of this mismatched couple. The allusion to Blake is an implied rebuke to Edwin's trivialized existence; it also exposes the academic travesty of the youth culture. Iris, a modern handmaiden of the goddess-narrator, hounds poor Edwin to death; he dies of a heart attack, running away from the horrifying spectre of her hermaphroditic child. Iris is joined by another marginal campus figure: a sculptor who makes mountainous figures out of trash. To destroy potentially dangerous evidence, he sets Locke's corpse on fire under a culvert—a Vietnam incendiary image, as well as a mocking echo of mythic immolation.

The novella, at times a powerful sociopolitical critique, virtually collapses under the weight of symbolic overload. Yet it provides a dramatic prologue for *Angel of Light,* a novel which draws upon a complex design of mythic and literary allusion. As an example, the parodic echo of Blake's *The Marriage of*

Heaven and Hell in *Cybele* expands into a major intertextual reference in Oates's "Oresteia."Taking up the clues of prophets, poets, and mythmakers, she sets forth to explore the contemporary sociopolitical labyrinth. But unlike the crazily asymmetrical sybilline vignettes, *Angel of Light* displays fearful symmetries. The nine sections are arranged in alternating sequence, moving between the contemporary debauch and the more naive milieu of the previous generation. The carefully plotted echoes and overlays suggest the inevitability of human action: Oates's version of classic fate.

Kirsten and Owen Halleck's plan to kill their mother and her lover, Nick Martens, moves with the inexorable logic of Greek legend. Brother and sister are moved by Blake's "hellish" proverbs: better students than Iris, they quote him correctly (*AL*, 291–92). For them it is no idle academic gloss; Blake inspires their urge to enact their desire for revolutionary justice. In the aftermath of their father's disgrace and suicide and their mother's infidelity, as hostages in a world of shadowy assassins, it is understandable that the betrayed children see Blake's proverb as justification for retribution.

If they misread Blake, however, they understand Aeschylus all too well. In *Angel of Light* Oates takes up a mythic quest herself, determined to reorder, rework, and revise. Her novel is an ingenious intellectual exercise: her own drama of contraries; a battle between generations. "I wanted to deal with a myth in which children felt estranged from their parents . . . and were led to avenge their parents," she explains.[13] Like Blake, she is attuned to opposition: the violence of the youth culture, both invigorating and self-destructive; the need to purify a corrupt social order; the killer's passion which shades mysteriously into a lover's compassion. As she draws parallels between titanic and historic struggles—at Troy, at Harper's Ferry, on the steps of the Pentagon—she also dramatizes the moral confusion of the enfeebled individual human actor. *Angel of Light* is a drama of self-deception; fathers as well as children are betrayed by their credulity. The dead father, Maurie Halleck, has been betrayed by his belief in external agency: his commission as Minister of Justice; his reliance upon the marriage contract and the friend's handshake; but most of all, his expectation of divine intervention and visitation—"All his life he has awaited a sign but of course no sign came. For he had imagined it outside him" (*AL*, 509).

Clearly, in the way Oates has come to define the genre, this is academic fiction, reflecting the passions of the young and newly tested, the force of imposing cultural symbols and traditional visions, and the resonance of a host of influential texts. *Angel of Light* is prefaced by a dedication which sets forth Oates's academic and artistic intentions:

This novel is for Robert Fagles,

> *in honor of his service in the House of Atreus;*
> *and for our lost generations—*

In the intriguing epigraph, Oates pays her artistic respects to three influences. One is Hemingway, perhaps the most curious of her "demonic" mentors. Elsewhere she describes her debt to Hemingway's craft:

> As a sophomore in high school . . . I accidentally opened a copy of Hemingway's "In Our Time" in the public library one day and saw how chapters in an ongoing narrative might be self-contained units, both in the service of the larger structure and detachable, in a manner of speaking, from it. So I apprenticed myself, with my usual zeal, to this beautiful and elusive new form. (Stories, 15)

In *Angel of Light* Oates, like Hemingway, focuses on the young and the betrayed, the generation with "the self-consciousness of being lost, being special, 'damned,' casually committed to self-destruction."[14]

The epigraph also identifies this novel as Oates's homage to Aeschylus. But as she takes pains to indicate, Oates chooses to read the classic trilogy through the eyes of a special scholar and mediator. Her Princeton colleague Robert Fagles, translator and critic, is a third imposing influence on *Angel of Light*.

In his preface to the Princeton translation of *The Oresteia,* "The Serpent and the The Eagle," Fagles, in fact, finds in the ancient text a demonstration of the ongoing process of artistic revision. He writes convincingly of the power of mythic renewal; the classic "rite of passage from savagery to civilization" must be reimagined by every age:

> Aeschylus insists that each generation create a new alliance between the forces in contention for its world; and he presents their conflict in a range of ways, from cosmic to intensely personal . . . the potency of creation . . . the force of love-in-hate that impels our rude beginnings toward our latter-day achievements.[15]

The Greek dramatist himself had underscored the parallels between ancient wars and modern Athens, and in *The Oresteia* "makes old myths new." And if this were not enough to inspire Oates in her own work, Fagles also invokes Blake in his vision of Clytemnaestra's children: "They have heard Blake's Proverb of Hell: 'Sooner murder an infant in its cradle than nurse unacted desires' " (Fagles, 7). Like Fagles, Oates seems convinced of the persistent rhythms of ancient blood-feud; she creates a new alliance between the house of Atreus and the fratricidal tragedy of John Brown.

This novel thus provides almost too much quarry for the reader with purely academic pursuits. Yet Oates is intent on giving her long deferred novel the density of myth. The Hallecks and their circle exhibit classically swollen ambitions in *Angel of Light*. Their minds have been shaped by the trivium and quadrivium, by old-fashioned pedagogues (although one Socratic mentor vanishes mysteriously, to reappear as a modern Washington shape-shifter). The very complexity of Oates's weave turns mythic illusion into a deliberate tangle: Maurie Halleck is the classically-wronged husband, but is he the warrior, brought low by wife and lover, or the bandy-legged Vulcan, betrayed by Venus? At one point in the novel, three young wives watch a seemingly endless tennis combat, retelling—as well as symbolically reenacting—the legend of the Judgment of Paris. Yet no Paris comes to judge. To make her didactic intentions clear, Oates has one of her fictive goddesses voice a complaint at being locked into this timeless pattern:

> I hated [Greek legends] when we studied them in college—in ancient Greek— because they're so crude and merciless, and I think because they tell us such implacable truths about ourselves. Truths that don't seem to change across the centuries. (*AL,* 386)

Such reference illuminates some of the novel's darkest passages; it also gives the novel a curiously elegant note of parody. Clytemnaestra betrays her husband by appealing to his vanity, having him walk on a rug consecrated to the gods; in this novel, Owen, the avenger, is invited by his homoerotic seducer to step on a mysterious Uruguayan flying carpet woven of birds' wings. Oates provides a mocking academic evaluation of Maurie Halleck's state of mind by recording his response to Greek drama during his final anguished days:

> He lies awake much of the night, reading the Bible, trying to read Sophocles, Aeschylus, Euripedes . . . at first in Greek . . . and then in translation; but it is very difficult to concentrate. The Greeks sound at times too contemporary, he wonders if he is misreading the text. (*AL,* 71)

Failing his human and literary assignments, he is finally "unable to read Aeschylus. . . . Aeschylus requires extreme concentration and a great deal of courage" (*AL,* 504). Maurie enforces his own death sentence after this terrible *reader's* block.

Isabel Halleck, a fabled beauty, thwarted by her own unacted desires, emerges from the trivial pursuits of Washington society as a modern Clytaemnestra. Like her mythic model, she holds her husband responsible for the death of a daughter; but Oates's classical reference again is savagely reductive. Ironically, Isabel's child has died of congenital defects; in the Greek myth, the child has been sacrificed to propitiate angry gods. She has not "technically" become the mistress of Nick, her "demon" lover (*AL,* 245) and this work's Aegisthus. Literally, they have not murdered the hapless, worshipful Maurie; but, as Isabel cries out to Nick, their unconsummated but passionate desires and Nick's political sabotage make them responsible for his drunken plunge into a weedy Virginia swamp: "We did it, Isabel is whispering, we killed him, we'll be punished. . . . You killed him that day you lied to him—it's as simple as that." (*AL*, 539–40)

Responding to their father's disgrace and death, Isabel's daughter and son seek "justice" (*AL*, 578), imagining themselves the agents of divine furies but more often acting as dupes of anarchists and egoists. Kirsten is an anorexic and neurotic Electra, a school girl who is not well served by the curriculum or governesses of Eyre. The real life of her great-great-grandfather, John Brown, becomes somehow trivialized as a term paper topic. But Kirsten pursues a grandiose obsessive quest to fix responsibility for her father's death: "She was a fact-finder, an interpreter. A kind of translator. She listened, she watched, she took note, she observed. But she did not judge" (*AL*, 193).

She is also tortured by a secret: like Joyce's young artist, Kirsten has refused to kneel and pray with her God-mad father before his death (*AL*, 73, 169, 222, 506). To assuage her guilt, she imagines herself in his watery grave, gasping in the nauseating underwater seepage. Wasted, bruised by encounters with her mother's admirers, Kirsten, like Electra, survives the novel's bloodbath, finally more victim than victimizer.

In contrast, Owen Halleck—Oates's Orestes—is a parody of his mythic counterpart. A pampered and effete collegian, bound for "HLS" (Harvard Law School), Owen is embarrassed by his sister's excessive behavior; he is not convinced of the truth of her accusations. His attitude changes when he is taken up by an aging pederast, Ulrich May, and seduced into becoming a terrorist-hero. His plot eclipses hers; he enlists Kirsten in May's revolutionary cadre, a group reminiscent of Patty Hearst's symbionese liberators. With little genuine moral conviction and overweening vanity, Owen drives himself toward his bloody act of vengeance, surprising and bludgeoning his mother in her bath (another parodic mythic echo). Ironically, he is too maddened, drunk, and dazed to escape when the deed is accomplished, although what was *"once already imagined"* in Blake's echoing phrase *"is now proved"* (*AL*, 292, 428). Regressing to an infantile state, he crawls under old bedclothes, and dies in the explosion of a bomb he has planted in his family's house.

Thus, Oates's intertextual strategies create a work of almost perverse contrariety. The halls of the powerful are booby-trapped by the deluded heirs-apparent; modern children are vulnerable to unpredictable assult; love is reduced to a tennis love-set. In *Cybele,* the king must die, victimized by his own sexuality; under the reign of an unforgiving goddess, there is no redemption. Fagles speaks of the Oresteia as a fable of democracy. But Oates revises the mythic tradition in *Angel of Light* to serve her own designs.

Owen cancels out his mother's guilt and his own; more significantly, however, Kirsten fails to complete her assignment. She seeks out her mother's demon-lover, Nick; she arranges a seduction; she unsheathes her knife and stabs him as he reaches for her in a breathless, perspiring embrace. Preparing to escape, she hears Nick's agonized gasps, but cannot finish him off; her act of violence has also been an act of love. Running to the street, she muffles her voice and telephones for help. On his part, the slowly recuperating Nick lies about the incident, unwilling to betray his murderous assailant.

The novel's epilogue is not set in the palace of wisdom, the city of Greek measure; civilization is neither redeemed nor condemned; the guilty are not punished. Kirsten is spirited off in the custody of distant relatives to cooler northern regions. Nick Martens survives to live out a solitary life amid the raucous birds on some primitive shore. Healing, he writes letters to Kirsten. The first is a curious academic lesson, describing a primitive rite very like those dedicated to Cybele, which had fascinated Nick and Maurie in their school days:

> We'd both been studying Latin and we had both read about some brutal religious practices—secret rites—rites of what we would now call initiation—in which young men were terrorized and exhausted to the point of hysteria, so that they lost their sense of the self's boundaries, and identified with the very victim of the sacrifice. . . . They passed over into what they were killing—they were the victims. Victims—it was a form of sympathy we can't understand. (*AL,* 604)

That very lesson has begun to permeate some deeper consciousness. Nick had confessed to the crimes once blamed on Maurie Halleck. Now he prowls the shore, conscious of the fragility of his own boundaries and the unreliability of human measures of size and range and sanity:

> A trotting dog in the dunes can acquire, within a fluid instant, the size of a deer; a tern dipping overhead, the proportions of a hawk. Algae in a puddle trapped on a ledge might be darkly scarlet as blood, and then, as the light shifts, as the clouds pass overhead, it reverts to the hue of seaweed, and suddenly there is nothing to see.

> Nick cannot be surprised any longer by such changes. One minute he is dwarfed by the immensity of sand, the next, he feels himself towering ten feet tall, his shadow bobbing like a clown's. (*AL,* 604)

As a schoolboy, on a trip with Maurie and two other classmates, Nick had experienced the world of nature as a great and insatiable maw; responding, the boys had been filled with rapacious and bestial hunger. Hours later, at the mercy of raging rapids, Maurie had almost drowned; the stronger Nick had saved his life. Now, panting, weak, bearing the scars of murderous violence, and tasting his own mortality, Nick is no longer able to work his will. Vulnerable to mirage, he mistakes shadows on the waving grass for ghostly lovers;

churning seaweed for a flailing swimmer. As Minister of Justice, Maurie Halleck was driven to suicide by the impossible terms of his office. At land's edge, Nick Martens humbly abandons his own search for worldly justice. At the same moment, he releases his assailant—and victim—from the prison of his own memory and will. He writes Kirsten a last letter: *"I won't ever attempt to find you,* he tells her, *I see that our exiles can never touch. I can't even imagine you now"* (*AL,* 605). Through the hellish agency of Kirsten, "a frenzied angel of wrath" (*AL,* 603), Nick has awakened to a world beyond human understanding. It is a world where angels often seem devils, a realm bathed in duplicitous light.

Oates resists the safety of closure, and promises her demon-hero no state of grace. Tragically, his vision has come too late, and Kirsten's sacred rage has virtually destroyed them both; Nick must live out the terms of mortality and exile in a world of contingency and change. Yet Oates has also weakened the grip of the tyrants of the mind and spirit in the curious coda of *Angel of Light.* She has revised one of our oldest texts; she has also renewed her energies for the novels to come. Unlike Aeschylus, it is her intention to keep the furies' energies alive.

In *Image-Music-Text,* Roland Barthes declares that texts are not singular but irrepressibly plural: "A text is made up of multiple writings, drawn from many cultures and entering into mutual relations of dialogue, parody, contestation. . . . "[16] While Barthes's description could cover all of Oates's work, it is especially suggestive of the narrative design and theme of *Angel of Light.* In her earlier novels, Oates dramatized the almost unendurable tension between the shapely world of books and the disorder of human history—especially the torturous journey of the self. But in this novel, written over several decades, she finds an uncanny metaphoric fit between poems of Blake and Aeschylus and stories of recent vintage. *Angel of Light* is her strongest protest against the loveless anarchy which fired campuses in the sixties. Although vastly different in setting, structure, and time, it also resembles *Bellefleur* in its resurgent vitality, its cacophony, and range: its paradoxical vision of the creative force unleashed by hellish violence.

In the novels which follow, Oates resumes her experimental exploration of the American literary past. Sensitive to their mutual relations and intertextual alliances, she moves from the twentieth to the nineteenth century, testing and expanding the boundaries of her own artistic residence. She is also ready to confront an issue of particular concern in the eighties: the complex relationship of literature and gender.

8 Woman's Place

A Bloodsmoor Romance, Mysteries of Winterthurn, Solstice, and *Marya: A Life*

"Who, in our midst, is so hardened of heart, as to be *immune* to Romance, in its numerous masks & costumes?" (*BR,* 568). With the rhetorical extravagance of her nineteenth-century "scribbling" sisters, Joyce Carol Oates returns to her project of imaginative reconstruction in *A Bloodsmoor Romance* (1982), a sprawling reenactment of turn-of-the-century American history, with a full assortment of costumes and masks. Once again, her intentions are not only to imitate, but to subject a traditional genre—in this case, the genre of romance—to critical review. From its opening scene, a dramatic balloon abduction of a less than dutiful daughter, to the final pages, when that same child sees a patriarch's dream go up in smoke, *A Bloodsmoor Romance* is a curious act of revision. Oates demonstrates a scholar's knowledge and an excellent ear; her parody is apt and exhaustive. Yet, like *Bellefleur,* this voluminous novel moves perilously close to self-erasure.

It is also Oates's first explicitly feminist novel, although it is not her first foray into the realm of feminist critical controversy. *Do with Me What You Will* (1973), dedicated to the president of N.O.W., attacks society for promoting a sleeping beauty ideal. While her consciousness is raised, Oates's heroine awakens and acts in a world still shaped by egoistic masculine aspirations. The novel received mixed notices from feminist readers, uneasy at its orgasmic turning point. Oates drew further critical fire in 1973 for the view of androgyny she had presented in lectures and essay-reviews. She defended her position in a letter to the *New York Times Book Review*:

> Surely . . . anyone . . . might acknowledge the difficulties that arise when language (or a single term, "androgyny") is evoked to gain an emotional response. . . . I use it myself, to discuss certain ambiguous conceptions. . . . "Balance" might do as well. . . . The synthesis of "masculine" and "feminine" impulses has always been the ideal of all cultures and all individuals.
>
> I am more concerned about a polarization of the sexes . . . along crude, blunt, old-fashioned lines. A polarization in which the "masculine" forces in our society lose their restraint—and begin yet another assault on the "feminine."[1]

Repeatedly, Oates has called herself a "feminist"; she has also resisted being "ghettoized" herself as a "woman writer." In 1979, she declared that the very need for such a work as *The Penguin Book of Women Poets* was "insulting" to women. Yet in the same essay, she acknowledged her sense of the disjunction between masculine and feminine experience: "Though I don't believe that there is a distinctly "female" sensibility, I know, of course, that there has been a distinctly female fate."[2]

Most recently, in her essay "(Woman) Writer," published in her anthology of essays by writers on writing, *First Person Singular,* Oates protests the differential treatment accorded male and female artists:

> A "Woman Writer" is an anomalous thing, lacking a counterpart, a grammatical equivalent, a mate. For there are no "men writers." Persons of either sex who write define themselves as writers, but roughly half of us are defined (by others) as women writers. Problems of a metaphysical nature arise.[3]

Yet, despite her protests, it is not only the female fate but the implications for the woman writer that Oates explores in her own Victorian romance.

The literature of Victorian America has offered a rich resource for writers and critics especially intrigued by the interplay of two major and seemingly antithetical tendencies: moralistic and escapist. The genre of romance, which flourished in the second half of the nineteenth century, in fact embodied both: the admonitory and didactic Victorian spirit and the extravagance of the gilded age. Hawthorne, Poe, and Melville, and indeed the entire transcendentalist club, employed romance to reflect their own vision. Some twentieth-century readers—Chase, Lawrence, Fiedler—thus consider romance *the* American form: singular, self-assertive, didactic, utopian, and implicitly masculine.

Contemporary feminist critics such as Gubar, Gilbert, Auerbach, Miller, Heilbrun and Showalter offer quite different readings of the romance: a subversive "heroine's text", or the devious mask of a "madwoman." In their view, Victorian romance not only satisfied the popular taste but enforced "The Cult of True Womanhood," tightening woman's domestic bondage through a deviously palliative and escapist strategy.

Such historians and literary critics have returned to American Victorian writing to present a new picture of our cultural past. Observing the pervasiveness of etiquette books and fictional romances, Carroll Smith-Rosenberg suggests that together they give compelling evidence of woman's "intolerable threat" to male culture: "From the mid-nineteenth century on," she declares, "woman had become the quintessential symbol of social danger."[4] If women as well as men employed the conventions of romance to impose order, it was a cover for a peculiar sort of "disorderly conduct." Rachel Blau DuPlessis is more explicit in identifying romance as "a form of sexual feudalism" holding woman in thrall. In contrast to their more duplicitous nineteenth-century sisters, she sees woman writers of the twentieth century openly assailing castle walls, breaking through narrative boundaries, resisting conventions, "writing beyond the ending."[5]

DuPlessis does not discuss Oates or her Bloodsmoor adventure; nevertheless, her description matches Oates's own narrative performance. In reimagining American romance, Oates dramatizes the conflicting claims of "canonical" critics and feminist revisionists. She recreates the expansive forms, language, and thematic obsessions of popular and classic nineteenth-century American literature in *A Bloodsmoor Romance;* she also exposes a buried pattern of constriction, a pervasive and oppressive social subtext. Soaring in rhetorical crescendo, ludicrously appointed female characters (heroines, writers) are handmaidens of an aggressively male culture. In literal and figurative house arrest, they are dwarfed and hobbled by sexual ignorance, elaborate rules of conduct, yards of crinoline, and whalebone corsets. Significantly, however, Oates's novel defies literary etiquette. On the final pages, the storyteller abandons the reader, after pushing the tale beyond the predictable romantic finish of death and marriage. Demonstrating both Oates's familiarity with and "immunity" to the genre, her fourteenth novel is best seen as an anti-romance; a work of feminist resistance.

Oates telegraphs her intentions in the preamble—by now a familiar practice. *A Bloodsmoor Romance* is dedicated to her Princeton colleague Elaine Showalter, whose study, *A Literature of Their Own*, reexamines English women writers and their ambivalence in the face of romantic conventions. Speaking through her narrative persona in the acknowledgements, Oates identifies a few of the other diverse sources for "this definitive chronicle": nineteenth-century American advice and marriage manuals, popular magazines *"Devoted to Literature, Industry, and Religion,"* and two treatises concerning pseudo-science, from our own century. The epigraph is Emily Dickinson's first published poem, a valentine—which again should be taken "slant" rather than at sentimental face value.

The most compelling voice of the novel, however, is not Showalter's or Bates's or Dickinson's, but the narrator's. Appropriately anonymous, she is also "authorized," a character in her own right, one of Oates's most interesting creations, a garrulous, excitable and intrusive "maiden lady of advanced years" (*BR,* 595). Representing that league of women who issued a flood of best sellers to an enthusiastic American audience, she is attuned to the dominant rhythms of the age: "Even those of but limited imagination," she gushes, "could grasp the fact that *change,* of every kind, was swift impending!" (*BR,* 85). An adept nineteenth-century literary spinster, she has also set her canny eye on the century to come. Through her agency, *A Bloodsmoor Romance* holds competing worlds of value in imaginative tension. Beyond the variegated threads of history and fable, her own performance is itself the major romance of Bloodsmoor.

Oates's choice of persona demonstrates an apparent shift of artistic sympathy. In a *New York Times* piece in 1980, Oates characterized the work of such prolific and popular nineteenth-century woman writers as "brainless moralizing romances,"[6] akin to our latter-day "Harlequins." Yet as she immersed herself in the Victorian fiction of E.D.E.N. Southworth and Susan Warner, preparing to write her own romance, Oates found herself impressed by their "wonderful passages of detail"; she told an interviewer it was "extraordinarily revealing . . . as if you opened a door into that world." Oates described the fun of attempting to reproduce their rhetorical extravagance, recommending it to others. But in a more serious vein she expressed her respect for those women whose very style, at once decorous and extravagant, posed an unanticipated challenge. Oates had come to view her experiment in romance, born of a more general interest in American social change, as a way to expose the unspoken premises of the genre and the culture it reflects.[7]

Oates has used the metaphor of courtship to describe her previous imitations; this novel seems an especially artful arranged marriage. Oates again presents a novel which is academic in more than one sense. Still working like a crazy-quilter, she constructs her romance with snippets of biography, popular science, philosophy, and newspaper stories, detailing the history of an American Adam and an assortment of Eves. Her hero is a self-styled transcendentalist pathfinder, the inventor John Quincy Zinn, a composite out of the pages of Twain, Cooper, Emerson, and Thoreau. She makes conscious use of other American literary classics. Deirdre Zinn is lifted from the first pages of the authorized account to reappear as one of the celebrated mediums who flourished in this credulous age; she is also a fictive kin of the Veiled Lady in Hawthorne's *Blithedale Romance*. John Quincy Zinn is orphaned after his Yankee pedlar father, a rapscallian true to type, is tarred and feathered by an angry mob. The solicitous narrator explicitly identifies the allusion to Hawthorne's ironic allegory, "My Kinsman, Major Molineux." Another Hawthorne tale, "The Birthmark," is invoked and revised in the story of Samantha Zinn. Serving as John Quincy's laboratory assistant, she is coerced into becoming an experimental animal, testing his prowess in cosmetic repair. Zinn at least proves himself more adept than Hawthorne's Dr. Aylmer: he removes his daughter's birthmark without killing her. His crime against his child's integrity and his monstrous pride nonetheless mark him as a stereotypic American villain (and frequent Oates target), a madman of science.

Oates again deliberately blurs the boundaries of fiction and reportage, challenging our definition of romance as a world elsewhere. Springing from the *Bloodsmoor* pages are three generations of Zinn/Kiddemaster family residents, rooted in Pennsylvania soil. They mingle with historical figures:

Darwinists, dour and sober representatives of the American Philosophical Society, reporters from the *Atlantic Monthly,* dress reformers, political assassins (Guiteau), spiritual charlatans (Madame Blatavsky), and literati (Mark Twain). Adopting the strategy of incorporation she used in *Bellefleur,* Oates again describes a metamorphic realm. But in the lexicon of John Quincy Zinn and an expanding Victorian society, change is progress—loveless, the product of natural struggle and survival. The secular lords worshiped in his world shift from Emerson to Edison to Einstein; acolytes become demonic. It is all too easy for his fictive friend and associate Charles Guiteau to step out of his imaginary laboratory and into history as the assassin of President Garfield. Zinn's own "romantic" work is ignored: his time machine, his attempts at designing an instrument of perpetual motion. Yet it is even worse when he does attract national attention: he is commissioned to create a vehicle of capital punishment worthy of a technically superior society. (He obliges by inventing the electric bed. His wife Prudence, understanding the sadistic motives of Congress better than he, changes it to a less easeful chair.) From his viewpoint, the American romance is ended. By the final chapters of the novel, he has become a mirthless and monomaniacal alchemist.

The inventor's Adamic fable is thus radically inverted in *A Bloodsmoor Romance*: like Zinn's laboratory, it is bounded by woman's estate. For while the loquacious narrator is authorized to concentrate on his history, she seems more fascinated by the adventures of the female members of the family. The novel in fact serves as an oblique tribute to another literary predecessor: appropriately, several readers have suggested that *A Bloodsmoor Romance* is Oates's *Little Women.*[8]

Louisa May Alcott's novel, published in 1868 (the authorized account of the Zinn family begins just a decade later, in 1879), has recently generated some controversy of its own. Critics have begun to study the relationship between Louisa May and her father, Bronson Alcott, the eccentric transcendental pedagogue whose domestic experiments certainly influenced his literary daughter. More interesting, perhaps, is the discovery of her secret life as the writer of pseudonymous sensational fiction. Taking these issues together, Madelon Bedell suggests that *Little Women* itself has been misread as a decorous conduct book or girlhood romance: "*Little Women* is not about being good, nor even about growing up, but about the complexities of female power and the struggle to maintain it in a male-dominated society."[9]

In this context, *A Bloodsmoor Romance* can be seen as a reading of a nineteenth-century text from a twentieth-century perspective, playing with resemblance and discordance. Most obviously, the Zinn sisters (Constance Philippa, Malvinia, Octavia, Samantha, and the adopted Deirdre) are little women with a vengeance. They nurse romantic, escapist fantasies like those of Alcott's March family, and even display many of the same superficial character traits, although in comically exaggerated form. Thus, Alcott's tomboy inspires Oates's transvestite, Constance Philippa; the aspiring actress becomes Malvinia, a notorious showgirl; the romantic angel of virtue is portrayed as Octavia, a target of vice, abused by both husband and son. Alcott's heroine is a brainy nonconformist; one of Oates's little women is similarly out of place in the idiom of romance, whether woman's domestic sphere or the inventor's laboratory. Samantha Zinn finally takes matters into her own hands, moving into the world of commerce and practical science. Alcott's most romantic figure suffers a stereotypic and tragic early death. Oates seems to reimagine Beth March as Deirdre, the Zinn who is ghost-ridden but incredibly resilient, returning from the edge of impossibility in Oates's parody. Under cover of the narrator's apparently prayerful imprecations, the adventures of the Zinn little women—a company which includes mad grandmothers and maiden aunts—are indeed the contests for authority, identity, and power which Bedell describes. Counterpointing the world of public event, they present Oates's inside story of Victorian romance.

The Civil War is an important reference point in the fiction of both Oates and Alcott, revealing significant connections between the two artists: they are women conscious of the disjunction between romantic conventions and "the heroine's text." While the war rages, mothers and daughters are forced to take the place of sons, fathers, and lovers. Yet in the novels of Oates and Alcott, the old patriarchal order is not restored after the war ends. When the soldier-fathers each return, they are given no hero's welcome. Permanently displaced and spiritually maimed, they live on as brooding peripheral figures in the family drama.

There are other telling parallels between Oates and Alcott. Bedell provides a sinister view of Louisa's father, Bronson Alcott, who used Louisa as a guinea pig, not only to record but to modify his daughter's behavior from the moment of her birth. Her portrait of Bronson Alcott suggests he is the model for Oates's eccentric pedagogue John Quincy Zinn:

> Although he was an important member of the Concord school of thinkers, his name is usually included as an afterthought . . . as a footnote rather than part of the main text. . . . So egocentric as to be almost a megalomaniac . . . he entered into one venture after another—first as an experimental educator in a number of schools, and then as a philosopher.[10]

Clearly, Oates makes extensive use of her literary ancestor's work and personal history. Bloodsmoor's utopian tinkerer, Zinn, like Alcott, is an inept provider, otherwordly dreamer and, most significantly, given Oates's perennial academic interests, a cracked pedagogue—one of the novel's many teachers. Yet Oates presents him in a different role than the didactic narrators who sermonize about proper conduct or the imperious patriarch, Judge

Kiddemaster of Bloodsmoor, who boasts a well-stocked if rarely consulted library of "transcendental utterings" and "books and periodicals . . . pertaining to scientific discoveries through the ages and inventions" (*BR*, 46), along with "the calfskin-bound classics of English, French and American literature" (*BR*, 225). Ironically, John Quincy Zinn approaches the judge as a would-be scholar but is misread as a suitor; he leaves the judge's chambers betrothed to his daughter Prudence, a schoolmistress herself and a proto-suffragette. Concerned about perpetuating the family name, the canny Judge Kiddemaster understands that Prudence is immune to schoolgirl romantic fare, but is uniquely vulnerable to the teacher's rhetoric. The narrator reveals she has been seduced by John Quincy Zinn's treatise (again, modeled after Alcott's journals) *Out of the Mouths of Babes: A Teacher's Day-Book*. Her celibate resolve is shaken by this "*barbarian prince, a native American genius, a revolutionary of the spirit . . . our Rousseau*" (*BR*, 85).

Oates offers an extended definition of native romanticism in her ironic parody of transcendentalist philosophy. John Quincy Zinn's treatise is a romance of teaching, and an American one at that: it is a way to achieve the "American destiny" (*BR*, 198). He describes "a new Garden of Eden" open to his young charges, a technological paradise graced by telegraph, reaper, steam engine, and Whitney's "interchangeable parts" as well as the yet-to-be invented submarine, horseless carriage, and airplane. His school is a "tinker's paradise," for "*America . . . and Invention* are near-synonymous!" (*BR*, 208). Again, like Bronson Alcott, he thinks of his teaching as Socratic discourse; in practice, it is a set of rote responses, a transcendental catechism. His syllabus includes readings from Newton, Galileo, Poe and Oates's ever-present William Blake, supplemented by his own romantic Darwinism:

> What is called, boys and girls, an *invention,* is but the dramatic climax of a vast accretion of details, insinuated as it were, into Time, by the grace of Eternity. An invention is an *Evolution,* very closely resembling a biologic and geologic process. (*BR*, 210–11)

Prudence obviously has been moved by the erotic overtones of Zinn's account. He romanticizes his charges, imagining that they possess an innate capacity for goodness: "*The child knows what the Teacher must recover*" (*BR*, 92). Displeasing their parents, he spares the rod, longing to "dance with them" himself:

> He knew only, and at once, with an emotion that caused tears to spring to his eyes, that *education* might fairly be equated with *loving* and that one could not succeed in educating when one has failed to love. (*BR*, 203)

But Zinn's story takes a bewildering turn after the optimistic conclusion of

Out of the Mouths of Babes. As his authorized historian discloses, he is driven
from his backwoods haunts, dismayed by the outcome of one of his experiments (one child is sent into another dimension while tinkering with his time
machine). More serious (for no one seems to miss his hapless sorcerer's apprentice) is the growing hostility of the rural community to his preaching.
Like Vernon Bellefleur, and like his own father, he is the target of sneering,
unlettered village vigilantes. In one of this novel's many ironies, he must run
for his life from his utopia into bustling urban America. Judge Kiddemaster,
on his part, knows that his line, if not his life, depends on his taking protective custody of this backwoods dreamer and ideologue.

The Oates thus has picked a range of targets for her romantic satire. However
subversive Alcott's hidden text may be, on the surface, her heroines in *Little
Women* display conventional attitudes. They are genteel and of course impe-
cunious: "It's so dreadful to be poor," Meg March complains on the first
pages of *Little Women.* In the first scene of *A Bloodsmoor Romance,* Malvinia Zinn haughtily intones, "the poor are so dull, and so tiresome, and, I
am sorry to say, so boring" (*BR,* 54). The Marches are literally confined to
their cozy cottage, romantically close to high estate. The Zinns live in a bizarre construction, the Octagon House; they also have access to their grandfather's luxurious manor. Indeed, the novel begins with their debut at
Kiddemaster Hall. Almost immediately, however, as the narrator notes with
anxiety, the Zinn sisters are offered new and shady options, from the wicked
stage to the experimental laboratory to the parlor seance to the wild west, air-
borne through a necromancer's abduction or the spiritualist's transgressive
flight. Oates's narrative imitates a romancer's lively, almost breathless,
prose; yet the colorful threads of her story follow an atypical itinerary.

The infidelity of this novel reflects Oates's perennial desire to create expansive and multivarious texts. In *A Bloodsmoor Romance,* the author pulls together not one but two major strains of American romance, reinscribing the
"brave, tumultuous" masculine adventure into woman's equally tumultuous
"domestic" text, and revising both through this curious conjunction. Leo
Marx, for example, suggests one key to the vision of the American romantic
hero is the image of "the machine in the garden," both repellent and seductive.[11] In *A Bloodsmoor Romance,* Oates reflects a similar ambivalence about
technology in her history of John Quincy Zinn; but she also expands the issue
to show the impact of American science on women's lives. Zinn's machinations frequently violate the integrity of adoring women and children; he actually seems to prefer the company of a monkey to that of his own daughters.
Obsessively pursuing a formula which could result in the earth's holocaust,
Zinn slips out of his patriarchal role into Frankenstein attire with almost horrifying ease, leaving a nearly impossible task of reclamation to daughters and
narrators.

The perverse mechanistic ideology of Victorian America is also reflected in Oates's picture of a new American type whose work is hazardous to women's health: the gynecologist. As she presents the specialist in "female complaints" in *A Bloodsmoor Romance,* Oates again demonstrates her familiarity with social history and feminist theory.[12] Like their real counterparts, her doctors dispense stern proscriptions to the Bloodsmoor women, warning them against intellectual pursuits (including the reading of romances); they regard the female body as a diseased machine. Through their efforts and the support of a cadre of feminine advisors, women view their sexuality as "The Mark of The Beast," with both hilarious and horrifying results (*BR,* 435, 442, 444). Again, the narrator's discomfort with such topics is a "mark" of her own conditioning and a measure of the Victorian mind, suggesting a radical discontinuity between social rules and woman's experience.

As the narrator spins each daughter's story, she emphasizes such contradiction: beneath the embroidery, she shows a darker ground, a pattern of sexual repression and social conformity. Counterpointing her advocacy of proper conduct and conventional wisdom there are signs of some irremediable disorder. Deirdre's mysterious abduction, for example, is meticulously described but never fully explained; the narrator herself expresses frustration at the indecipherability of experience, and the resulting impossibility of narrative closure. Deirdre's history, in fact, demonstrates again and again the perversity of a masculine drive to deriddle and debunk spiritual phenomena. Nonetheless, she continues to be employed by haunted victims in a credulous age. Tested by "scientific" investigators, Deirdre loses contact with her spirit-voices, but at the cost of mental breakdown. In a further and grimmer irony, her skeptical male inquisitors suffer madness and even death in the course of their attempt to unmask the hapless medium. Like many a romantic character, Deirdre is also a foundling; yet the revelation of her true parentage, another romantic convention, does not bring about a happy end. Rather, in her last appearance, she is the novel's Cassandra, the little-regarded and helpless witness to a vision of future nuclear dilemma.

Ironically, Deirdre is almost as terrorized by a nightmare of Victorian domesticity: she constantly imagines herself being stabbed by the wickedly sharp embroidery scissors of her step-sister, the lovely Malvinia Zinn. Frustrated indeed, but not to the point of murderous assault, Malvinia longs to escape her needlework and the confines of Bloodsmoor. Soon she does run off with a handsome actor, Orlando Vandenhoffen (a mocking allusion to Woolf's famous androgyne). Malvinia is another of Oates's narcissistic goddesses; like Karen Herz, like Elena Howe, "she was forever checking her image in mirrors" (*BR,* 264). In this novel, however, the narrator interposes a disapproving glance: a woman's self-love is incompatible with the Victorian ideal. Even worse, as the embarrassed story teller confesses, Malvinia has inherited the curse of the Bloodsmoor women: her own zesty sexual appetite, liberated as soon as the lights go out. The supposedly "demonic caprices of her body" (BR, 463-64) make her especially terrifying to would-be lovers, who, despite their seductive rhetoric, seem no more desirous of feminine response than a group of necrophiliacs. In the novel's funniest and wildest scene, her most famous wooer, Mark Twain, runs from a hotel boudoir, unclothed and undone by the chortling and devilish Malvinia. Believing herself wicked and lost, the loveliest Zinn sadly quits the scene and the stage to become "Miss Malvinia Quincy, Spinster Instructress of Elocution, Music, and the Thespian Arts" at one of the novel's ubiquitous and presumably virtuous female academies (*BR,* 535). When she reappears to take part in the novel's last chapters, she has found an old admirer: not Twain, but a tweedy professor. (The waggish author has rescued her from the seminary to cast her in the romantic role of faculty wife.)

If the young Malvinia feels marked with sin—the sign that old Judge Kiddemaster looks for on all children born beneath his roof—Samantha is marked by a literal birthmark like that on her father's face. Removing it, John Quincy Zinn cannot erase their resemblance: Samantha enters the world of science. The narrator warns her readers that such inappropriate occupations make a woman unattractive—a point seemingly proven when this brainy Zinn falls in love and is suddenly pretty. Unfortunately, Samantha's beloved comes from "a lamentably obscure" family (*BR,* 404): he is the child once sent spinning into the future by Zinn's time-travel apparatus! The narrator is not surprised when Prudence Zinn arranges Samantha's betrothal to the highborn but syphilitic heir to the DuPont munitions fortune. The self-possessed Samantha, however, reacts with outrage: she persuades her lover (Hareton—another literary allusion, this time to Brontë) to elope; they leave the laboratory and the Octagon House for a simpler life, sustained by Samantha's own practical inventions. Her father by now is working on torpedoes and instruments of detonation. Samantha instead stakes out patents for inventions which will gladden twentieth-century sisters: baby-strollers and disposable diapers.

Oates reserves her most mischievous attack on Victorian sexual ideology for the story of the oldest Zinn daughter, Constance Philippa. A tomboy like Jo March, Constance has climbed trees and fearlessly waded through streams, half in love with a schoolgirl neighbor. The narrator is disturbed by her bad manners, and especially by the ribald ballad Constance perpetually hums: "A fox went out. . . . " (The refrain mockingly evokes "The Fox," D. H. Lawrence's tale of homosexual romance.)

Constance Philippa does not openly resist the arrangements Prudence makes for her betrothal to an impressively titled if piggish German baron. Yet as her wedding day approaches, she is more and more terrified of the

marriage bed; however unconventional her girlhood has been, she is as ignorant about her sexuality as any ordinary Victorian woman. Begging for en-
lightenment, she is met with her mother's chilly silence and even more
mystifying euphemistic advice from "Wedding Day Books" designed to substitute sentiment for information. By the time of her nuptuals, she is in a state
of madness. On her wedding night, she disappears, leaving her own effigy, a
dressmaker's dummy, to consummate the marriage. Oates's view of the an-
aesthetic effect of Victorian convention—the transformation of healthy girls
into hollow women—is strikingly represented by the array of dummies
standing upright in the Zinn/Kiddemaster sewing room long after the living
models have left the scene.

Oates finds other Victorian conventions ready-made vehicles of satire as
well as useful plot devices. In a scene out of many a popular romance, the
Zinn sisters are summoned back to Kiddemaster Hall. The occasion is the
reading of the will of another "scribbler" and advice-giver, Aunt Edwina. She
has left orders that all of her nieces be present, and they assemble according
to formula. Yet everyone is startled by the appearance of one Philippe Fox,
a tanned and beardless young man who has come back from the West to represent Constance when the will is read. In a scandalized whisper, the narrator
tells us that Philippe was once Constance Philippa, but now is "of the masculine persuasion," physically altered by his/her practice of wearing men's
clothing! Like many otherwise well-educated Victorian women, and seemingly as many men, the narrator shows an incredible naivete about sexuality
and human physiology.[13]

The legend of Constance/Philippe Fox is part of the novel's larger exposure of gynecology as a Victorian pathology. More than one woman comes to
a tragic ending in *A Bloodsmoor Romance,* cramped, starved, and dosed with
laudanum and other more lethal potions aimed at controlling her "wild, scattered unproductive thoughts" (*BR,* 374). The anorexic fate of Grandmother
Kiddemaster is thus more than a variation on a familiar Oatesian theme. The
narrator reports with awed regard, "this good lady had gradually conquered
appetite in all its insidious forms" (*BR,* 235). Physicians blame her resulting
death not on fasting but on "ovarian neuralgia." The narrator is a wide-eyed
post mortem witness: the corpse of this hunger artist weighs forty-three
pounds, and after years of whalebone corseting, the inner organs are either
nonexistent or "of a miniature, or atrophied, nature" (*BR,* 238). Irrepressible
or insane (or both), Grandmother leaves a curiously subversive legacy to the
angel in the house, Octavia Zinn, a mad triumph of woman's work. While
Octavia bursts into grateful tears, the deadpan narrator describes the star-
tling gift for us: a hand-crocheted antimacassar, "somewhat above the conventional in length, being 1,358 yards, or some three-quarters of a mile." As
the narrator points out with apparent seriousness, such an item "would pre-

sent problems of practicability" (*BR,* 238)! Rejecting Christian Science in her last days because of Mary Baker Eddy's "deficient" prose style, Grandmother Kiddemaster has her own mischievous last word.

Oates's portrait of the supposedly dutiful Octavia represents the novel's subtlest feminist satire. Octavia is the narrator's confessed favorite; proving herself a modest daughter and compliant bride, she endures the perverse sexual practices of her "respectable" husband and the vicious behavior of that "innocent," their son Little Godfrey. Shocked as she has been by the wanton behavior of Malvinia and Constance, the narrator seemingly does not question Octavia's wifely or maternal obligations. A dutiful reporter, she describes in meticulous detail the accidents which result in Octavia's liberation. Acquiescing to her husband's sexual fetishes, she inadvertently strangles him. Always the good hostess, Octavia also cannot leave her guests in time to save Little Godfrey from a watery death (he dies in the act of trying to drown John Quincy Zinn's pet monkey in the Kiddemaster well). Again, the narrator lets us draw our own conclusions.

Significantly, she presents Octavia's story as a ludicrous Victorian romantic parody which seems exemplary in more realistic modern terms. She is genuinely loving and tolerant, keeping track of her wayward sisters after her parents disown them. Generous of spirit, she avoids the miniaturization of little women like her Grandmother; she is able to forego feminine remedies, opium-laced nostrums provided by mothers and doctors, and meet the world on its own terms. At the end of the story, Octavia has made the best match: her loving second husband is that figure of romantic fiction and repressed girlish fantasy, a dashing Irish stable boy, now grown to be a dynamic and respected member of the modern Bloodsmoor community. With him at her side, among her sisters (and "brother"), Octavia waits for Great Aunt Edwina's testament.

It is at this point, despite her sustained performance, that the narrator raises her own complaint, feeling somehow unequal to her task. Unable or unwilling to bring the other stories to an optimistic resolution, unable to write beyond the prescribed ending, her history seems to take a vertiginous swerve. Deirdre's sudden shift in fortune could provide a romantic way out of this story; the other sisters have found appropriate husbands; the new "brother" brings the novel full circle with a dashing abduction scene, rescuing his former schoolgirl love from the literal prison of her loveless marriage. If none of these happy endings suffice, the lengthy sentiments read by Aunt Edwina's lawyer might certainly provide an apt Victorian close. If this novel were a true romance, Great Aunt Edwina would have the final moralizing word from beyond the grave.

Another scribbling author, although clearly not a spinster, Aunt Edwina speaks *ex machina;* she has carefully orchestrated the family reunion, seeking the perfect audience to immortalize and authorize her own effusive confession. She is another of the novel's significant points of reference. In contrast to the nameless narrator, she is a celebrity—like one of those immensely popular woman writers who perpetuated the cult of true womanhood. Her very rhetoric marks her as an accessory to a system aimed at trivializing female pursuits by absurd exaggeration. Yet Oates also shows the cost of such collusion: Aunt Edwina has also been a victim of that system. Living out the terms of Victorian romance, accepting the gynecologist's opinion of her sex, she has abandoned Deirdre, her daughter, for the life of an invalid; she has been rewarded by a public reputation (unlike Dickinson, she is "somebody") but has suffered from private deprivation. She has turned her unspent energies to the production of hundreds of pages of pulp fiction and good conduct guides; her testament has been planned as her last publication, one final Victorian entertainment, both lurid and pious. Her bequest comes rather late to rescue Deirdre, recovering from the ravages of psychic battle and lifelong rejection. The lovelessness of her real history is pathetically at odds with the sentiments of her last lecture: a disquisition on "what constitutes a lady":

> Is not a Lady one who, tho' being of the female persuasion, ne'ertheless feels, in her pulsing veins, the *moral strength* (if not the physical), of the male? Nay, and is not a Lady one who, tho' dwelling in a humble rustic cottage, or in a marbl'd palace, ne'ertheless submits to Our Saviour's enjoinders, as to charity, and love, and compassion, and giving alms to the poor. (*BR,* 561)

Unaware of the gulf between lady and woman, infatuated with the rhetoric of repression, coyly aware of her own hold on this imagined audience, Aunt Edwina lectures about defiance as a way to glorify her own posthumous confession:

> I believe it is not remiss to state that a Lady is one who, in defiance of the opinions of conformist society, and even in defiance of the wishes of her own family, is courageous enough . . . not only to acknowledge her sinful failings, but to make redress for them, to the best of her ability. (*BR,* 561)

Significantly, in *A Bloodsmoor Romance* Oates thus exposes the curious duplicity of Victorian style: the congruence of verbal extravagance and moral prudery, the countercurrents that simultaneously repress and inspire "little women." Beyond the exuberant entertainment and masterful acts of mimicry, Oates is concerned with the nature of the corresponding strain on the feminine imagination. Brontë's Victorian romance, *Wuthering Heights*, in Oates's reading, is a work of metamorphosis, tracing the cultural construction of the female through a series of fragmentary and sometimes mutually disconfirming stories.[14] Similarly, Oates's *A Bloodsmoor Romance* displays the disharmonious finish to traditional romance narratives.

After the family reunion and the so-called happy endings (six, if we are to count the flight of Prudence from Kiddemaster Hall to the cause of Dress Reform), the narrator returns to the unfinished story of John Quincy Zinn. The final scene is in the sorcerer's workshop, a realm of black magic. On the eve of the twentieth century, John Quincy Zinn lies wasted, dying, too weak to return to the laboratory to retrieve his final formula. Deirdre, his only caretaker, a virgin still, agrees to seek the foolscap bearing the formula (we suspect it is $E=mc^2$). But candles waver in the draft—perhaps she again is medium for spirits—and the formula is lost in a sudden blaze. Along with this terrifying scrap, the fire consumes Zinn's other grotesque projects, such as his designs for a "single Great Eye," a horrendous fusion of Emersonian metaphor and Orwellian prophecy, which would provide the nation with a mechanism for "moral surveillance" (*BR, 395*).

It remains for the narrator to bring this history to a satisfactory close. Yet she has also undergone a series of changes as profound as those of her fictive charges. As *A Bloodsmoor Romance* unfolds, her voice subtly alters from a gregarious and gushing confidante to a self-conscious artist disturbed at the limits of fiction: "Ah, to omit—to be forced to omit," she cries (*BR, 520*). Once an accomplice of Aunt Edwina, confident in her perception of the moral contours of the universe, the virtues of Victorian hearth and home, the heroism of the self-reliant genius, her eye for detail has given her a view of human evil too close for comfort. As the threads of her romance intersect and knot, the narrator experiences an uncharacteristic reluctance to continue:

> Upon rising from a night of troubl'd dreams, yesterday morn, I had fully hoped to plunge at once into this chapter, despite my wanness of countenance, and a deep revulsion of the soul. (*BR, 522*)

Distrusting her "enfeebl'd powers," she claims the timidity mandated by Victorian culture for women who write is a barrier to the production of great novels. It also seems to explain this writer's block:

> Indeed, I am bound to confess here that I have, upon several occasions, shrunk from taking up this strand, in my intricate fancywork, out of that timidity of my sex, that has rendered us so generally unfit for the creation of great works, like those by Mr. Dickens and Mr. Balzac, and, in our own clime, Mr. Melville—a timidity that has its unapologetic basis in natural *ignorance,* and *innocence,* of the cruder aspects of life, and a gracious wish that naught but "rainbows of unearthly joy" . . . irradiate our literary attempts, as, it is devoutly hoped, they irradiate our lives. (*BR, 522–23*)

Fancywork indeed, a coy device, an artful pause to enhance the mystery and sensation of romance, it also must be viewed in relationship to the last act of *A Bloodsmoor Romance,* set not in the cozy rooms of "little women" but in the fiery laboratory of the once-heroic John Quincy Zinn.

Hardly innocent or ignorant, two "timid" women, medium and scribbling spinster, share a remarkable and chilling vision of the turn of the century. Deirdre allows John Quincy Zinn's formula to burn, hoping to retard the onset of the atomic age: "should it *not* be duplicated," she thinks, "will I not then have *saved the world*? Spared us, from the madman's dream?" (*BR*, 614).

But it is the narrator, ever more tentative behind her stylistic furbelows and mocking masks, who puts an end to this resurgent act of feminine fantasy. She draws back from the seduction of romance in her final chapter of less than a page which concludes this teeming, voluminous account. In mocking humility, the narrator defers both sentimental ending and apocalypse with a knowing wink. "The Twentieth Century is not *my* concern," she reminds us, as she bids "love's fond adieu." Clearly, it is one way to bring romance to an end: abandoning "gladsome *certitude*" along with the "thankless task" of exposing the *riddle* of men's and women's lives to future scribbling sisters (*BR*, 615).

Oates rises to her own challenge in the next volume of her "long range experimental project," her investigation of "those marvelous genres" of the literary past. In *Mysteries at Winterthurn* (1984), she tries her hand at another peculiarly American artistic invention: the detective story. A new and idiosyncratic sleuth, inspired by Emerson but sired by Conan Doyle, Xavier Kilgarvan, takes center stage, propelled by the same indefatigable desire to deriddle the universe displayed—and defeated—in *A Bloodsmoor Romance.*

Oates continues to experiment with voice in this parodic novel. Her romance displays stylistic bravado, visible in effusive dashes, italicized asides, and frequent exclamation points; the detective story begins in the same hyperbolic mode. Yet as the mysteries deepen, the quality of narration seems to shift: Kilgarvan's last cases are described by an avuncular raconteur who takes the reader into his confidence, promising to restore order. His certitude seems misplaced: Kilgarvan violates the conventional demands of detective fiction in his last adventures. Part of the mystery in Oates's novel thus lies in the act of narration itself.

Oates's romantic alter ego had resisted the seductions of sentimental plotting, deferring closure. The rhetoric seemed contagious: Oates herself felt the effects of a writer's block as she wrestled with the crime-detective form.[15] She was also keenly aware of the limits such a "tightly plotted novel" imposed on her own sensibility. "To write a detective novel," she told an interviewer, "one has to almost become a different person!"[16] Marks of that difficult passage are evident to any reader who moves from the extravagance of *A Bloodsmoor Romance* and the "first person breathless" style to the cooler prose of the armchair connoisseur of detection, the bemused narrator of *Mysteries at*

Winterthurn. The reader is left to struggle with a narrative voice in *Mysteries at Winterthurn* that seems at first indistinguishable from the gushing romancer who bids us *adieu* in the earlier novel. In the editor's note which prefaces the second case study, the narrator seems less intrusive, although he declares he stands ready to violate the "purest standards of the genre" (*MW,* 155) in order to follow Kilgarvan's unusual exploits. But in the final section of Oates's detective three-decker, he has become a master of detachment. By then, both narrator and hero have survived the turn of the century, a time of cataclysmic change. At ease in his cozy digs, the narrator can sort through the paraphernalia of violent crime without a perceptible shudder. But his very impersonality and prescience separates him from his hero, Kilgarvan, whose chosen vocation has embedded him in the terrifying, riddling world.

Aping her scribbling sisters, the narrator of *A Bloodsmoor Romance* seems most in character when she is feigning innocence and resisting the demands of fact: *I am ignorant of all detail, and wish to remain so.* This apparent modesty gives her license to supply fictions of her own making, altering the contours of the world she finds offensive: "For is not the artist . . . obliged to serve the higher moral truths, in his or her craft? Is he not obliged to *better* the world, and not merely *transcribe* it" (*BR,* 581). The detective story narrator of *Mysteries at Winterthurn* seems moved by antithetical impulses, "possessed of a near-insatiable passion for authenticity, down to the most minute, revealing, and lurid detail" (*MW,* 3). He is authorized to dispel ambiguity and confusion; to offer vivid and truthful representation and ingenious and satisfying solutions. Such a compact between reader and author creates the climate of the detective-thriller. Yet Oates's work itself questions the validity of these generic obligations. Optimism is succeeded by bafflement; the detective's confidence soon seems a confidence game.

If it is tempting to see *Mysteries of Winterthurn* as the obverse of *A Bloodsmoor Romance,* it is even more interesting to note the many points of convergence. Taken together, these two novels demonstrate one of Oates's most interesting literary discoveries: the uncanny connections of detection and romance. Both affirm the drive for control, whether they project a world elsewhere or fix the mind's eye on the riddle of reality. In devising this pair of experiments, Oates reveals a Gothic grimace beneath the mask of ratiocination: the Janus-face of the nineteenth-century American imagination.

Oates is performing duplicitous acts of imitation: she is also mischievously accurate in her mimicry of minor genres. Her romance draws on popular novels for its picture of the mind of Victorian America; similarly, her detective story is indebted to the "whodunits" and blood and thunder thrillers turned out by dime novelists a century ago. In both cases, she lays claim to the American past not only through literary allusion and scholarly documentation, but by reentering and recreating the popular imagination. It is a complex artistic enterprise, the act of a playful antiquarian and ventriloquist who is also a serious critic.

Mysteries at Winterthurn is again more than artful parody. As in all of her novelistic experiments, Oates reinvents literary forms in order to peel back their polished surfaces, exposing deeper levels of reality. In Oates's view, both the Gothic romance and its nineteenth-century double, the detective thriller, are deceptive cover stories, foredoomed strategies in the face of a faithless and threatening world.

In *Mysteries of Winterthurn,* a novel of multiple reversals, the man of reason is doomed by both his affections and his own mental powers. Kilgarvan's scrupulous attention to detail is also directed within: too perceptive, he is all but trapped in "numerous inexplicable fissures and ravages" (*MW*, 158), witness to atrocities and reversals of justice. In this novel, artistic ingenuity is also linked with darker realms. Oates's perennial symbol, the labyrinth, is again the region of perverse artifice. More obviously, the *trompe l'oeil* paintings which decorate the Kilgarvan bridal chamber menace the vulnerable dupe—and the more knowing observer. Uncannily true to life, they come to represent the author's own strategy as she both imitates and tests the power of artistic suggestion.

The pattern of *Mysteries of Winterthurn* is established in the first episode. After a grisly and mysterious crime involving his wealthy cousins, the neophyte sleuth tests his vocation and tries his hand at solving the mystery. However apt his investigative powers, his efforts lead instead to his own undoing. An alert private eye at the outset, he displays progressively clouded vision as he falls in love with Perdita Kilgarvan, his pretty cousin. She teases him cruelly, leading him to a secret room and then locking him in, compromising his privileged position and leaving him full of doubts. Unable to dismiss the signs of incestuous abuse, Kilgarvan protects his cousin's honor by deliberately withholding "unspeakable" (*MW*, 137) evidence. Surely violating his professional code, he even burns all "offensive notes" (*MW*, 151) to frustrate further investigation, leaving the narrator to provide a lame apologia—but no solution.

The three case histories thus describe two oddly antagonistic processes of investigation, as both Kilgarvan and his chronicler circle a realm of deepening mystery. The narrator constructs a context for definitive explanation, which never materializes. Consistently, at the point when justice should be rendered, Kilgarvan swerves: juries bring in irrational verdicts, exculpating the guilty; vigilantes hound and lynch the blameless; the investigator all too often is conscious of the resemblance of predator and prey. Ultimately, he discovers the depths of his own criminality. When the anthologist and his detective part company, they are clearly worlds apart.

Like her narrator, Oates has collected the paraphernalia of crime detection. One authentic touch is the frontispiece, a map of Winterthurn. Oates has found cartography a rich source of symbolic reference in other novels: the cosmic circles of *With Shuddering Fall,* Stephen Petrie's family atlas in *The Assassins,* the persistent survey of Emmanuel Bellefleur, the terrorist's design in *Angel of Light.* In *Mysteries at Winterthurn* she exploits a detective story convention, a sketch intended to mark off the imaginative terrain, imposing rule and direction on the inchoate and disorderly. Yet the maps in this novel create more mystery: they fix points of confusion and scenes of unsolved crime. Ironically, they underscore the irrational state of Winterthurn, where mindscape is not attuned to landscape. Trusting his ability to traverse this charted territory, Xavier Kilgarvan first is nearly trapped in a secret dungeon. In the second adventure, reaching for a carefully planted piece of evidence, he slides into quicksand unmapped on any chart and toward a terrible death. Having touched bottom and escaped (we never learn precisely how), he seems permanently confused about his direction. His third adventure leads him to the lurid underground chambers of a house of sybaritic pleasure symbolically named The Hotel Paradise, a disturbingly labyrinthine edifice. Hoping to unmask a murderer in those steamy passages, Kilgarvan is confronted with the traces of his own guilt.

In the mapping of *Bellefleur,* the cartographer's faults are geological; in *Mysteries of Winterthurn,* the falls are mythological. Indeed, the novel spills over the tidy boundaries of its own maps and covers, a work of expansive exploration traced across a stretch of fictive time and through an evolving and shifting narrative perspective. Essentially, it dramatizes the issue at the core of detection: the nature of belief.

Questions of faith in this novel take historical, theological, and imagistic form. For example, one of the denizens of Winterthurn voices his contempt for the anachronistic "peasant religion" of the community:

> . . . for did they not live in an enlightened era, in the closing decades of the nineteenth century, with fresh advances in science and invention and Logic being made on all sides? (*MW,* 134)

Ironically, Oates has put these rationalist sentiments in the mouth of Kilgarvan's uncle, Simon Esdras, an elderly sot, an absent-minded professor, and academic crackpot. The tractates of Esdras on the "probable" existence of the world attract the attention of a genuine American philosopher, Charles Peirce; but at closer look, his theories cancel themselves out by a mere movement of quotation marks from one word to the next. Oddly akin to the romantic tinkerer John Quincy Zinn, Simon Esdras feels it is his duty to *"invent a revolutionary Logic,* imbued with the fresher air of the New World, and free of all Old World and Attic muddle" (*MW,* 131). When he ventures beyond the bookshelf and inkwell, Esdras become quixotic and addled, foolishly fond of his own Roxana. His skepticism (and penury) lead him and his bride to a wedding night in the haunted family bridal chamber. His frail reason proves no match for the *trompe l'oeil* spectacle and its gruesome powers of suggestion: morning finds him mutilated and his fortune-hunting young widow quite mad. As if to prove his radical nihilism true, no explanation surfaces for the night's ghoulish revels; mind—projected in painterly nightmare —has conquered matter.

The enlightened Esdras thus reflects Oates's penchant for academic satire. More subtly, Kilgarvan's willful blindness is born in books (both great and popular) and nurtured in the academy. As a student at Harvard, he is drawn to the theories of the unconscious described by Professor James. But he is even more influenced by the models of rationality professed in ivy halls:

> He had come to see that all the academic disciplines were paradigms of the detective's search for Truth: that life itself might be imagined as a pursuit,—a hunt—an impassioned quest—requiring both diligence and bravery, and not a little resignation. (*MW,* 206)

Like a Bloodsmoor pedagogue, he sets forth with robust optimism. Harvard has given him a degree of self-reliance: Xavier Kilgarvan's business card is even engraved with Emerson's phrase, "I make my circumstance" (*MW,* 389). He has also adopted Emersonian articles of faith, believing that "crime, if not the criminal heart itself, might someday be eradicated by the *intelligent, pragmatic,* and *systematic unification of the numerous forces for Good* (*MW,* 194). He struggles to maintain that optimism as he pursues his exalted but "inordinately lonely . . . pursuit" (*MW,* 199), feeling called to do battle with the forces of irrationality: "for what might *not* be explained by the supernatural, or the unknown?" (*MW,* 125).

Yet even early in his career, Kilgarvan also wonders that "events . . . seemed to proceed not only with a logic of their own but with a logic *antithetical to his wishes"* (*MW,* 60–61). As he grows older, he is more baffled by the unreliability of appearances and the limits of human observation: "crimes of greater cunning and subtlety were likely to be committed by persons who gave every impression of being wholly human, and civilzed" (*MW,* 215). Following the deductive models set forth in all of the detective stories he has read, he is again and again confronted with "the intractability of the phenomenal world" (*MW,* 104), its refusal to disclose its darkest secrets.

Oates again takes up the complex and allusive threads of nineteenth-century American literature. Emerson is not alone in providing intertextual linkage. The opening mystery centers on a reclusive and heterodox poet, the oldest Kilgarvan sister, whose dashes and deliberate rhetorical eccentricity in poems carefully penned and bundled proclaim her a Dickinson heiress. (Iphegenia's work, posthumously published, is to provide a steady and even handsome income for her surviving sisters.) Another Emily—Brontë— seems the spectral author of the ghost stories which haunt Winterthurn dreams. (Indeed, Oates's own essay on *Wuthering Heights,* appearing shortly before this novel was published, serves as an interesting gloss for the portraits of Winterthurn's passionate spinsters.) Louisa May Alcott is again a palpable influence: Kilgarvan and his brothers are a provocative set of "little men"; and Alcott's own exotic sleuth, M. Dupres, is one of many literary models for Kilgarvan to follow. (Unlike Oates. Alcott found the detective genre sheer recreation.[17]) Certainly Poe's vision of detection casts hallucinatory shadows across this novel's pages: teasingly reimagined in the lurid and eerily animate bridal chamber decor, it is more subtly represented by Kilgarvan's obsessive identification with his criminal prey.

Latin American as well as North American writers have left distinguishing prints on *Mysteries of Winterthurn.* Kilgarvan's father is a solitary toymaker, a Gabriel García Márquez figure. The influence of Jorges Luis Borges is detectable in Oates's fissures of unreason; the subversive myths of ratiocination she develops in this story may be inspired by "Death and The Compass," Borges's detective story in which solving the crime will cost the sleuth his life.

Oates's novel also shows its kinship with a post-modern genre, variously called the "anti-detective" form, the "metaphysical detective" story, or what Stefano Tani describes in a recent study as the "doomed detective" narrative.[18] Clearly, the detective genre is an ideal vehicle to display the failures of perception which cloud the contemporary private eye. In this context, the detective story is no longer a reassuringly low genre or academic recreation. Frank McConnell goes even farther, to suggest that the anti-detective hero lives out a modern myth: living on the margins, an outsiders, who "chooses to enter the dark mazes of crime and passion" with an oversized mission: "a pawn in Knight's clothing." McConnell seems to anticipate Oates's Winterthurn scheme: a scenario of failure:

> As society's own sense of the extent and depth of its criminal impulses grows, the detective does not so much solve as resolve the "problem" of the crime, mediating among the claims of public order, private decency and the inescapably fallen nature of both spheres of existence.[19]

Kilgarvan's acts of mediation not only distinguish him from stereotypic detectives; they lead him to the shocking recognition of his own culpability.

In *Mysteries of Winterthurn,* Oates also continues her critique of nineteenth-century attitudes toward women—in this novel, revealed in ubiquitous modes of assault. She exposes the misogyny which masquerades as medicine: Dr. Hatch, like the gynecologists of Bloodsmoor, treats female complaints as if being female were itself a disease, overdosing his charges with opiates and sternly advising them to avoid intellectual pursuits, including the reading of "meretricious romances" (*MW*, 82). In the course of the novel, as Xavier is drawn into the murkiest realms of the psyche, the society above ground engages in bloody acts of racism, sadism, anti-Semitism, and xenophobia; but the most frequent and horrifying crimes are those against women. Even his beloved Perdita is a bloodstained victim. In Winterthurn, songs of innocence echo in crimes of violence: once again, half-voiced folk ballads are evidence of subterranean plots.

Haunted, Oates's heroines and heroes wind their way through inner latitudes, toward the deepest and most wordless levels of mystery. Xavier Kilgarvan survives his terrible physical falls, yet each brush with death undermines his sunny belief in self-reliance. Inside the confident Harvard graduate is a child crying in the dark for his mother (*MW*, 143); his hope to banish crime and evil is virtually erased as he sinks in the foul trap at the "Devil's Half Acre" baited by his enemy:

> Xavier came to see that this was no merely local and finite a space into which he plunged, but the *primordial, everlasting, boundaryless* Universe. Here, no World existed, for "existence" was but a phantom: this inchoate sprawling lapping sucking substance predated all extension in space, and all time. . . . *This, then, is the greatest of Mysteries,—to which there is no solution.* (*MW*, 259)

The narrator spins his final story, boldly affirming the principle of detective fiction, "that infinite Mystery, beyond that of the finite, may yield to human ratiocination" (*MW*, 353). But his hero lies sleepless, tortured by his own guilty secrets, raising his own lament for the terrible unsolved riddles of life: "Ah, the bitter mysteries of Winterthurn!" (*MW*, 392).

Oates draws on academic sources to bring her literary experiment to an end. The first is Esdras, her philosopher-buffoon. Now supposedly celebrated by young Bertrand Russell, his solipsistic texts echo, along with Iphegenia's poems and folk ballad refrains, in the consciousness of Xavier Kilgarvan:

> Who,—or what—am I?
> Who,—or what—am "I"?
> "Who,"—or what—am I?
> Who, or "what"—am I? (*MW*, 476)

To the narrator's dismay, Kilgarvan prefers a romantic text, the problematic words of Thoreau (the lines are from *Ktaadn*):

> Talk of mysteries!—Think of our life in nature,—daily to be shown matter, to come into contact with it,—rocks, trees, wind on our cheeks! the *solid* earth! the

actual world! the *common sense! Contact! Contact! Who* are we? *where* are we? (*MW,* 476)

Thoreau's challenge seems too vehement to the armchair detective-narrator; yet Xavier is reborn through their passionate agency, moving out of fictive range. Oates's doomed detective relinquishes his dramatic but cursed role, marrying his Perdita at last (the lady, and not baby, Bunting), taking his place as husband and father; exchanging *mystery* for "naught but mere *Life*" (*MW,* 482).

McConnell suggests that within the anti-detective genre, there is no means to resist "the potential chaos of crime" which always haunts the margins of sanity. The hero-detective at best is engaged in "a holding action" negotiating the claims of society and "the dark reality of the beast within."[20] In his last days as a detective, Xavier Kilgarvan imagines his own fate in similar metaphoric terms:

> The shifting of the Earth's poles,—this inexorable slide to the winter solstice— roused in the hapless detective . . . a frequent sensation of panicked despair; for in him, still, was the child-soul, paralyzed by the specter of greedy and all-embracing night. (*MW,* 452)

Close to madness, he shudders at the darkest mystery, death itself, impervious to mortal efforts. His Puritan forebears imagined themselves as puny creatures, dangled over infernal realms by an implacable deity. After his unwanted view of human guilt, Kilgarvan's vision is even more vertiginous: he thinks of himself not as a spider, but "a mirror suspended above an abyss- . . . possessed of no content, and reflecting nothing save motion. And now, alas, that motion appears to have stilled—!" (*MW,* 471). In a scene curiously reflective of the final pages of *A Bloodsmoor Romance,* Kilgarvan rouses himself from deathly torpor to gather "labyrinthine charts, graphs, and maps" and consign them to a New Year's Eve blaze (*MW,* 472). Unlike his ancestor, Poe, the maddened investigator swears off alcohol and averts total breakdown. Thoreau's words, the solicitude of friends, and the redemptive possibilities of human love rouse him to life, moving him beyond catatonia.

Interestingly, Oates returns to the image of stillness and stoppage, the self's holding action, in the novel which follows, *Solstice* (1985). Thus, while it appears that Oates has again interrupted her ongoing project to offer a work modern in theme and even "post-modern" in its self-conscious exploration of the art of fiction, *Solstice* is linked with strong and invisible bonds to Oates's nineteenth-century literary imitations.

Although *A Bloodsmoor Romance* and *Mysteries of Winterthurn* both were concerned with woman's history, *Solstice* has created new critical controversy because of its even more explicit focus on feminist issues. Oates continues to insist that she ought not to be "ghettoized" as a woman writer.[21] Yet, clearly, *Solstice* is a woman's text; one reader, Ildiko de Papp Carrington, suggests it is another of Oates's vehicles of satire: this time, "a parody of the plot and themes of the contemporary feminist novel".[22]

Oates does not seem to undercut the actions of her heroines, or hold them up for ridicule. On the other hand, *Solstice* does indeed draw upon a wealth of contemporary feminist works. Chief among these is Doris Lessing's novel, *The Golden Notebook.* In her introduction to the second edition, Lessing describes a relationship of author and reader in many ways akin to the view Oates expresses in her critical essays:

> Writers are looking . . . for an *alter ego,* that other self more intelligent than oneself who has seen what one is reaching for, and who judges you only by whether you have matched up to your aim or not.[23]

That alter ego may be the common reader or empathic critic; it may be a fictive persona. In *The Golden Notebook,* it is a character of the author's own devising, "tallish, bit-boned" Molly Jacobs, a "hoyden in lean trousers and sweaters, and then a siren" in gleaming green eye makeup, a sometime actress (Lessing, 9). It is also Anna Wulf, a writer, "small, thin . . . brittle," who "deliberately efface[s] herself," playing the foil to the more dramatic Molly. Beyond the precarious terms of their endearment, *The Golden Notebook* becomes a powerful parable of art, another holding action against the brutality and chaos of the world. This also is Oates's central intention in *Solstice.*

Like Oates, Lessing exposes the wiles of the self-aggrandizing artist, denying that such "towering egotism . . . has to be forgiven" in the name of art. Unforgiving herself, she brings her own authority to bear against the "monstrously isolated, monstrously narcissistic, pedestalled paragon" (Lessing, xii). Lessing deliberately shows her agent, Anna, struggling against stillness, an artist's block; to survive, she must fight for a new mode of expression.

In *Solstice,* Oates again demonstrates her powers of subversive imitation, creating her own pair of female alter egos: teacher and artist, critic and creator. The teacher is Monica Jensen, tiny and bright, bearing the visible scar tissue of recent divorce. She has made an eastward journey, joining the faculty of Glenkill Academy, an exclusive Quaker boys prep school, as a teacher of writing and literature. The artist, Sheila Trask, is Monica's obverse reflection: dark where she is light, rude when she is decorous, slovenly while Monica is fastidious. In other ways, the pair seem alike; both are women without men, thus outside of the conventional partriarchal order. Sheila is the widow of Morton Flaxman, a well-known sculptor. (With characteristic allusive intentions, Oates has named him for the friend and patron of William Blake.) One of his large works, enigmatically named "Solstice," stands on the Glenkill campus. Oddly enough, Monica had become quite familiar with his sculpture during her New York days:

> She wasn't unstintingly enthusiastic; the heavy white masses, the unbroken lines and featureless curves, the mere *semblance* of living, primitive forms, had always vaguely troubled her, weighed upon her vision, as she sat with a cooling cup of tea—one cup after another, in fact—in the sculpture garden of the Museum of Modern Art, trying to find a way out of the cul-de-sac of her life. (*S*, 4)

Sheila Trask is an artist in her own right, a woman with a "hoydenish charm" (*S*, 21), a painter at the verge of celebrity. She is in the throes of producing a major work: a group of canvases for a one-woman show intended as a form of defiant self-assertion, a project of subversive mythmaking:

> The series was called "Ariadne's Thread." It had to do, Sheila explained, with the idea or memory of a labyrinth, not the actual labyrinth—"in which," Sheila said mysteriously, "we don't always believe." (*S*, 37)

> Ariadne's thread: the labyrinth as a state of mind, a region of the soul: heroic effort without any Hero at its center ("This is only about Ariadne's thread, this has nothing to do with Theseus," Sheila said angrily). (*S*, 53)

Yet her project remains unfinished; like Anna Wulf, she is frustrated and blocked. Her canvases lie "haphazardly about the studio," reflecting the underside of a painter's craft: "intimations of clouds, a network of nerves, the brain's secret convolutions." Oates shares Lessing's vision of work in progress as "a map of the mind," a glimpse of the primordial sources of creativity itself (*S*, 203–4).

She thus dramatizes the inner and outer lives of her two central figures who together, as artist and audience, lover and beloved, make creation possible. In public, Sheila is disruptive, disrespectful, in a perpetual state of rage. She craves attention like a desperate child; yet it is no child that descends on Monica Jensen, demanding to be comforted, and admired, vampiristic although she promises no attention in return. Fascinated from the moment of their first meeting, Monica drops the thread of her own life to pick up Sheila's clues, and at first to forgive any egoistic transgression.

Lessing's artist works in a variety of forms and voices (the several notebooks expand the literary convention of the diary), taking her characters into history and across two continents. In her own reimagined "golden notebook," Oates is concerned only tangentially with political or historical reality; her novel moves into inner latitudes, the region where art comes into being. After Monica and Sheila are introduced, the novel follows a sinuous path, the pattern of yin and yang, the attraction and repulsion of energies. The very play of contrariety is the generative force of their relationship, although at times it is difficult to know whether it will redeem or destroy them.

Oates's satiric eye remains focused upon the academy, her favorite target, shrunken to Lilliputian proportions in *Solstice*. Like another Oatesian alter ego, Brigit Stott of *Unholy Loves,* Monica finds that the academy itself trivializes its valuable pursuits by putting authority in the hands of unimaginative tutors and sanctimonious administrators. Monica herself has taken part in the American schoolgirl's dream: an aging ex-prom queen from Alix Kates Shulman's pages. Fingering her scar (ironically, the mark of accident rather than a passionate blow), she is a pathetic rather than tragic victim of a man's world; when, like the heroine of Margaret Atwood's *Surfacing,* she tells the sorry tale of her abortion, she does not set the stage for new beginnings.

Once again, Oates writes a work based on teasing literary marriages and infidelities. Carrington's suggestion that *Solstice* is a parody of feminist fiction seems off the mark: Oates has joined her own energies to the contemporary feminist critique. Her portrait of Monica thus exposes the loveless reality of Monica's golden touch:

> Monica saw herself unsentimentally as a woman, a former *girl,* who had the power—derived from where, she couldn't have guessed—to convince others, for a while, of her goldenness, her specialness. The emotional logic of loving *her.* (*S,* 9–10)

But if she has outlived her value in this tawdry design, Monica continues to find an imaginative place in literature: she at least can hymn the loss of her youthful goldenness in Shakespearean metaphor and cadence ("Golden lads and girls all must,/ As chimney-sweepers, come to dust" [*S,* 9]).

She also seems the perfect complement to the artist in residence of sleepy Bucks County, a foil for the aggressive and flagrant *poseur.* At one point in the novel, Sheila plays a wanton's part, bar-hopping, taking a false name, and traducing the half-willing Monica to join the masquerade in ever more dangerous forays to rural taverns. At last, painfully out of character, Monica leaves the ugly show in self-disgust and genuine fear. Sheila, apparently immune to the tweak of conscience, keeps her perverse, nightside self teasingly alive.

Always attracted to doubles, Oates presents Monica and Sheila as emblems of the divided artistic self, twin personalities who at first hold radically different views of the nature of the creative enterprise, and the value of texts and tradition. After their initial meeting, Sheila Trask prowls through Monica's house, impressed with her new friend's library:

> Sheila began to muse aloud, saying she envied Monica her books, these particular books (orange-spined Penguin copies of the Brontës, Dickens, George Eliot, Trollope), they were so dog-eared and worn, so marked with underlinings and annotations, it was obvious their reader had not simply read the novels but had lived through them.(*S,* 21)

Yet books are alien objects to Sheila. Flaxman, her sculptor husband, had believed "there was something wholly sane about a book . . . because there is something finite about it. The book, no matter its length, encompasses a complete world. It *is* a world" (*S,* 21). On her part, she regards fiction as false and insubstantial. "It displaces virtually no space in this world":

> Of what value was a novel, Sheila asked, if one couldn't live through it?—if it were only a matter of words skillfully arranged? She was herself so caught up in her work, not trapped exactly, but caught up, immersed, for years she had been obsessed with "figuring certain problems out visually," she had all but abandoned reading. (*S,* 21)

Ironically, then, she has no use for the very novels which fascinate Monica Jensen—and the author of *A Bloodsmoor Romance* and *Mysteries of Winterthurn,* Joyce Carol Oates:

> She had certainly abandoned these leisurely, massive, world-embracing Victorian novels. . . . The printed line, after all, is so orderly and chaste, so chronologically determined—that is, the reader is obliged to read line by line, page by page in sequence; very unlike the visual image, which assults the eye out of nowhere, in a manner of speaking, with no preparation, and no power over the viewer to demand from him more than a moment's casual contemplation. (*S,* 21–22)

Conversely, Monica at first is visually illiterate, like one of the well-meaning but "unintelligent . . . uninformed" museum goers who are the object of Sheila's unmitigated scorn. She finds modern art "flat, sterile, and oddly unimaginative." Instead, she is nourished by the literary heritage and its repository of shapely verbal texts. Sheila, defiant, flaunts her bookless freedom; she claims she *is* "the present tense" (*S,* 22).

It is more than idle wordplay. The story intensifies as the two women draw near one another, almost magically attracted, reaching curious points of juncture and intersection. At times, Sheila seems the bully; in her presence, Monica feels herself becoming wordless, aphasic. Yet the painter is as strongly influenced by this golden girl, whose daylight aura seems all at once to be reflected in her half-completed canvases. Pulled in opposite directions, spun back toward one another in passion's silent grip, artist and acolyte move past forces of division, in league against the fearful artist's block.

Even more curiously, in the process they seem to exchange roles. Sheila darkly treatens suicide, abuses and starves herself in defiance of Monica's nurturance; she refuses to answer her friend's frantic calls and abandons her at Christmas without a word. Back in town and in touch with Monica, she carelessly and cruelly exposes Monica to the designs of potential exploiters and rapists, and almost assuredly costs her the Glenkill position. Yet after

Sheila offers a rare and rough but affectionate goodnight kiss, Monica takes up Ariadne's thread, finding a way to penetrate the artistic paralysis.

In Oates's later novels, the power of art is often rendered as invasive and manipulative: the moral and formal obligations of genre shape and limit an artist's design. Yet even in her tightly plotted and over-determined detective tale, there are glimpses of a more imposing creative force. Investigating lurid clues Xavier Kilgarvan pulls out his sketchbook, and then pauses in his search, abandoning himself to a half-wakeful reverie. At once, he is privy to the imagination's rich realm of disclosure: "did it not seem that, by these efforts, he could suddenly *see more?*—that it might be his privilege, in the next minute or two, to *see beyond?*" (*MW*, 65). Across centuries and changing custom, Monica has a burst of creative insight like that of the doomed detective. Still wondering at her friend's embrace, she drowses; and all at once, she "sees" and "is" Sheila's final canvas:

> That night she dreamt of the most extraordinary painting, fluid, three-dimensional, throbbing with life: Sheila's painting perhaps, but only partly imagined, still in the process of being transcribed. Monica was staring at the painting yet at the same time she was in it; swimming in its sweet radiant warmth, in its fleshy-sweet erotic warmth, scarcely daring to breathe because the sensation was so exquisite, so precarious, so forbidding. (*S,* 201)

In Sheila's selfish grasp, Ariadne's thread grows taut and seems to snap; but Monica—midwife, muse, vicarious artist, ideal reader and alter ego—fights against the dying of the light. Love, to paraphrase Kafka, is the ax that breaks the frozen sea within. Oates describes her feverish struggle as a secular conversion; Monica finds herself attuned to the power of pure visionary creation:

> There was a distinct internal logic to the series which one began to feel but it would have been impossible for Monica to talk of it. To murmur that the canvases were beautiful—powerful—compelling—lyric—or "lyrically violent" . . . seemed quite beside the point. All that was significant about them was interior, secret, indefinable; they possessed their own integrity, they *were.* (*S,* 204)

The two collaborate in a wordless realm:

> Sheila detested the very notion of a conceptualist art—words were an admission of failure. So, in the studio, hour upon hour passed in absolute silence. It was a place where language did not determine action. It was a place, Monica sometimes thought, prior to language. To enter it—to dare to enter it—was to surrender the power of words, and to submit to another sort of power altogether. (*S,* 204)

Resisting, brawling, clawing, in an agonized spasm of creation, Sheila

Trask finally brings her work into view, framed and hung. Almost perversely, in the ebb and flow of force that marks this novel, Monica Jensen cannot—will not?—attend the opening and exhibition. The vampiristic, egocentric artist seems to have drained and depleted the teacher's energies, robbing her of the will to survive. Too wasted now to meet her classes, to judge (she allows a student to "disgrace" himself in a poem about his own homosexuality, read to the prudish academy faculty), unable to eat, she has a breakdown.

It is both literally and figuratively a time of solstice. As the word suggests, this story has come to a standstill. On the other hand, it may be a turning point. It is hightly significant that *Solstice,* which has been Monica's narrative all along, concludes with Sheila Trask's bullying, impatient, roughly affectionate words.

This novel is again framed by the words of Emily Dickinson. Her first published poem, a light-hearted valentine addressed to a world of young lovers, is an ironic epigraph for *A Bloodsmoor Romance.* Oates chooses "After great pain, a formal feeling comes" as the more chilling epigraph to *Solstice.* It is itself an arresting poem about the soul's terrifying "hour of lead," death's irresistible seduction, the letting go. Oates has used this poem before in the more unlikely academic context of *Unholy Loves.* In *Solstice,* it sets the stage for a different sort of drama, focusing not on the isolated artist in deserted, echoing libraries, but on a contentious, threatening, demanding, loving col - leagueship.

Solstice is a curious painterly novel: grinning death's head images reflect against the windows of the house of fiction. It also seems bathed in Dickinson's uncanny "slant of light," which paradoxically eludes exact verbal paraphrase. Indeed, images of light seem keys to the novel. Monica generates her own golden glow; sitting beneath the "pitiless skylight" of Sheila's studio, she becomes aware as she has never been before of the power of "formal feeling," the play of sign and color and shape. She cannot find verbal equivalents; she tells herself that "beauty is after all only a matter of light; of gradations of light; degrees of seeing" (*S,* 160). More and more out of touch with verbal discourse, both teacher and artist are vulnerable to the tug of deathly stillness: Sheila dreams of "contentless forms, wave-motions, hairline fractures as of . . . great blocks of ice" (*S,* 227); Monica imagines falling "into the depths of one's own body, retreating to a small snug well-lit place deep in the brain . . . a languorous deathly sleep, the most delicious of sleeps" (*S,* 231). The dream-images are at once intoxicating and sinister: suggesting but not disclosing future possibilities.

In her artful reworking of nineteenth-century genres, Oates has exposed a fundamental incongruity in those narrative conventions: they seem at once to shape, constrain and misrepresent the world and work of women. In *A Bloodsmoor Romance,* the gushing storyteller, confronting her own subversive tendencies, prudently withdraws; in *Mysteries of Winterthurn,* once the detective-hero embraces domesticity, he and his uncomprehending narrator part company. In *Solstice,* Oates turns from parody to prophecy: she acts as Ariadne, uncoiling clews, moving through torturous turnings and dangerous passages, past the leaden hour, the block, evading the still point of closure. She also paints an oddly familiar yet disturbing picture of female intimacy. As Monica and Sheila, teacher and artist, draw upon each other's energies, they seem to violate conventional expectations both of women's relationships and of the novel itself.

Correspondingly, some readers have voiced their uneasiness at Oates's apparent refusal to either mirror or ratify expectations based on gender. Joanna Russ rebukes Oates for appealing to prurient appetites; Oates takes ironic issue with her reading and premise in *The Women's Review of Books.*[24]

Such comments testify to Oates's contrariety. *Solstice* evokes the subversive presence Nina Auerbach describes in *Communities of Women,* a curious mythic counterforce in Western literature and culture:

> As a recurrent literary image, a community of women is a rebuke to the conventional ideal of a solitary woman living for and through men, attaining citizenship in the community of adulthood through masculine approval alone. The communities of women which have haunted our literary imagination . . . are emblems of female self-sufficiency which create their own corporate reality, evoking both wishes and fears.[25]

By necessity, such fictional women do not reinforce conventional assumptions; their resistance turns them into amputees or exiles. Auerbach provocatively suggests that "as a literary idea, a community of women feeds dreams of a world beyond the normal" (Auerbach, 5).

If *Solstice* reflects such unsettling dreams, Oates's next novel, *Marya: A Life* (1986), seems centered in a harsher daylit world. This is a *Künstlerroman,* an inside story drawn both from the author's life and from her earlier fictional landscape. The novel's opening and closing chapters are again set in that backwoods region which she has called Eden Valley and Childwold. Here she names it in ironic tribute not to Milton or Nabokov but to Yeats: Innisfail.

Oates's seventeenth novel is another portrait of her alter ego: a young woman who moves from that rural scene into the world of the academy—resisting her female fate by entering a privileged community of men. While Marya is awarded marks of approval—scholarships, good grades, graduate admission, tenure—she remains an outsider, exiled from her own creative sources. The longing for community haunts the novel, framing as well as fracturing the narrative, shadowing the heroine's conventional academic path. As Oates takes up the strategies of realist and parodist, chopping the

novel into a series of foreshortened anecdotes, she emphasizes the discontinuity of women's school experience. From early grades to her later life as a
college professor, Marya is in residence—but never at home.

She is dispossessed even in preschool days. In the violent opening scenes
of the novel, Marya is dragged out of "a night of patchy dreams" (*M,* 1) and
driven to Innisfail to view the battered and bloody corpse of her father. Her
slovenly, maddened mother abandons her and her brothers to an aunt and
uncle's foster care. Attempting to obey her mother's parting advice, Marya
dons a passive and tearless mask; once again, such passivity seems to inspire
sexual abuse. In this "child's paradise" of junked automobiles and broken
promises, the ceaseless and random threat of assault only deepens Marya's
nightmarish sense of abandonment.

Terrorized by the cruel "secret logic" (*M,* 23) of the playground bully, she
seeks the sanctuary of the schoolroom. Oates described a similar moment in
her own life: when bullies attacked, she fled from "brutish Nature" to the
classroom's "magical confines" (Stories, 15, 16). In *Marya: A Life,* more subtle forms of assault are practiced in that protected environment. When the
heroine enters the class of a wacky high school pedagogue, Brandon P.
Schwilk, the experience is at first exhilarating; he initiates her into the mysteries of Blake, Dickinson, and William James, and awakens her own passion
for language and creative expression. Longing for her teacher's approval, she
submits stories to him, only to be humiliated and betrayed when he reserves
his praise for her spelling. In silent fury, Marya resorts to the devious vengeance born of early playground experience. Ironically taking her cue from
the teacher, she turns on him to demand literal explanations of his soaring
pedantic metaphors, inciting the savage laughter of insensitive classmates
and quickly transforming the classroom into an arena of cruelty. Marya's
subversive ploy is unwittingly self-destructive: she not only destroys
Schwilk's "capricious authority," but her own schoolroom haven.

Seeking less eccentric and more rigorous tutors, Marya turns to the church,
becoming a Catholic convert and an acolyte to a dying priest. Awed by Father Shearing's powers, she becomes a self-styled sacrificial lamb, silencing
her own questions to act as his amanuensis and medium. The experience
ironically narrows her sights: she worries that his gift of philosophical and
critical expression may be an "entirely masculine skill" (*M,* 95). The priest is
progressively devoured by cancer; his death leaves her outside the circle of
belief, the inheritor only of his beautiful watch, now an emblem of mortality.

The pattern of the novel seems clear. A dutiful pupil oddly out of place,
Marya is frustrated in her attempts to mirror and please her tutors. Repeatedly she makes a spectacle of herself in a community with very different expectations for women. It is no surprise that her ringing high school
valedictory address, a social critique with priestly echoes, offends the local

audience. The incident could almost be taken from the biography of Willa Cather, whose precocious valedictory marked her graduation from the conventional mentality of small-town America. Similarly, the proud Marya refuses marriage and domesticity in order to "give birth to a new self" through academic study and scholarship. The response of the community of men is ugly, practiced, and ritualistic. Lingering too long at the farewell party organized for her the night before she is to go to college, Marya is assaulted by a gang of drunken boys who subject her to a brutal shearing, cutting off her beautiful waist-length hair.

At college, Marya's winged aspirations are clipped as well. She lives in the garret of a dilapidated house for scholarship girls, in exile on the campus periphery. Like her housemates but not truly part of any company, she worries about funds and anticipates failure. Gifted students around her inexplicably *do* fail; there are no viable female role models here. Receiving good grades, Marya is uncertain that she deserves them. She is further humiliated by the sorority parody of sisterhood. Indeed, all academic agencies seem to conspire to devalue her ideals, assigning her a morally and intellectually confining role:

> The university piously preached an ethic of knowledge for its own sake— knowledge and beauty being identical—the "entire person" was to be educated, not simply the mind; but of course it acted swiftly and pragmatically upon another ethic entirely. Performance was all, the grade point average was everything. (*M,* 135–36)

Yet top performance only deepens Marya's self-doubt; she becomes more manipulative and devious. What is worse, the attempt to please academic mentors depletes Marya's creative energies. The Innisfail libraries had left her hungering for the great poetic texts; poor Schwilk had owned and offered (but never produced) the only copy of William Blake in town. But in Port Oriskany college, she feeds her appetite warily, by now conditioned to serve as acolyte but never celebrant:

> She made her way with the stealth of the thief, elated, subdued, through another's imagination, risking no harm, no punishment . . . the books she read greedily seemed to take life through her, by way of her, with virtually no exertion of her own." (*M,* 134)

For Marya, the artist's prized negative capability is subtly translated into self-erasure. Like Oates, she comes to believe that "a writer's authentic self . . . lay in his writing and not in his life" (*M,* 135); yet unlike Oates, Marya fights off her desire to yield to the ravishing power of art:

> She half-way feared to write anything that wasn't academic or scholarly or

firmly rooted in the real world . . . once she began she wouldn't be able to stop; she was afraid of sinking too deep into her own head, cracking up, becoming lost. (*M*, 154–55)

Terrorized, she admonishes herself, "Give up. Don't risk it. *Don't risk it*" (*M*, 175). Oates issues a stinging and ironic rebuke to her own academic community: to remain safely in residence, her heroine must abandon the passion of the artist for the decorous language of academic scholarship:

> There was another kind of writing—highly conscious, cerebral, critical, discursive—which she found far easier; far less dangerous. She was praised for it lavishly, given the hgiest grades, the most splendid sort of encouragement. She should plan, her professors said, to go on to graduate school. (*M*, 175.)

Yet Marya feels like an imposter as she advances from community college to the "atmosphere of privilege and academic rigor" of the ivy league: "She was an alien here. . . . She felt her presence in a way subversive, a tactical error on the part of others" (*M*, 190–91). Although she is at least as qualified as her male graduate school peers, she is assigned other roles: copyist and clerk, house-sitter, mistress. Maximilian Fein, her graduate advisor and lover, is another Oatesian academic type—a self-infatuated scholar who parades his own ego in place of literature:

> Fein goaded her by saying that scholarship as well as art was very likely, at bottom, only play and improvisation and illusion; it *played* at meaning in order to justify its extraordinary demands of time, spirit. . . . (*M*, 228)

Privately angry but publicly acquiescent, Marya moves from her earlier excitement at the academy's "feast of books" (*M*, 188) to the far more limited satisfactions of a "claustrophobic community" (*M*, 217).

Oates raises an eloquent and angry protest against the mutilation suffered by women in the academy in *Marya: A Life*. By the time she becomes Professor Knauer, Marya has learned to move like a woman with bound feet, minimizing her own needs and original insights. Interestingly, her first dependent scholarly project is a feminist endeavor: she plans to work with the very community of women which inspired Oates's *Bellefleur, A Bloodsmoor Romance,* and *Mysteries of Winterthurn*:

> She wanted to study "magical" narratives in nineteenth-century fiction . . . apocalyptic romances of a sort. . . . She wanted to pay a good deal of attention to neglected writers, to unknown woman writers, in whose work radical and even revolutionary themes might be discovered, beneath, or behind, the formal conventions of a genre. (*M*, 241)

As Oates's alter ego, Marya takes up the role of cultural critic and commentator, observing to herself that "professors in the humanities spent their lives rigorously analyzing texts, classical and otherwise, but displayed a curious reluctance to examine the 'text' in which they played out their own lives" (*M*, 242).

Yet her energies are reined in sharply. When her chairman shares his "frank doubts" about her "areas of scholarship" (*M*, 247), she covers her tracks, displaying work which will win her contract renewal, "shrewd enough to say nothing at all about her nonacademic writing, or to allude to it in in the slightly disparaging way in which such writing is generally alluded to, in her profession" (*M*, 259). In this game, winner takes nothing. Marya is nauseated by her own complicity; she thinks, with her penchant for irony, "perhaps the initiation into her profession was in fact a powerful emetic" (*M*, 263).

The next episode, Marya's tenure decision, is an odd mixture of lampoon and hallucination: Oates's own brand of academic fiction. On the day of tenure decisions, Marya agrees to take a bicycle ride with a colleague to relieve their mutual anxiety. The holiday excursion soon turns into a deadly contest, like the tenure fight itself. Her erstwhile lover sadistically leads Marya far beyond the limits of her physical endurance, and she takes a horrendous downhill fall. While she goes off, shaken, to wash her lacerated leg, he "cheats" and calls the college for the committee results. In an ironic reversal, it appears that Marya has won the prize but he is denied; their relationship ends as abruptly as the chapter.

Marya's dogged insistence that she can set her own intellectual course is mocked at every turn of the plot; indeed, it seems a wishful misreading of the novel's epigraph: "My first act of freedom will be to believe in freedom." When she chooses to leave the academy, Marya immediately surrenders her autonomy to another imposing male tutor: the influential editor of a journal of politics and public opinion, Eric Nichols. He is married; she becomes his lover, interpreter, and thus, the creature of his imagination. Even after Nichols dies, she is bound to his will; his voice echoes in her mind, goading her into radical protest, forcing her to confront the sickening spectacle of human cruelty on an international scale. Covering an international conference as his posthumous surrogate, she collapses, unable to bear witness. Her journey out of Innisfail comes to a dead end, leaving her without role or voice.

The energy of much of Oates's fiction comes from literary marriage and imaginative appropriation; in this novel Oates might better be accused of breaking and entering, employed creative larceny to dislodge convention, to expose the struggle for power masked by manners. The motif of theft functions at the level of both form and theme. Most obviously, everything Marya treasures is stolen from her as she moves fearfully through a world of predators. Fighting to sustain herself in exile, she is robbed of money, pens, the fine watch which is her Shearing legacy. In a community that seemingly is devoted to individuality, Marya's privacy is never respected; the contents of her desk are frequently rifled. Marya herself is guilty of petty shoplifting; she is also prey to thieving fantasies, in which she is the criminal. In a wry and wicked variation on this theme, even when she is installed in a professorial office, her tenancy is disturbed by the disrespect and trespass of an irreverent black custodian. In residence, but not the artist she might have been, she becomes the novel's most problematic thief, robbing herself of the fullness of her own life.

Marya's breakdown forces her to review those assets she has not lost to ever-thieving time. Years of creative possibility have been lost in translation; at thirty-six, she has the problematic "solace" of emptiness, a welcome absence of mirrors which relieves her of the necessity of confronting her own "troubling image," and renders her "invisible to herself" (*M*, 285). Yet the world of books has left her something: she can summon up the spirit of her poetic tutors and prophetic demons. In an allusion to Blake, she thinks "energy is sheer delight," roused to seek new levels of awareness, "swift and happy as a ray of light" (*M*, 285). (Her own name, Marya, seems an uncanny anagram of Nietzsche's buoyant phrase.)

In the last pages of the novel, Marya is drawn back to a wedding in Innisfail. Returning to the scene of her first loss, she is now earnestly in search of the mother who abandoned her; she has placed an advertisement in the paper, and her aunt, having seen it, confides to Marya her mother's whereabouts. It is a stunning revelation. Far from libraries or conference rooms, in a seedy Innisfail cafe, Marya is all at once conscious of the power residing in the community of women:

> The moment was oddly light, blurred; not so strained as one might imagine, served up as it was in the tacky old Royalton Cafe, at eleven in the morning, amid chatter from other tables—women shoppers, mainly. . . . Marya was staring at Wilma, who was busy buttering a croissant. She wanted to ask how long Wilma had known but she decided against it, the words might have struck the wrong note. Instead she said, laughing, weak, breathless, "My mother is alive. . . . " (*M*, 308–9)

No text or male advisor has prepared her for this assignment. Having written to her mother (tellingly, the much-rewritten letter is not shared with the reader), she waits in terror, and is rewarded with a reply. Here, at last, is the new life she once went to school to seek: holding the envelope, she fearfully shakes out its contents, a snapshot of her mother, a woman with Marya's own features. "Marya, this is going to cut your life in two," she tells herself, waiting for the letter itself to come into focus, awakening from one set of nightmares into a vision that remains wonderfully indistinct, "as if a dream secret and prized in her soul had blossomed outward, taking its place, asserting its integrity, in the world" (*M*, 310).

Interestingly, in her essay, "My Friend Joyce Carol Oates," Elaine Showalter reads Marya's life as a representative feminine text, drawn from woman's community: "The community of women is not idyllic, but torn by rage, competition, primal jealousy, ambiguous desire and emotional violence, just like the world in which women seem subordinate to and victimized by men."[26] Providing her own vision of the "community of women," Joyce Carol Oates is sensitive to violent forces which promote amputation and exile. Yet she also finds the "dreams of a world beyond the normal" providential. Cutting off *Marya: A Life* at a moment of rebirth, she provides no happy ending, no conventional closure. Instead, Marya recovers her hopeful and questing spirit in the world of her mother: open to the terrifying but tantalizing revisionary challenges posed by a woman's unfinished text.

Conclusion
Missing Views, "Last Days"

In a recent essay, Roger Shattuck declares that contemporary fiction is in crisis because of an "unnarratability principle." Facing a world of "fragments," "shards," and "cock-and-bull stories," some writers respond with an array of narrative devices which evoke cinema more than the novel:

> ... digression, parody, marginal discourse, reflexivity, fragment, miscellany, theme and variations, *ecriture,* palimpsest ... short anecdotes, comic asides, deadpan refrains, and dissertations on far-fetched topics. ...

At best, Shattuck argues, these self-conscious performers produce "astutely shuffled works" and the readers who join them are always in the process of "gathering odds and ends." As an example, he quotes the narrator of Renata Adler's *Pitch Dark,* who describes the novelistic act as reductive and "atomic":

> It's all bits and pieces. A book should confine itself to small discrete units of experience and not try to arrange them on levels and in sequence. It's an art of juxtaposing quanta. To go further means to blow one's cover.

Such writers are no longer storytellers but "shrewd ventriloquists" who practice a minimalist art of "removal," a "realism of the schizoid." Their work has gone far beyond the wordplay of *Tristram Shandy,* incorporating the vision of Einstein and Eisenstein: a "montage of attractions," without concern for character or redeeming social value. Groping for the old verities, Shattuck cries "our fate, our very life, depends on stories." He charges that post-modern strategies of collage, montage, and "slant" or cinematic structure actually mask a "fear to narrate," or "advanced writer's block." Worse, they induce a reader-chilling "Medusa process."[1]

It seems almost irresistible to view the filmic properties of post-modern narrative—montage, short takes, temporal dislocations—as sheer self-display, representations of what fiction ought *not* to be. Shattuck calls for a contemporary aesthetic of narrative "fusion," using a surgical metaphor: fused, the damaged spinal column generates substitute tissue in a vigorous act of self-repair. Artists such as Kundera and Márquez provide such political and ethical frameworks, turning assemblage into meaningful moral statements (Shattuck, 3–4).

Joyce Carol Oates also confronts the contemporary question of "unnarratability" in her fiction and essays. Like Shattuck, Oates draws back in alarm from the spectacle of post-modern literary fragmentation. Like Márquez, she attempts to celebrate the multivalence and pluralism of contemporary life. For Oates, the artist is bound by the imposing authority of the story-telling process:

> The rhythms of narrative, the very phenomenon of narrative itself
> . . .surely they correspond to some deep rhythms of our own unconscious, even
> physical, in origin; and a highly self-conscious . . . art that rejects "plot" is in
> danger of rejecting the very origins of art's impulse. (Ballads, 560–61)

Yearning to be true to form and yet original, the artist in Oates's view labors "to set down words with such talismanic precision, such painstaking love, that they cannot be altered—that they constitute a reality of their own, and are not merely referential" (Stories, 15). To fuse her new narratives, she depends on old-fashioned voices, and reappraises "unworthy" or homespun arts. Oates's own work displays a search for forms which are intimately attuned to the rhythms of felt life as well as the deep structures of narratability (Stories, 15).

In this context, her literary revisions are not purely academic: they are witty but serious attempts to reinvoke particular states of consciousness; imaginative sequels rather than mere parodies. Oates has also tried to present counterstatements to the pervasive myth of the isolated artistic self:

> It may come to seem obvious to people in the future—that unique personality
> does not necessitate isolation, that the "I" of the poet belongs as naturally in the
> universe as any other aspect of its fluid totality, above all that this "I" exists in
> a field of living spirit of which it is one aspect. . . . Hopefully, a world of totality
> awaits us, not a played-out world of fragments. (NHNE, 139–40)

Even earlier than Shattuck, she attacked the fabulators for writing a literature of "particles . . . self-conscious 'cities of words' . . . that ricochet off one another more often than they do off reality" (NHNE, 183–85). As a critic, Oates continually admonishes her contemporaries to acknowledge their communal role.

But when Joyce Carol Oates's critical articles of faith are applied to her own work, many paradoxes emerge. Most obviously, her novels afford only the rarest glimpse of the ideal self-actualizing personality. Calling for visionary art, she experiments in revision. The prophets who appear frequently in her work, from Wonderland's activists and gurus to the mediums and inventors of A Bloodsmoor Romance and the spiritual seekers who play central roles in *The Assassins* and *Son of the Morning,* face the world's ridicule and a sense of failure.

Admitting her own defeat in *Wonderland,* Oates revised and radically foreshortened that novel's conclusion and moved away from dreamscape; in consequence, her *Wonderland* became a "death trip." The novels of the following decade, in contrast, have traced the itinerary of a new traveler. She revisits her own terrain in *Childwold,* pitting her young artist against an older fabulist; she attacks her pedantic colleagues but reaffirms the value of artistic residence in *Unholy Loves. Angel of Light* draws on Thoreau, Blake, and Aeschylus; *Bellefleur* is literary patchwork and legendary assemblage. No genre seems immune today to her revisionary energies. But the very breadth of her work continues to trouble critics eager to "place" Joyce Carol Oates.

In a sense, Oates's short fiction provides the best view of both her intentions and her artistic practice. Many of her stories show the marks of academic residence. Some are outright imitations: she calls them by their original titles. As she reimagines the work of other storytellers, Oates invites speculation about artistic genius and originality. Her own stories emerge in modern dress or in a contemporary cultural context; playing with form, she also raises moral concerns. Instead of the literature of "quanta," Oates attempts to arrange literary "marriages." In the best of them, such as her version of James Joyce's "The Dead" (see chapter 6), or Chekhov's "Lady with a Pet Dog," Oates demonstrates her own creative and synthetic powers, her own "negative capability."

Oates is not only drawn back to the work of mentors and masters, she also returns to the scene of her own fiction, haunted by particular characters and scenes, aching to revise. Indeed, Oates considers revision an essential part of her creative process:

> The rhythm of writing, revising, writing, revising, etcetera, seems to suit me. I am inclined to think that as I grow older I will come to be infatuated with the art of revision, and there may come a time when I will dread giving up a novel at all.[2]

At this point, however, she seems equally infatuated with the act of reconstructing and reimagining fictive designs.

Interestingly, again, many of the short stories which she writes and rewrites are literally academic; some, in fact, are obliquely autobiographical. But one group of her sketches and stories seems especially important as a revelation of her complex academic concerns and her literary practice. In 1965, when Oates was a professor at the University of Detroit, she met an extraordinary student, Richard Wishnetsky. Richard was to attain special and horrible notoriety. The mystery of his personality as well as the failure of academic mentors to understand and save him became a burden on Oates's own conscience. Characteristically, she turned to art to mediate her inner conflicts.

Reviewing her work, we find more than one version of Richard Wishnetsky's violent and tragic history. Her first, an essay, appeared in *The Detroit Free Press,* March 6, 1966, only weeks after the young man strode to the front of Shaarey Zedek Synagog and shot Rabbi Morris Adler, then himself. As the newspaper editor observed in a headnote, Joyce Carol Oates was "troubled" by the "intensity of his thoughts, the compulsion of his ideas." She seemed not only impelled to voice her own anguish but to serve as a kind of apologist for the young assassin in her article, "Richard Wishnetsky: Joyce Oates Supplies a Missing View."[3]

When she wrote the article, Oates was in a privileged position to address the questions of a shocked community: the position, literally and figuratively, of the artist in residence. Wishnetsky, a student at the university where she was teaching and writing, had sought her out:

> One day in the spring of 1965 a young man came into my office at the University of Detroit and introduced himself as Richard Wishnetsky. . . . He had a certain urgent, harassed, slightly embarrassed look . . . he was to remark later, when I knew him better, that a good day for him was a day in which nothing catastrophic had happened.

Oates was almost perversely impressed; in this account, she finds him from the first "argumentative in a way sometimes admirable in students" with a "brilliant, keen sense of humor—one certain mark of sanity." Apparently under the sway of his powerful personality, she admires his "audacity" as well as "those occasional tender moments of self-illumination that made him unforgettably human." As a professor, she is excited by his qualities of mind; she is both fascinated and repelled by "his obsession with ideas." To defuse her own mounting sense of danger, she minimizes his stream of literary consciousness, attempting to be "flippant":

> I told him that ideas have but a tenuous relationship to real life and that one should not become deranged over them; they are not that important. He dismissed this contemptuously. Ideas were the highest creations of man, the only reality. . . .

Professor Oates had accused Wishnetsky of being too literal; nonetheless, she approves of his determination to become a "scholar, a man of ideas." Could she have read his enthusiasm with a less naive and more clinical eye, Oates suggests that she might have prevented the tragedy ("It was all there on that first day—the latent violence, the scornful refutations, the sense that the majority of people are wrong and therefore contempitible."). His obsession with ideas might have served as a symptom of future disaster, to an "orthodox psychiatrist"; Oates instead analyzes his classroom performance on strictly academic and literary grounds:

> He came one day to visit my class and this was the first time I had seen him in a situation involving others. He shocked the class—which probably felt sorry for me—by talking wildly and with dizzying generalizations, wrenching the discussion from *The Damnation of Theron Ware* to Goethe, Shakespeare, Aristotle.

> Like Dostoyevsky, whom he greatly admired, Richard was violent, righteous, a "punisher." . . . His identification with the hero of . . . *The Pawnbroker* drove him nearly to hysterics . . . and he identified rather violently with the hero of *The Collector;* while everyone else sympathizes with the girl, imprisoned by a madman, Richard identified with the "collector" himself. . . . "She didn't try to love him."

Oates is fascinated by his use of religious metaphor: his identification with "The Sacrificed One," with his "messianic" gestures. Too late, however, she recognizes his statements are not figures of speech but figures of terrible truth:

> In all our discussions I was deluded, because I could not understand that what I as a professor talked about all the time—every teaching day—these grandiose problems of life, death, God, fate, etc. etc. were being taken in absolute seriousness by Richard. He was really living these problems out, while my colleagues and I made coin by them, so to speak—transforming writers' personal anguish into refined classroom discussions among students with good teeth and good manners and highly ordinary plans for the weekend. In this world, Richard was entirely alone.

This, then, is the "missing view": an eye-witness account gradually stripped of its objectivity and distance, becoming an act of confession, a plea for absolution, and ultimately a profound critique of the academy. Not yet collected or reprinted, this early essay provides a striking view of Oates's sense of the moral limitations of her residence.

She remained more than "vaguely troubled" by the Wishnetsky incident and her own role as his unwitting accomplice. Versions of his character can be found throughout her work. Richard is one model for the maddened terrorists and self-styled messiahs whose lives she mirrors in her novels. More interestingly, Oates reimagines his story in two important pieces of short fiction, attempting to come to terms with this American type and in effect, indicting the academic realm which inspires such violence in its most precocious and gifted acolytes.

"In a Region of Ice" appeared in 1969; the events and characters of the story are clearly life-studies and "missing views." But the narrative also has the opaque quality of parable. As tightly structured as the required curriculum, it unfolds in the semester's relentless chronology as the central characters navigate through successive social and imaginative frames. Richard is Allen Weinstein, a brilliant and insistent intruder into the university preserve, manic and disruptive in the classroom, a breaker of precedents and rules. It is not surprising that he catches the professorial figure off guard. Sister Irene, beginning a new position in the sanctuary of a Catholic college, is bewildered by the demands of the profane world:

> She had no trouble with teaching itself, once she stood before a classroom she felt herself capable of anything. It was the world outside the classroom that confused and alarmed her. . . . At times she had the idea that she was on trial and that the excuses she made to herself about her discomfort were only the common excuses made by guilty people. But in front of a class she had no time to worry about herself, or the conflicts in her mind. She became, once and for all, a figure existing only for the benefit of others, an instrument by which facts were communicated. (*RI,* 11–12)

Sister Irene's territory seems mapped into distinct regions. Beyond the outer limits, inchoate, raw, immune to human concerns, is the world of nature. The human circle is marked off by highways and the manicured suburban boundaries of "expensive people." Within, behind ivy walls, the university stands: a privileged location, an asylum for the marginal figure; a sacred archive of canonical texts. Even that realm is subdivided into offices and corridors, laboratories and libraries, and the most sacrosanct area of all, the classroom.

Sister Irene's house of fiction is thus a labyrinth; the academy, deep within its winding and narrowing passages, is a very safe "new world" (*RI,* 11). "In the Region of Ice" at one level is early Oatesian critique of academe, an exposure of the sterility and seductions of the author's vaunted, albeit small, moral universe. The idealized vision of the religious acolyte and the teacher-scholar seemingly converge in Sister Irene: a mediator and mentor, a curator and connoisseur. But as Oates's story shows, in the university, where intellectual passions can inspire surprising terrorist demands, balance can mask imbalance: such poise may be a form of self-deception as well as a failure of nerve.

Drawn into the fray by the punishing, braying, brilliant Weinstein, she is attracted by his agile mind; at the same time, she is shocked by his emotional commitment, and turns to a colleague for help. What had been a flippant comment to Wishnetsky by Oates herself becomes the sign of intellectual blindness in Sister Irene, the dissociation of sensibility, an academician's unpardonable sin:

> "He's an excellent student," she insisted. "I'm very grateful to have him in class. It's just that . . . he thinks ideas are real." Sister Carlotta, who loved lit-

erature also, had been forced to teach grade-school arithmetic for the last four years. That might have been why she said, a little sharply, "You don't think ideas are real?"

Sister Irene acquiesced with a smile, but of course she did not think so: only reality is real. (*RI,* 15)

Sister Irene is a quintessential academic: dedicated, reverential, disinterested in the best sense. But neither her professional training nor her profession of vows has prepared her for Weinstein's urgent application for admission to a more intimate and sacred space. She *does* admit him to her Shakespeare class, she allows him to bend and break her rules. Finally, she responds to his bullying and disruptive intrusion with an almost erotic intensity of her own.

Oates clearly has ambivalent feelings about her place of residence as she reimagines Wishnetsky's tragedy. Her story centers on acts of misreading and misinterpretation, a series of curious verbal transactions. The very subject matter which Sister Irene presents in the classroom with clarity and cool detachment becomes desperately real, transformed into an urgent coded message from Weinstein, his last application for sympathy and assistance. Committed to a sanitorium, given shock treatments to control his immoderate passions, he sends Sister Irene a letter carefully designed to baffle caretakers and censors. He praises his captors; he anticipates a "different life" after therapy. He also alludes to a play by Shakespeare, the tragicomic *Measure for Measure,* best known by students and scholars, and thus already encoded for an academic elite. Stunned, Sister Irene translates his hope as utter despair: "She knew what Weinstein was trying to tell her" (*RI,* 20). He has referred to a speech by Claudio, condemned to death: a desperate plea to his sister to sacrifice her virginity and save his life. Turning to Shakespeare's text, "cold with fear," she locates Claudio's description of the "different life" that awaits him in a "thrilling region of thick-ribbed ice . . . howling . . . horrible"—the kingdom of the dead. Moved and frightened, she resolves to honor Weinstein's single request, to share the message with his father.

Unlike Oates, who had maintained a professorial, if fascinated, distance from her student, Sister Irene decides to act. In a salvific role, she voyages out of the protection of the cloistered classroom into a world she knows at this point only through metaphor:

In her troubled mind the city traffic was jumbled and yet oddly coherent, an image of the world that was always out of joint with what was happening in it, its inner history struggling with its external spectacle. (*RI,* 21)

It is a case of pupil educating professor in the most literal sense of the word, leading her out into new realms of experience. No longer able to believe that "the convent's rhythm of life had nothing to do with the world's rhythm" (*RI,* 18), she finds herself moving to Weinstein's frantic beat with a new sense of vocation: "he was making her into a Christian, and to her that was a mystery, a thing of terror" (*RI,* 19). In both physical and spiritual passage as she drives toward the Weinstein home to warn the parents of their son's suicidal intentions, she feels a new kinship with the suffering Christ:

> She understood now the secret, sweet wildness that Christ must have felt, giving himself for many, dying for the billions of men who would never know of him and never understand the sacrifice. For the first time, she approached the realization of that great act. (*RI,* 21)

The demands of the waiting world inflame her imagination. Out of her element, she is filled with ontological insecurity like one of R.D. Laing's divided and terrorized selves; "a flicker of something close to madness" (*RI,* 21).

But this new incendiary impulse is diminished when she enters the Weinstein suburban chalet; facing his mother, observing the stylish and expensive furnishings, her own passions chill: "Sister Irene could not stop shivering" (*RI,* 22). When the elder Allen Weinstein rushes into the room, she is further dismayed and deflected from her mission and purpose: "Sister Irene stared at him and in that instant doubted everything" (*RI,* 22). That doubt even extends to her own interpretative and critical authority. When she shows him Allen's letter, he rejects her reading. She explicates the text as a suicide note; he insists on taking his son's words literally. As if she were introducing the concept of narrative irony to a naive student, she insists, "he means the opposite of what he says." "Then he's crazy!" Mr. Weinstein responds. She has failed at all levels: as teacher, as advisor, as an apostle of Christian love, as rescuer. Sister Irene retreats to university and convent, embarrassed by the Weinsteins' praise for her concern.

Sister Irene reenters the cloister and classroom refuge; the story whirls to a close. In his last act of desperation, Weinstein escapes his therapists and authoritarian father and comes to her once more; aroused, she aches to reach out to him. Yet when he demands money from her and holds out his hand, she shrinks from his touch and coldly refuses to assist. His suicide by drowning—a "wasteland" death by water a few months later in the cold and silent Canadian north—is no surprise. Pacing the university corridors, she cannot discern if she is safe or trapped, innocent or guilty: "If she could have felt guilt, she thought, she might at least have been able to feel something" (*RI,* 28).

"In the Region of Ice" is an imaginative translation of the Wishnetsky case into academic allegory. In her journalistic account, Oates had already moved far beyond matters of fact to explore the disjunction between real life and the academy. Shaken by Wishnetsky's conversion of words into action, Oates had confessed her own unwitting but fatal insensitivity. In this short story, in which the university no less than the human heart is a region of ice, Oates's confession has larger implications.

Framing her fiction in essentially religious terms, Oates suggests that in a secular society it is the critical interpreter who serves as the medium of conversion. Her point is not merely academic; life itself is at stake. Thus, when Sister Irene fails to convince Mr. Weinstein of the truth of irony, young Allen is doomed; forces of sterility and madness gain ascendancy; lines of defense are obliterated in a mind-chilling act of self-erasure.

True to form, "In the Region of Ice" is not Oates's last word on the subject. "Last Days," a short story published in 1984, is another attempt to supply "missing views." Wishnetsky is renamed Saul Morgenstern, bearing even closer marks of kinship with his actual model: he is an outsider, a prodigy, a wandering Jew, in residence for a time at a Catholic university; he is similarly God-mad, in the grip of messianic compulsion. Like Wishnetsky, Morgenstern has carefully planned a ritual of sacrifice, to be performed in a synagogue. He sees himself as "scourge of God," a prophet of apocalypse in a world which has lost its sense of sacred texts and divine imminence. To rouse this modern congregation he plots violent and outrageous acts: he will kill the rabbi; he will kill himself; he will become a vehicle of transcendence.

Saul is a brilliant student and a writer as well. Significantly, he wants to supply all missing views himself; his last days are spent revising penultimate texts and preparing his own posthumous interpretation. He drafts an exhortation to be delivered in the synagogue on the fateful Sabbath eve; he draws up a "Last Will and Testament" in Biblical style: *"As I cannot and will not continue to live in this abomination of hypocrisy I will make you an outright present of my life to satisfy your blood lust"* (*LD,* 33). Saul's intentions, like Wishnetsky's, have been shaped both by revealed religion and academic practice; they are framed in literary and linguistic terms, which for him are the terms of reality. He wants to become part of an eternal text. If the art of prophecy seems antique and hermeneutical or talmudic response has become a closed book, Saul's purpose is to revise the table of contents; he reassures himself, *"He cannot fail, he has entered History"* (*LD,* 33) as he drives to his violent ending.

Saul Morgenstern is another of Oates's young terrorists, figuratively if not literally failed by the modern academy; they are memorialized in her version of "The Dead"; she has dramatized their destructive urges in novels like *Wonderland* and *Angel of Light*. Again, Oates is ambivalent about this American type—the ideologue, the fanatic, the strident, half-mystic, half-terrified adolescent. She transcribes Saul's thoughts as the testament of a monstrous egoist who sees other people as twins of himself. Following him on his assassin's route, she registers his appetite for accolade. Yet she also provides compassionate evidence of his irrepressible idealism, his daring, his intensity, his personal force. A demiurge out of Blake or Freud, Saul signals his refusal to accept the diminished terms of modern existence and the amoral and materialistic ethic that fuels contemporary society. He flaunts convention and regulation: he tears his Rhodes Scholarship award into bits, purchases his death weapon without difficulty from a sleazy profiteer, and with a parodist's keen ear, he establishes his freedom from institutional constraints. He is wise to the psychiatrist's euphemistic jargon; his fugitive status ("unauthorized leave") is translated to "convalescent" as soon as he supplies the name of a therapist who will attest to his "reasonable adjustment" (*LD,* 33). Quixotic and irreverent, Saul shows his close kinship with his real and fictive prototypes, Wishnetsky and Weinstein.

But the story also shows the shift in Oates's academic and critical position since she encountered Wishnetsky in the traumatic sixties. One mark of transition is her technique. Her earlier story was tightly plotted, unfolding out of the labyrinths of Sister Irene's brain. Saul Morgenstern's "last days" are seen through a cracked and brittle surface, told in manic fragments incorporated in a third-person composite. As in several of her later novels, there is no single or still point of observation, but many witnesses, none of whom is able to get Saul's story straight.

Rather than offering a chronological narrative, Oates focuses upon a crisis in the process of personality, a marginal state very close to madness. The setting is again the university, a problematic theatre for such drama; yet, given its attention to the world as a verbal construct, a singular source of metaphor.

"Last Days" depends for its most striking effects not on linear plot, but on juxtaposition, parody, and paradox. Classic values and academic virtues are trivialized and standardized; scholarly effort is reduced to self-promotion. The academy confirms Morgenstern in his madness. Pushing through the disbelieving world with the force of unspent spiritual passion, Saul perversely attains his goal: to be inscribed in the book of congregational life, entering its pages through the violence of suicide and assassination.

The cracked prophet is a parody of an artist as well: he imagines himself immortal because no "syllable, not a wince, will be lost." He has left a definitive text for future academic and lay readers:

> He has penciled in last-minute corrections in his fastidious hand, the manuscript awaits its public, he can hear beforehand the envious remarks of his friends and acquaintances and professors. (*LD,* 39)

Tragically, since he has no inner measure to assess his own self-worth he becomes a grotesque publicist. Striding to the *bimah* to deliver his exhortation, he is flooded with light; he feels the thrill of election and revelation. But the illumination comes from the synagogue's recording equipment. Filled with ever more dubious joy, Saul exults that his final performance will be video-taped! "Am I the Messiah, he wonders, with so many eyes upon me?" In the story's last image, he stands at the altar, gun in one hand—and microphone in the other.

In a mad finale, Oates thus supplies more missing views of Richard Wish-netsky's tragic predicament. Her newspaper essay had provided insight into his academic and spiritual history; "In a Region of Ice" had exposed the ste-rility of cloistered realms of privilege. Oates's third version, "Last Days," is a view from another enclosure: the mind of an academic terrorist, a gifted student who has put the resources of language and the imagination to the ser-vice of his own self-inflation. No professors offer refuge to Morgenstern dur-ing his passage; not the classroom but his own tortured soul is the locus of any possible translation and conversion. Responding to the story, Erica Jong declares that Oates is "the poet laureate of schizophrenia."[4] Certainly, the au-thor has by now established the multiple possibilities of a "true" story.

In light of Oates's larger project of imaginative revision, it is evident that this story by necessity has no closure. But a work of fiction must end some-where. Oates resists the pull of finality in "Last Days" by bringing her narra-tive to the moment *before* Saul begins to fire his weapon. It is a strategy she has used in other works, notably *Bellefleur,* in which the story loops back in time, arriving at a moment of suspended judgment, a point of juncture when the story might have moved in a different direction. As readers, of course, we already know the final act; but Oates is intent upon making us more con-scious of marginal states, times between the acts.

Oates also undermines our desire for well-made Aristotelian plots and nar-rative finish by a shift in attitude and tone. Morgenstern is clownish rather than deeply tragic; his death, to be preserved on videotape, seems an absurd caricature. Oates becomes a comic ventriloquist, doing the university in different voices. She provides a series of comic prophecies which not only are an ironic contrast to her hero's apocalyptic yearnings, but satirize the acad-emy as well. In their own imitable accents, we meet the pedants, revisionists, and critics who will seize upon the life and death of Saul Morgenstern, hop-ing to promote their own interpretations. No longer a "region of ice," the uni-versity has become a realm of vampires, insensitive to the agonizing plea of the living; they wait instead for a figure like Saul Morgenstern to perish so that they may publish.

Oates does not exempt herself from critical scorn, but is first in line for rue-ful self-parody: mirrored as a woman "on the periphery of 'Saul's circle'" who will write an account of the event for the student newspaper: "over-long . . . impressionistic . . . 'The Tragedy of a Lost Soul.'" Even more to the point,

Dale S_____, though not present at Adath Israel this morning, will write an article called "The Enigma of Saul Morgenstern, Sacrifical Assassin," to be published in late May in the Sunday supplement of the larger of the two newspapers: a controversial piece that draws so much attention Dale is led to think (mistakenly, as it turns out) that he might have a career in journalism of a glamorous sort. (*LD,* 38)

Saul will be preyed upon by an interdisciplinary host: he will be mentioned in a footnote in a much-revised dissertation on American assassinations published by Oxford University Press. Another scholar is trapped in his own obsessive need to provide the definitive missing view: he of course will never reach closure, because he is flooded with data. He cries, "*there is too much to say.*" Oates invents another hapless writer in residence in her last act of self-mockery:

Rose P_____ will stubbornly revise a short story over the years, presenting it in various awkward forms to writing workshops in the university's extension school, and rejecting all criticism with the angry rejoinder, "but it happened like this, it *happened exactly like this.*" (*LD,* 38)

It would be a mistake to consider this only as deft mimicry or fabulation. Nor are these mocking fragments meant to erase her previous accounts of Wishnetsky's perilous predicament. In a sense, each version is a palimpsest, reinscribing another design over the old ground. The self-emending texts in themselves give evidence of the author's perennial desire to reimagine and revise, to invite critique and collaboration.

"Last Days" mocks the pretensions of academe in its own language. But however arch or self-conscious Wishnetsky's story has become, it pushes beyond the level of spectacle and performance, exposing Oates's continuous and central concerns. In chilling or defiant or mocking voice, she raises sobering questions, challenging the academy to live up to its verbal contract. Saul, Allen, and Richard together represent the youthful and transformable contemporary self: the prodigy, the self-styled terrorist. Indeed, believing that ideas are real, they are too often sacrificed and exploited by the community of mind and spirit that gives lip service to their enthusiasm, but maintains ironic distance. Seriocomic, a collage of contending voices, the Wishnetsky project remains tantalizingly unfinished, open-ended, part of Joyce Carol Oates's ongoing quest for missing views.

Paying homage or proposing marriage to writers and artists of the past has never caused Oates any "anxiety of influence": as a scholar and teacher, she also finds self-criticism and revision indispensable. She is most concerned with breaking the hold of traditional categories that limit the self as well as the artist. Her example is an implicit critique of academicians who pursue "ceaseless classifications . . . exhaustive, hubristic attempts to dissect reality and conquer it" (*NHNE*, 272). No fabulator, she seeks signs of continuity rather than fracture; she also insists that the artifact as well as the artist's own vision are susceptible to transformation. "Marriages and infidelities" are most appropriate metaphors for Oates's sense of visionary possibility.

In her novels, in complex and even contradictory ways, Oates has tested the mediating influences of literary conventions, drawing upon the treasures of her academic environment: ideas, books, the reflective life, the anguish and agitation and energies of the young. Each of her novels thus offers a vision of the history of the literary tradition as well as the history of the beseiged self. For Oates, her characters' sense of doubleness is akin to the artist's double consciousness.

Clearly, Oates values the powers of the rational intellect. She would agree with Thoreau, who claims in *Walden,* "with thinking we can be beside ourselves in a sane sense." She is equally aware of the perilously fragile membrane between that sanity and the madness which may erupt in the widening space between imagination and reality, the sacred and the profane. The chaos loosed on the world may set it into perpetual motion—the mad quest in *A Bloodsmoor Romance*—or build to holocaust proportions; the entry to a promised mystical passage may be buried in the society's debris. Alice's twentieth-century *Wonderland* return seems to be a grim reentry. Yet, while the magnificent claims of the old Bellefleurs are consumed in the fury of aerial bombardment, they continue to exist in patchwork threads and scraps of the crazy commonplace. When her doomed detectives give up their search for rational solutions, they open the way for loving resolution.

From her first days as a teacher and writer, Joyce Carol Oates has attempted to establish a region open to the call of tradition and the demands of politics and history; a space in which she can experiment in genre, theme, and voice, testing and regrouping her imaginative forces. From first to last, that place has been the university. Oates finds it an inexhaustible source of metaphor and reference.

Yet because of her portrayal of a violent world, critics continue to debate her curious double allegiance. Most recently, reviewing her recent work, Denis Donoghue voiced a concern about her "obedience" to "circular laws of other fiction."[5] Donoghue's comment evokes an earlier remark of the master, Henry James, who also spoke of the writer's performance in terms of imaginative legislation:

> To improvise with extreme freedom and yet at the same time without the possibility of ravage. . . . The thing was to aim at absolute singleness, the clearness and roundness, and yet to depend on an imagination working freely, working . . . with extravagance: by which law it wouldn't be thinkable except as free and wouldn't be amusing except as controlled.[6]

Clearly, James views such rules as dynamic, rather than restrictive: the limits imposed by the patterns of genre and terms of reality on the artist's soaring fancy. Similarly, Oates's obedience is part of a process of imaginative absorption, revision, and recreation. Beyond "quanta," beyond the fractured surface of the atomic age, and beyond the allusive echoes, Oates finds her own voice as a resisting and at times *dis*obedient reader, testing the elasticity of art's laws; fulfilling her contract as writer in residence.

Afterword

Pursuing the phenomenon of Joyce Carol Oates over three decades, we come back to our original questions, conscious that they must remain open-ended: How can we grasp her ambitious project, assess her significance, see her not only as an amazing American original, but in a broader context? How are we to make sense of her beyond the often-contradictory reigning estimates—not as eccentric, not as a kind of literary parodist, not as a staggeringly prolific producer of best-sellers, but as an artist who provides a new angle of vision about both our intellectual heritage and our contemporary cultural disarray?

Clearly, Oates has become an imposing presence on the public scene, in the critical press and classroom, and in the interpretive community. She continues to exhibit an insatiable appetite for ideas; a reverence for the sacred arts of poetry and fiction; and the deliberately profane intentions of the probing cultural critic. She has thus accepted her residential status in the fullest sense. She not only teaches, writes, and publishes, but is continually refreshing her work through a series of lively experimental projects of imaginative revision, drawing upon academic resources at the same time that she challenges the privileged status of the canon with new readings.

To paraphrase the title of one of her best-known short stories, "Where is she going? Where has she been?" She has already contributed a collection of criticism, poetry, and fiction which would fill several library shelves. Her early work reflects the cross-currents of American literature: homage to English forebears; reexamination of the strategies developed by the American realist and the philosophy of the naturalist and existentialist. Her later work (after *Wonderland*) is most centrally a refutation of the fabulational or postmodernist enterprise, a counterstatement to the fashionable fiction of "quanta," randomness, ellipsis, and contingency. Yet she shares with her avant-garde contemporaries the sense of being caught between the acts, groping for words in an Orwellian world, seeking a structure to honor reality in a time marked by discontinuity. Pushing beyond the superficial delights of fabulation (she is not entirely immune to its seductions), Oates directs her own powers of imaginative recreation at a multilayered and irreducibly real world. It is a world in which she continues to insist that poetry *does* make things happen.

Oates's novels, taken together, represent an imaginative critical history of American fiction. Her own search for form has led her through the looking-glass of the modernist aesthetic. Reworking her own narratives, she resists all acts of closure. Branded once as too conventional, it should by now be clear that she has instead taken up "exhausted" or superseded conventions with serious intent: in her fiction, parody and plagiary assume moral and social dimensions. If her novels have a characteristic structure, it is a window, rather than a mirror or frame, allowing us to see through our cherished fictions. Paradoxically, it is her openness to a range of influential texts that frustrates easy critical estimate. As Daniel Howard declares,

> Oates's fiction is of all kinds the most original and distinctive: not free of influences but fully assimilative of the suggestions of a wide and rich tradition. ... Thus, in a sense, because she is so well-read, all traditional writers are behind her.[1]

Various and multiform, at once serious and playful, Oates's work continues to defy our academic gravity, our passion for classification.

Joyce Carol Oates is more than an iconoclast or subversive reader. She also brings us news of an emerging aesthetic strikingly akin to the stylistic and mythic tendencies of contemporary women's art. Lucy Lippard describes that art in her own recent studies: whatever its individual shape and size, it is intriguing and even surprising in its texture, more "web" than "artifact," and profoundly "inclusive." Antiminimalist, it has the profusion of collage. Women's art today is aimed at "knitting the fragments of our lives together."[2]

Lippard is concerned with the visual and plastic arts. Susan Wolfe and Julia Stanley make a case for an emerging literary aesthetic in remarkably similar ways, examining the work of women writers who "strain to break through the limits of English" and, in the process, open new poetic territory. In this wrestle with convention, feminist literature calls the tradition and language itself into question:

> The natural imagery of growth, proliferation, and evolution replace nature as object and product. Flux, not stasis, characterizes experience. Labels and abstract nouns as viable perceptive categories give way to active, process verbs and concrete nouns, the language of touch. ....[3]

In this context, it is clear that Oates's work is representative of a strong and significant current of contemporary thought. Lippard, Stanley, and Wolfe might be describing the very images, and certainly the trajectory of Oates's novels; her movement from controlled and bounded cultural patterns and the long-standing Western idealization of heroic mastery to a literature and language of asymmetry and incorporation; the shift of her designs from the Miltonic circle to an art of assemblage, revisable, in motion, fluid as cinema, eccentric and various as a crazy quilt.

In the process, Oates has reinvented the relationship of the artist and the academy, described decades ago by Kazin, Levin, and others as parasitic and problematic. Saul Bellow, himself a novelist in residence, speaks of the comforts of academic life with considerable scorn:

> The Universities give sanctuary for delicate people who need it. And the Universities also have their sassy con-artists and noisy promoters. I never had much use for sanctuaries.[4]

But while Bellow sneers at academe as the refuge of would-be artists and intellectuals, it serves a different function, both literally and metaphorically, for Oates. She delights in the world of mentorship, the enchanted realm of galleries and dictionaries and archives. Her love affair with the academy has been a lifelong phenomenon, paralleling her infatuation with the writer's craft. Curiously, she was first drawn to the confines of the classroom as a terrorized victim seeking safety. In an autobiographical reflection, she tells us that as a child, she had been singled out for punishment by local bullies in an area misnamed a "playground":

> Such systematic, tireless, sadistic persecution had the consequence of making me love with a passion the safe, even magical confines of *home* and *schoolroom* (cynosures of gentleness, affection, calm, sanity, books) and, later, *library*. For outside these magical confines the true brutes, or merely brutish Nature, awaited. (Stories, 16)

Obviously, this personal experience has found its way into her work, most notably in *Marya: A Life.* Such a sense of sanctuary is cherished by many of her frightened and vulnerable characters, unprepared for the brutal realities of existence. But Oates again and again dramatizes the betrayal and failure of the passive or, in Bellow's word, the "delicate" self. Her fiction registers multiple acts of invasion, some brutal, some annihilating, but some life-inspiring and regenerative. At this point, too, she envisions the academy not only as a sanctuary but as the center of disturbance. Oates thus finds it a remarkably appropriate setting for her work, an imaginative space in which a sense of the sacred persists in the midst of the world's most profane demands. The dream of a moral universe that Heilbrun describes and Auerbach's description of the darker dream born in woman's community also inspire Oates's fiction and criticism.

Perhaps the most fruitful approach to the phenomenon of Joyce Carol Oates is mythic, in the sense of that word developed by Estella Lauter in her recent and important study, *Women as Mythmakers.* A revisionist herself, Lauter demands a reevaluation of our mythic categories and images; she demonstrates through a variety of visual and printed texts that today, when we seek the mythic through the conventions shaped by centuries of Western thought, we are met with the spectacle of loss. In the press and confusion of modern life, legend becomes merely fiction, no longer a force to inspire and sustain us and join us to the pageant of the heroic past. That extraordinary mythographer, Joseph Campbell, for instance, declares that we no longer have any "mythogenetic zones," disturbed and baffled as any Oatesian map-maker by the radical erosion of our imaginative and cultural terrain.[5]

Many of our most influential poets and philosophers seem to agree. In his study, *Storytelling & Mythmaking,* Frank McConnell describes that pervasive modern angst and ennui, finding in contemporary literature and film a curious and often sorry echo of the myths that have sustained Western culture. He suggests Eliot's *The Waste Land* as a representative text:

> . . . a collection of mock-heroic citations from the noble past, each of which painfully indicates the distance we have fallen from the great ages in which their utterance was possible. . . . The technique of the poem is a frantic searching, a rummaging about among the monuments of culture for a saying, a line, a text that will open the sterility of the shriveled prophet to the rain . . . it is a parody beyond the point of parody. . . . [6]

In contrast, just as Oates observes that the Renaissance ideal of the autonomous hero is a deathly anachronism, Lauter considers our patriarchal myths outmoded and sterile themselves. Lauter's feminist mythic aesthetic is highly suggestive of the direction of Oates's fiction and the energies which move her as an artist and critic:

> If the central issue of myth for men has been to triumph over the threat of nothingness, then the central issue for . . . women . . . is significantly different. Tentatively, I would describe it as a tension between the multiplicity of being (experienced often as an overflow of images, feelings, or thoughts) and the manmade structures that are supposed to order being. . . . Instead of a wasteland, we have here a landscape teeming with interwoven forms of life.

Lauter goes on to speculate about the future of women's art, and the necessity for new images, patterns, valuations, and definitions:

> The job of myth under such circumstances would not be to fill the void of nothingness but to overcome the restrictions on being we have built into our symbolic code.[7]

Again, this seems to describe Oates's central intention. Certainly, the belief in the permeability of codes, conventions, and boundaries is at the heart of Oates's work. Her vision of a community of discourse, resting upon no fixed geographic place, may even serve as a "mythogenetic" region in Campbell's sense. Looking to the mythic past populated by titans and shamans, he laments the loss of myth-creating and nurturing outposts. Yet Oates's own residence in itself belies such an absence.

Thus, naming Joyce Carol Oates an "artist in residence" does not restrict her to conventional categories or relegate her to some elite and privileged sanctuary. Like Bellow, she has no patience for sassy academic con-men and noisy self-promoters; she even reinvents the minor genre of college fiction to expose her confreres and their hubristic pretensions. A moralist, she has more soberly registered the end of academic innocence and the invasion of the cloister. She has protested the abuses of looters and tricksters in her midst; she has testified to the predicament of young and vulnerable acolytes and prodigies, transformed into the terrorists of our own lost generation. More importantly, perhaps, she has unmasked the restrictions of our "symbolic code," questioning long-accepted dogmas and violating decorum.

In the largest sense, then, her position as artist in residence becomes a compelling metaphor for her past achievement and her future direction. Redefined on her terms, it also is a model for contemporary American writers. Sustained by the intellectual community at many levels, as critical commentator, as mentor, as student, as teacher, open to the play of multiple texts and the call of the world, Oates has recovered and reopened mythic space. She rejects the self-referential satisfactions of contemporary fabulation, what the late John Gardner labelled "literary gimcrackery." Her own imaginative realm resonates with literary and extraliterary influence, our culture's vital signs. In the face of the violent and explosive pressures of modern life, Joyce Carol Oates offers her creative and critical work as regenerative art; a process of revision and mediation; "a kind of massive, joyful experiment done with words . . . submitted to one's peers for judgement."[8]

Notes

Introduction

1. Oates makes extensive reference to Blake's ideas throughout her work. Blake's sense of the creative power of "contraries" often seems to inspire her own visions of the liberating force of violence. In her collection of critical essays published in 1981, *Contraries* (New York: Oxford University Press), Oates suggests that the artist, a "gnostic intermediary," is moved by powers which seem antithetical and subversive:

> The 'Contraries' of which Blake speaks in *The Marriage of Heaven and Hell* are in fact the very energies of Blakean 'Delight'—the Eternal Delight that rests in motion, in strife, in passion, in revolutionary violence. Energy, as Blake says, is the *only life* (pp. vii–viii).

2. Oates made this widely quoted remark in an interview with Walter Clemons in his *Newsweek* cover story "Joyce Carol Oates: Love and Violence," 11 Dec. 1972, p.72.

3. By 1972, when Oates had produced five novels, four collections of short fiction, and three collections of poems, she published a volume of critical essays, drawing this complaint from Roger Sale in the *New York Times Book Review* (9 June 1972, pp. 23–24). Since that time, the charge that she is "too prolific" has repeatedly been leveled by critics (most notoriously, in the 1983 *Harper's* attack by James Wolcott,"Stop Me Before I Write Again"). Oates has issued frequent rebuttals. In an interview taped in 1982, *A Moveable Feast,* she wryly advertised her "anachronistic" tendencies, observing that similar charges were never raised concerning Trollope or James: "writers did work fairly continuously . . . of *course* a writer *wrote"* in earlier times! At a conference at Goucher College in 1985, she voiced a feminist protest:

> No one criticizes John Updike because he writes too much. I think it's sexist. It's because I'm a woman. . . . I'm on a schedule many writers have. About a book a year. Maybe the world sees it as frequent. Is a woman considered prolific if she makes dinner every night? *(Baltimore Sun,* 24 March 1985, p. 8G.)

Oates is less amused about related charges that she does not edit her work. Frequently, she speaks of her "passion" to revise: "I do an infinite number of drafts sometimes of a page," she told an interviewer after the publication of her sixteenth novel, *Solstice,* in response to what has now become a habitual critique of her amazing productivity. "I do pages over and over again. If I get them right, then I move on to the next page. No, it isn't easy" *(Chicago Sun Times,* 3 February 1985, p. 27).

4. One of Oates's briefest but most important essays, "The Myth of The Isolated Artist" appeared in *Psychology Today* in May 1973 (pp. 74–75). It remains her strongest single statement about the artist's role as medium, working out of a communal sensibility much like the accepted model of the scholar in a scientific community.

5. In her "Guest Word" *(New York Times Book Review,* 4 June 1972), Oates criticized Barthelme for uttering this phrase:

> "Fragments are the only forms I trust." This from a writer . . . whose works

reflect the anxiety he himself must feel, in book after book, that his brain is all fragments . . . just like everything else.

Barthelme took amused note of what he considered a misreading, claiming that the phrase was not his own but "a statement by the character about what he is feeling at that particular moment. I hope that whatever I think about aesthetics would be a shade more complicated than that." In a characteristic gesture, he went on to invent a parody "recantation":

> New York, June 24 (A & P)—Donald Barthelme, 41-year-old writer and well-known fragmentist, said today that he no longer trusted fragments. He added that although he had once been "very fond" of fragments, he had found them to be "finally untrustworthy" (in Jerome Klinkowitz, *The Life of Fiction,* [Urbana: University of Illinois Press, 1977], a parody-interview with Barthelme, pp. 73–83).

6. Robert Scholes coined the term for those self-conscious, highly verbal contemporary writers who deliberately produce "fictional fiction" in his 1967 study, *The Fabulators* (New York: Oxford University Press).

7. Jose Ortega y Gasset, *The Dehumanization of Art,* (1925; translation, Princeton, NJ: Princeton University Press, 1968).

8. Alfred Kazin, "The Writer and the University," in *The Inmost Leaf* (New York and London: Harbrace/Harvest, 1979) pp. 242–52.

9. Discussed in "Transformations of Self: An Interview with Joyce Carol Oates," *The Ohio Review* 15, no. 1 (Fall 1973): 51–61.

10. For Oates, the sacredness of art resides in its communal dimensions. She thus chooses Whitman as a "spiritual father" for understanding "that human beings are not really in competition. . . . He knew that the role of the poet is to 'transfigure', and 'clarify'—and, in that way, sanctify." Clearly, her views put her at odds with the new Freudian critics, notably Harold Bloom, who theorize about the poet's fear of influence. In *A Map of Misreading* (New York: Oxford, 1975), Bloom takes issue with Oates's comments on Whitman, finding her homage "moving" but an "over-idealization of literature." He instead insists that critics acknowledge the "inescapable anxieties of competition" among poets (pp. 164–65).

11. Joyce Carol Oates, "Notes on Failure," in her 1983 collection of criticism, *The Profane Art* (New York: Dutton). She revises a traditional genre, the "defense of poetry"; instead of questioning art's utility and value, she questions the act and art of criticism, finding sacred qualities in the "art of reading":

> Why certain individuals appear to devote their lives to the phenomenon of interpreting experience in terms of structure, and of language, must remain a mystery. . . overlaid with a peculiar luminosity as if one were, and were not, fully inhabiting the present tense (p.111).

12. Oates, "The Myth of the Isolated Artist," p. 74.

13. Joyce Carol Oates, "The Death Throes of Romanticism: The Poetry of Sylvia Plath," reprinted in *New Heaven, New Earth* (New York: Vanguard, 1974), p. 119.

14. Joyce Carol Oates, "New Heaven and Earth," *Saturday Review,* 4 Nov. 1972, p. 53.

15. Joyce Carol Oates, "Art: Therapy and Magic," *American Journal* I, viii, 3 July 1973, p. 18.

16. Joyce Carol Oates, "'At Least I Have Made a Woman of Her': Images of Women in Twentieth-Century Literature," *The Georgia Review* 37, 1 (Spring 1983): 7.

1. Misreadings and Marriages

1. Oates describes this necessary opposition in the introduction to *The Profane Art* (New York: Dutton, 1983):

> Nearly all critics are conservative if only because they cannot presume to judge art by its own standards if those standards are new. . . . The artist, by contrast, really must follow his instinct into areas not yet mined by others. . . . What appears as disorder, instability, and frequent madness to the critic is in fact the creative activity itself. . . (p. 3).

2. Joanne Creighton seems to equate reader-response with an ability to appeal to a large audience. In that spirit, Creighton concludes that readers often do *not* respond to the mixture of visionary hypothesis and documentary realism in novels like *them* and *The Assassins;* she feels they are even more likely to be alienated by the "radically experimental style" of Oates's later work. Predicting that visionary concerns and experimental techniques will "lessen her popularity with a mass audience," Creighton nevertheless concedes that Oates "has apparently tapped some visceral 'reservoir of energy' in American experience *(Joyce Carol Oates* [Boston: Hall & Co., 1979], pp. 142–52).

3. Linda W. Wagner's introductory essay counters Creighton's concern about inappropriately blurred genres, suggesting that the multiplicity of styles and voices allows Oates to represent marginal states *(Critical Essays on Joyce Carol Oates* [Boston: G.K. Hall, 1979]).

4. Ellen Friedman goes beyond both Creighton and Wagner in asserting that Oates derives her power from sheer variety: "She is a writer obsessed with experiential plurality" *(Joyce Carol Oates* [New York: Ungar, 1980], p. 5).

5. Torburg Norman, *Isolation and Contact: A Study of Character Relationships in Joyce Carol Oates's Short Stories 1963–1980* (Goteborg, Sweden: Gothenburg Studies in English 57, 1984).

6. Alfred Kazin, *Bright Book of Life* (New York: Atlantic/Little Brown, 1973) pp. 186–204. See also his discussion of Oates in "Heroines," *New York Review of Books,* 11 Feb. 1971, p. 32; "The Literary Sixties, When the World Was Too Much with Us," *New York Times Book Review,* 21 Dec. 1969, pp. 1–3, 18; and "Oates," *Harpers* 243 (August 1971), pp. 78–82.

7. Harold Bloom, *A Map of Misreading* (New York: Oxford University Press, 1975), p. 164.

8. Ihab Hassan, "The Dismemberment of Orpheus" (lecture at the University of Notre Dame, 21 Oct. 1971).

9. David Madden, *The Poetic Image in Six Genres* (Carbondale: Southern Illinois University Press, 1969), p. 27.

10. Michael Wood, review of Oates's *Marriages and Infidelities, New York Times Book Review,* 1 Oct. 1972, p. 43.

11. Walter Clemons, "Joyce Carol Oates: Love and Violence," *Newsweek,* 11 Dec. 1972, pp. 72–77.

12. Walter Sullivan, "The Artificial Demon: Joyce Carol Oates and the Dimensions of the Real," *Hollins Critic* 9, no. 4 (Dec. 1972): 12. Sullivan's study is the most negative of the early review articles on Oates's work, largely because he finds it impossible to "place" her work in any literary genre or school.

13. Joyce Carol Oates, "A Quite Moving and Very Traditional Celebration of Love," review of James Baldwin's novel *If Beale Street Could Talk, New York Times Book Review,* 19 May 1974, p. 1.

14. Joyce Carol Oates, *New Heaven, New Earth* (New York: Vanguard, 1974), pp. 259–60.

15. Joyce Carol Oates, "Whose Side Are You On?" *The New York Times Book Review,* 4 June 1972, p. 63.

16. Oates, "Notes on Failure," in *The Profane Art,* pp. 106–20.

17. Ibid., pp. 110–11.

18. Oates, in an interview with Joe David Bellamy, "The Dark Lady of American Letters," *Atlantic Monthly* 229, no. 2 (Feb. 1972), p. 66.

19. Oates, quoted by Clemons, "Love and Violence," p. 77.

20. See chap. 7, n. 8, this volume.

21. Saul Bellow, quoted by Roberto Suro, "Bellow Mourns for Chicago Long Ago," *Chicago Sun-Times,* 2 April 1977, p. 5.

2. Eden Valley Residence

1. Walter Clemons, "Joyce Carol Oates: Love and Violence," *Newsweek,* 11 Dec. 1972, pp. 72–73.

2. Robert H. Fossum, "Only Control: The Novels of Joyce Carol Oates," *Studies in the Novel* 7, no. 2 (Summer 1976): 286.

3. Clemons, "Love and Violence," p. 73.

4. Ellen Friedman, *Joyce Carol Oates* (New York: Ungar, 1980), pp. 22–23.

5. See, for example, John Knowles, "A Racing Car is the Symbol of Violence," *New York Times Book Review,* 25 Oct. 1964, p. 5. He first describes the novel as a "swirl of sensual chaos," out of focus; yet he also is impressed by the novel's "unswerving fidelity to its theme." While he identifies the work's literary models, including Faulkner, he finally concludes that the novel displays "an originality and power which do not seem derived from anyone."

6. David Madden, *The Poetic Image in Six Genres* (Carbondale: Southern Illinois University Press, 1969), pp. 37–39.

7. Stanley Kauffman, "O'Hara and Others," *New York Review of Books,* 17 Dec. 1964, p. 22.

8. Clemons, "Love and Violence," p. 74.

9. Joyce Carol Oates, "Man Under Sentence of Death: The Novels of James M. Cain," in *Tough Guy Writers of the Thirties,* ed. David Madden (Carbondale: Southern Illinois University Press, 1968) pp. 127–28.

10. Friedrich Nietzsche, *Beyond Good and Evil,* trans. R. J. Hollingdale (New York: Penguin, 1973), p. 135.

11. George Meredith, "Ode to the Spirit of Earth in Autumn," in *The Works of George Meredith,* vol. 24 (New York: Scribners Memorial ed., 1910), p. 259. Oates may well have found telling parallels between Meredith's argument and the scheme of her first novel. Love exercises an almost sickly attraction for the poetic *persona* ("Death shall I shrink from, loving thee?") But Meredith's final lines shift from the romantic's dream to the realist's challenge: "Life thoroughly lived is a fact in the brain/ While eyes are left for seeing."

12. In her essay, "Frankenstein's Fallen Angel," the afterword to the Pennyroyal Edition of Mary Shelley's *Frankenstein* (Berkeley: University of California Press, 1984), Oates finds analogues between Milton and Shelley. When the "monster" draws back, stunned by his own reflection, Oates suggests Shelley is echoing Book IV of *Paradise Lost,* not the myth of Narcissus (p.246).

13. Rose Marie Burwell, "Joyce Carol Oates and an Old Master," *Critique* 15, no. 1 (1973): 48–58.

14. Walter Sullivan, "The Artificial Demon: Joyce Carol Oates and the Dimensions of the Real," *Hollins Critic* 9, no. 4 (Dec. 1972): 8–9.

15. Alfred Kazin, "The Literary Sixties, When the World Was Too Much with Us," *New York Times Book Review,* 21 Dec. 1969, p. 2.

16. Joyce Carol Oates, *New York Times Book Review,* 7 Sept. 1969, p. 2.

17. Joyce Carol Oates, "New Heaven and Earth," *Saturday Review,* 4 Nov. 1972, pp. 51–54.

3. Fabulation and Documentation

1. Walter Sullivan, "The Artificial Demon: Joyce Carol Oates and the Dimensions of the Real," *Hollins Critic* 9, no. 4 (Dec. 1972): 5.

2. Alfred Kazin, "Heroines," *New York Review of Books,* 11 Feb. 1971, p. 33. Also see Ellen Friedman's essay "The Gluttons Dream America," in *Joyce Carol Oates* (New York: Ungar, 1980), pp. 55–72, in which she suggests that gluttony represents human greed for "paradise on earth," and speculates that "Richard's bulk may be a comic correlative of heroic 'stature'."

3. Alice Martin, "Expensive People" (Unpublished paper presented at 1974 Modern Language Association session on Joyce Carol Oates), pp. 2–3.

4. Ibid., p. 3. The novel also deals with the idea of justice: a theme that Oates makes her central concern in *Do with Me What You Will.* In her earliest collection of short fiction, Oates presents a prototype of this story, "In the Old World." The hero is named "Swan"; he comes into town seeking punishment for accidentally putting out a black child's eye. But both victim and sheriff are embarrassed at his confession; Swan is sent home "not absolved of his sin or delivered of his punishment but simply in another dimension altogether" (Oates, *By The North Gate,* [1963; reprint, Greenwich, CT: Fawcett, 1971] p. 151). In passing from this realistic drama to the highly stylized *Expensive People,* Oates similarly has moved the issue to "another dimension altogether."

5. In her discussion of the novel, Joanne Creighton suggests that "since the story is in fact one of Oates's own previously published stories, it also breaks down the borders between the real author, Joyce Carol Oates, and the fictional one, Nada, inviting us to look for parallels" *(Joyce Carol Oates* [Boston: Hall, 1979], p. 59).

6. John Barth, "The Literature of Exhaustion," *Atlantic Monthly* 220, no. 2 (August 1967): 33.

7. John Knowles, in his essay-review "Nada at the Core," thus suggests that readers today "want the facts" *(New York Times Book Review,* 3 Nov. 1968, p. 5).

8. L. E. Sissman, "The Whole Truth," *New Yorker* 44, 6 Dec. 1969, p. 242.

9. Joyce Carol Oates, in "Transformations of Self: An Interview with Joyce Carol Oates," *The Ohio Review* 15, 1 (Fall 1973), pp. 52, 54, 60.

10. Joyce Carol Oates, personal communication, letter to E. Bender, 23 May 1974.

11. R. D. Laing, *The Divided Self: An Existential Study in Sanity and Madness* (London: Pelican/Penguin, 1965), p. 79.

12. Madonna Claire Kolbenschlag, "Joyce Carol Oates and the Centrifugal Imagination" (Unpublished paper presented at Midwest Modern Language Association meeting, March 1974), p. 16.

13. Oates, "Transformations of Self," pp. 57–58.

14. R. D. Laing, *The Politics of Experience* (New York: Ballantine, 1967), pp. xii–xiii.

4. Personality in Flight

1. Walter Sullivan, "The Artificial Demon: Joyce Carol Oates and the Dimensions of the Real," *Hollins Critic* 9, no. 4 (Dec. 1972): 5–6.

2. Joan Didion, quoted by Walter Clemons, "Joyce Carol Oates: Love and Violence," *Newsweek,* 11 Dec. 1972, p. 77.

3. Ellen Friedman, Joanne Creighton, James Giles, Rose Marie Burwell and this author focused on the novel at a special session (#505) of the 1977 Modern Language Convention. Papers included a study of the analogies between Oates's and Carroll's

"wonderlands," a discussion of the Jungian archetypes and Freudian symbology, and an analysis of the two endings of *Wonderland:* quite a range for a single novel. In the 1973 MLA session on Oates, Ildiko de Papp Carrington devoted her attention to *Wonderland* and Borges ("Monsters in Wonderland," unpublished).

4. Joyce Carol Oates, "New Heaven and Earth," *Saturday Review* 4 Nov. 1972, p. 54.

5. D. H. Lawrence, *Letters,* ed. Aldous Huxley (London: Heinemann, 1932) pp. 197–98. Lawrence writes, "You mustn't look in my novel for the old stable *ego* of character. There is another *ego,* according to whose action the individual is unrecognizable, and passes through . . . allotropic states which it needs a deeper sense than any we've been used to exercise, to discover are states of the same single radically unchanged element." He is, in effect, the first to describe the "protean" self.

6. Quoted by Jolande Jacobi, *The Psychology of C. G. Jung* (New Haven: Yale University Press, 1973) pp. 107-8.

7. Ralph Berets, in "Joyce Carol Oates' *Wonderland* seen as a Mythic Rite of Passage" (Unpublished paper delivered at 1973 Modern Language Association meeting), concludes that Jesse's journey toward Jungian individuation is frustrated; perhaps a deliberately ironic dimension of the novel.

8. Robert Jay Lifton, in *Boundaries: Psychological Man in Revolution* (New York: Vintage, 1970), describes a new paradigm of character, the self as survivor and shape-shifter, searching desperately for "imagery of rebirth. . . . The direction of Protean man's prophecy lies in new, fluid, threatening, liberating, confusing, and revitalizing personal boundaries" (pp. 37–63).

9. Ellen Friedman, *Joyce Carol Oates* (New York: Ungar, 1979), pp. 114–15.

10. Joanne Creighton offers an excellent summary of parallels between *Wonderland* and *Alice in Wonderland* in her study, *Joyce Carol Oates* ([Boston: Hall, 1979], pp. 82–87). She also compares Oates's vision with W.H. Auden's imagined"Wonder-World."

11. A. H. Maslow, "Autonomy and Homonomy," in *The Farther Reaches of Human Nature* (New York: Viking, 1971), pp. 163–64. He discusses "simultaneous and ambitendent urges to rule and be ruled, to dominate and submit" (p. 164).

12. Walter B. Cannon, *The Wisdom of The Body* (New York: Norton, 1919), pp. 20–21.

13. R. D. Laing, *The Politics of Experience* (New York: Ballantine, 1967), p. 88.

14. Joyce Carol Oates, personal correspondence, 23 May 1974.

15. In an autobiographical essay, "Stories That Define Me," *(New York Times Book Review,* 11 July 1982) Oates describes Carroll's work as the "sacred text" of her childhood:

> For some years my child-novels contained both drawings and prose, inspired, frequently, by the first great book of my life, the handsome 1946 edition of Grosset & Dunlap's "Alice in Wonderland" and "Through the Looking Glass," with the Tenniel illustrations. I might have wished to be Alice, that prototypical heroine of our race, but I knew myself too shy, too readily frightened of both the unknown and the known (Alice, never succumbing to terror, is not a real child) and too mischievous.

Oates discovers a more important distinction between herself and Alice:

> Though a child like me, she wasn't telling her own story. That godly privilege resided with someone named, in gilt letters on the book's spine, "Lewis Carroll." Being Lewis Carroll was infinitely more exciting than being Alice, so I became Lewis Carroll. One part of Joyce Carol Oates lodges there . . . (Stories, 15).

This view is far less sinister than Shelley's view of the text in *Wonderland,* and quite different in tone and philosophy from statements Oates made in 1974:

> The game is *being played* and we are participants, not really controlling the game, but fulfilling it in some existential, mysterious way (Creighton, p. 17).

Friedman also notes Oates's uneasiness about *Alice in Wonderland* and *Through the Looking-Glass* expressed to a creative writing class in 1977:

> She considers these two very misanthropic works that ask the "valid and terrifying" questions, "Is life really a game?" and "Is everyone cheating but me?" "In Carroll," says Oates, "life is a chess game; you eat one another in order to get to another square" (Friedman, p. 95).

Oates's most recent comments about her relationship to *Alice in Wonderland* are playful, but still ambivalent. Responding in the 1984 Christmas issue of the *New York Times Book Review* to the question, "What character in fiction would you like to be?" Oates remarks, "On cheerful days, why not Alice? . . . because she always returns" (2 Dec. 1984, p. 43).

16. Reference to the hardcover edition of *Wonderland* (New York: Vanguard, 1971), pp. 511–12.

17. Quoted in Joe David Bellamy, "The Dark Lady of American Letters: An Interview with Joyce Carol Oates," *Atlantic Monthly* 224, no. 2 (Feb. 1972), p. 64.

18. Joyce Carol Oates, personal correspondence.

19. Joyce Carol Oates, "Art: Therapy and Magic," *American Journal* 1, viii, 3 July 1973, p. 30 n.

20. Joyce Carol Oates, in "Transformations of Self: An Interview with Joyce Carol Oates," *The Ohio Review* 15, no. 1 (Fall 1973), pp. 58–59.

5. Beyond the Looking Glass

1. Rose Marie Burwell, "The Process of Individuation as Narrative Structure: Joyce Carol Oates's *Do with Me What You Will," Critique* 17, no. 2 (1976): 97.

2. In her 1982 critical study, *Woman and The Demon* (Cambridge: Harvard University Press), Nina Auerbach suggests that the mythology of the passive female, "meant to shackle female experience to male convenience," actually represented a means of "slyly empowering the subjects it seemed to reduce." See especially her discussion of the "sleeping beauty," pp. 41–43.

3. Virginia Woolf, *A Room of One's Own,* (1929; reprint, New York: Harcourt/ Harbinger, 1957), p. 35.

4. Ibid., p. 36.

5. See R. D. Laing, *The Divided Self: An Existential Study in Sanity and Madness* (London: Pelican/Penguin, 1965), pp. 39–52, for discussion of human "petrification."

6. Oates's fiction is often structured around points of stillness: not moments charged by a sacred awareness, but moments of paralysis in which the self is close to catatonia or death. She frequently represents these stopping points as statuary in her earlier novels: i.e., Jesse's desire to locate the "statue" in himself, in order to stop the protean slippage of his world. In this novel, as Elena seems to become as opaque and frozen as the statue before her, the image is close to Laing's petrified self. Oates's imaginary detective in *Mysteries of Winterthurn* equates this terrible stillness with the ultimate mystery, death. "Standstill" is the theme of her 1985 novel, *Solstice,* an imaginative projection of seductive and deathly cosmic rhythms, as well as an artist's "block"—which once again can be overcome through the power of love.

7. Joyce Carol Oates, "The Hostile Sun," in *New Heaven, New Earth* (New York: Vanguard, 1974), pp. 45–70. Oates later published the essay as a monograph (Black Sparrow Press).

8. Joyce Carol Oates, personal communication. These sentiments also suggest the meaning of one of the "academic" references in this novel, *Middlemarch*. Elena reads the novel after her separation from Howe; in turn, George Eliot's novel, in which the central female figure retreats from the possiblility of an autonomous life and accepts the necessities of living in time, prefigures Elena's decision to choose a life with Jack. Clearly, the critics who interpret the novel's ending as a surrender of feminist principle neglect or misread this important clue to Oates's intentions.

9. Joyce Carol Oates, quoted on jacket of hardcover edition of *Do with Me What You Will* (New York: Vanguard, 1973).

10. Joyce Carol Oates, personal communication.

11. See "Joyce Carol Oates: The Art of Fiction LXXII," *The Paris Review* (1978): 198–226 (interview conducted by Robert Phillips). The discussion of *The Assassins* is on pp. 210–11. Reprinted in G. Plimpton, ed., *Writers at Work,* with an introduction by Francine du Plessix Gray (New York: Penguin, 5th series, 1981).

12. Ibid., p. 210.

13. Ibid., p. 215.

14. Ibid., p. 212.

15. Joanne Creighton makes this remark, calling *Childwold* too "radically experimental." Ellen Friedman, on the other hand, seems more comfortable with the novel. In her essay, "The Victory of Eros," she provides a fine reading of *Childwold* as a novel of ideas, with Kasch serving as an intellectual tragically drawn into the "ineluctable reality of the physical world" (in *Joyce Carol Oates* [New York: Ungar, 1980], pp. 163–85).

16. Joyce Carol Oates, "New Heaven and Earth," *Saturday Review,* 4 Nov. 1972, pp. 53–54; But see also her earlier attack on Nabokov, Beckett, and Borges in "Whose Side Are You On?," *New York Times Book Review,* 4 June 1972, p. 63. As evidenced below, Oates's admiration for Nabokov's skill has always been tempered by her critique of his solipsistic stance.

17. Oates's presentation of the fabulator's inner states is a fascinating embodiment of theories of language and madness postulated by such contemporary critics as Bakhtin and Foucault.

18. See both "Whose Side Are You On?" and "New Heaven and Earth."

19. "Joyce Carol Oates," *The Paris Review,* p. 215.

6. Sacred and Profane Visions

1. Victoria Glendinning, "In Touch With God," *New York Times Book Review,* 13 August 1978, p. 10.

2. In "Author Joyce Carol Oates on 'Adolescent America'," *(U.S. News and World Report,* 15 May 1978); Oates claims she is writing her novel out of a fascination with the American phenomenon of "religious hysteria" (p. 60). But see also Oates's comments on the novel's gestation in *The Paris Review* interviews, "Joyce Carol Oates: The Art of Fiction" (reprinted in *Writers at Work,* ed. G. Plimpton [New York: Penguin Books, 5th Series, 1981] pp. 359–84). Oates suggests it is not historical but "rather painfully autobiographical, in part. . . . The religion it explores is not institutional but rather subjective, intensely personal . . . " (p. 210).

3. In her collection of short fiction published the previous year *(Night-Side* [New York: Vanguard, 1977]), Oates also dramatizes the crisis of figures in the grip of hallucination. As natural and supernatural elements intersect, sending the self "out of control," many of the stories seem to be preparatory studies for *Son of The Morning.* (The

title story, moving from science and seance to the welcome commonplace daylight realm, anticipates themes more fully explored in *A Bloodsmoor Romance* and *Mysteries of Winterthurn.)*

4. "Joyce Carol Oates," *The Paris Review* p. 201.

5. Ibid., p. 214.

6. "Author Joyce Carol Oates," *U.S. News and World Report,* p. 60.

7. "Joyce Carol Oates," *The Paris Review,* p. 213.

8. Ibid., p. 215.

9. Joyce Carol Oates, *A Moveable Feast*. Readings and interviews on audiotape. Columbia, MO: American Audio Prose Library, 1982.

10. Bernard Malamud, *A New Life* (New York: Farrar, Straus, 1961); Saul Bellow, *The Dean's December* (New York: Harper, 1982); John Gardner, *Mickelsson's Ghosts* (New York: Knopf, 1982). At the same time, novels like Amis' *Lucky Jim* and Lodge's *Changing Places* demonstrate a continuing interest in more conventional (and farcical) academic satire.

11. Remarks delivered at Society for Values Conference, Poughkeepsie, New York: Vassar College, August 1981.

12. Geoffrey Hartman, in *Criticism in the Wilderness* (New Haven: Yale University Press, 1980); he also suggests half-playfully that the critic is a hybrid, a demigod, a "Centaur" (pp. 214–25).

13. For a fuller discussion of this story and Oates's variations on her own academic themes, see the the final chapter of this study.

14. This pedant shows he lags behind the avant-garde; alluding to John Barth's famous phrase and essay, "The Literature of Exhaustion," he seems unaware of Barth's own "revised" definition of post-modern fiction, "The Literature of Replenishment."

15. David Kirby, "Sowing Their Oates," *Change Magazine* 12, 2 (Feb./Mar. 1980): p. 58–59.

7. Mythic Residence

1. Joyce Carol Oates, "How Is Fiction Doing?" *The New York Times Book Review,* 14 Dec. 1980, p. 3. In this brief prophecy of fiction of the eighties, she once again attacks the work of fabulation:

> The "self-referential" novel may be dead—was it ever alive?— but experimentation is surely not dead . . . perhaps in the 1980's critics will resist categorizing writers and chiding them for violating outdated expectations.

2. John Knowles, foreword to Harold Pinter's screenplay of *The French Lieutenant's Woman* (Boston: Little, Brown, 1981), p. xiii.

3. Oates's playful imitative experiments are even more interesting in the context of contemporary "intertextual" theory. See, for example, the work of Edward Said, who in *The World, the Text, and the Critic* (Cambridge: Harvard University Press, 1983) suggests that the author's business is not *de novo* creation but a kind of "combinatorial play": "Thus the ultimate, perhaps infinite goal of writing is a Book conceived of as a bibliosystem, a kind of activated library" (pp. 138–39). I am also indebted to one of my students at Notre Dame, Sun Bing He, for suggesting that the metaphor of "kaleidoscope" best represents the form of Oates's combinatorial play in *Bellefleur.*

4. Linda W. Wagner, ed., *Critical Essays on Joyce Carol Oates* (Boston: Hall, 1979), p. xviii.

5. Women's historians agree that quilting is as much an art as a craft. In *American Women Artists* (New York: Avon, 1982), Charlotte Streifer Rubinstein declares,

There is a common misconception that quilts were an anonymous collective effort, a somewhat haphazard putting together of random pieces by many women at a quilting bee. On the contrary, they were almost always designed by one woman and were often proudly signed and dated (p. 28).

6. Quilting has served as metaphor as well as handwork: see, for example, Marge Piercy, "Looking at Quilts," in *Circles on the Water* (New York: Knopf, 1982), pp. 170–71. Other studies of quilting as a significant women's art include Lenice Ingram Bacon, *American Patchwork Quilts* (New York: Wm. Morrow, 1973); Jean Gordon, "Early American Women Artists, *American Quarterly* 30 (Spring 1978): 54–69; G.K. Dewhurst, *Artists in Aprons* (New York: Dutton, 1979); Susan B. Swan, *Plain and Fancy* (New York: Holt Rinehart, 1977). For Alice Walker, in her short story "Everyday Use," the quilt serves as a way of joining aesthetics to utility. Oates also works with this complex image in her poem, "Celestial Timepiece" (in *Invisible Woman: New and Selected Poems, 1970–82,* [Princeton: Ontario Review Press, 1982], pp. 50–51).

7. Joyce Carol Oates, *A Moveable Feast*. Readings and interviews on audiotape. Columbia, MO: American Audio Prose Library, 1982.

8. Ibid. Oates seems more than capable of juggling novels-in-progress and centuries. In a 1985 interview, Oates describes the concluding volumes in her turn-of-the-century series: *The Crosswicks Horror,* to be published in 1987, academic in its setting (Princeton, at the time Woodrow Wilson was president); and a novel about confidence men and imposters, spanning the years 1910–1932, called *My Heart Laid Bare,* to be published in the following year (Marilyn R. Abbey, "Private Lives Don't Beckon to Joyce Carol Oates," *Chicago Sun Times,* 3 February 1985, pp. 24, 27). Yet she told another interviewer that she was busy with a novel set in the 1950s. She may have been referring to *Marya: A Life,* published in 1986. (Nora Frenkiel, "Joyce Carol Oates: The Quiet Writer of So Many Books," *The Baltimore Sun,* 24 March 1985, pp. 1G–6G.

9. Cara Chell explores the relationship between violence and women's fiction by Oates, Didion, and Piercy in "Writer as Terrorist" (Unpublished essay: personal communication).

10. Oates, *A Moveable Feast.*

11. Robert Graves, *The Greek Myths* (New York: Braziller, 1957). For *Cybele* references, see 18.3; 21.e, f; 29.3; 80.1; 158.4. The ambiguity surrounding this goddess is evident in the two very different translations of her name: "she of the hair" and "she with the axe."

12. See the exchange between Nancy Topping Bazin and Oates, *The New York Times Book Review,* 3 June 1973, "Letters."

13. Oates, *A Moveable Feast.*

14. "Man's Man? Woman-hater? Our Greatest Writer?" *TV Guide,* 8 Dec. 1984, p. 6. (Taken from an essay written as background for the television film of "The Sun Also Rises.")

15. Robert Fagles, "The Serpent and the Eagle," prefatory essay to the Princeton edition of *The Oresteia* with W. B. Stanford (New York: Bantam, 1977), pp. 13–14.

16. Roland Barthes, "The Death of the Author," in *Image-Music-Text,* trans. Stephen Heath (London: Fontana, 1977), pp. 143–49.

8. Woman's Place

1. "Balance Might Do As Well": an exchange of letters between Oates and Nancy Topping Bazin, *New York Times Book Review,* 3 June 1973. While Bazin defends her concept of "androgyny" and that of Heilbrun as a way to "destroy" the association of

masculine with male and feminine with female, Oates suggests that her own use of the word connotes "certain ambiguous conceptions."

2. Review, *The New Republic,* 21 April 1979, pp. 28–30. Oates concludes ruefully that the anthology is at least a "window" or "door" into previously inaccessible "areas of knowledge": "To be immortalized as a woman poet is second-best, of course, but it *is* better than nothing, which has been women's portion for too long."

3. Joyce Carol Oates, *First Person Singular* (Princeton: Ontario Press, 1983). She repeats that sentiment in her critical-autobiographical essay, "Stories That Define Me," indentifying her life as a "feminist story," although she adds, "I am not a radical feminist; I haven't that innocence either" (Stories, 15–16). Elaine Showalter responds to Oates in "Women Writers Are Women," *New York Times Book Review,* 16 Dec. 1984—an article which generated further comments from Oates:

> ... while women writers consider themselves solely writers, the world (very often including other women as well as men) persists in categorizing them as women writers. Hence we find ourselves in the position of denying a social fact. We are (women) writers who aspire to the condition not of maleness, still less androgyny, but of being, simply, writers (*New York Times Book Review,* "Letters," 20 Jan. 1985, p. 29).

4. Carroll Smith-Rosenberg, *Disorderly Conduct: Visions of Gender in Victorian America* (New York: Knopf, 1985). See also Sandra Gilbert and Susan Gubar, *The Madwoman in the Attic* (New Haven: Yale University Press, 1980); Harvey Green, *The Light of the Home, An Intimate View of the Lives of Women in Victorian America* (New York: Pantheon, 1983); Alfred Habegger, *Gender, Fantasy, and Realism in American Literature* (New York: Columbia University Press, 1982); Barbara Ehrenreich and Deirdre English, *For Her Own Good: 150 Years of the Expert's Advice to Women* (New York; Doubleday/Anchor, 1978); Nancy K. Miller, *The Heroine's Text* (New York: Columbia University Press, 1980); Nancy Cott's several essays, including "Passionlessness: An Interpretation of Victorian Sexual Ideology, 1790–1850," *Signs* 1, 2, (1978): 219–36; and Barbara Welter's often-quoted essay, "The Cult of True Womanhood: 1800–1860," *American Quarterly* 18 (Summer 1966): 151–74.

5. Rachel Blau DuPlessis, *Writing Beyond the Ending: Narrative Strategies of Twentieth-Century Women Writers* (Bloomington: Indiana University Press, 1985).

6. Joyce Carol Oates, "How Is Fiction Doing?" *The New York Times Book Review,* 14 Dec. 1980, p. 3.

7. Joyce Carol Oates, *A Moveable Feast.* Columbia, MO: American Audio Prose Library, 1982. For a more extended discussion of Oates's attraction to and ambivalence about "Popular Culture," the misrepresentation of women, and the exuberant fiction written by Victorian women writers, see her essay, "At Least I Have Made a Woman of Her," in *The Profane Art* (New York: Dutton, 1983), pp. 35–62. Oates declares that "the world of the popular-sentimental novel is not so alien as contemporary feminist readers might wish to think," and praises such writers as Mrs. Southworth for providing "sudden, illuminating, and altogether fascinating pictures of domestic female life, private life, sequestered from male eyes" (p. 42). Yet she concludes that "one cannot really fault the contempt of the 'serious' male writer for these vaporous female concoctions" (p. 43)!

8. For two very different responses to this novel—seemingly, along gender lines—see Diane Johnson's "Balloons and Abductions," *New York Times Book Review,* 5 Sept. 1982, pp. 15–16; and Denis Donoghue's "Wonder Woman," *New York Review of Books,* 21 Oct. 1982, pp. 12–17.

9. See Madelon Bedell's excellent introduction to *Little Women* (New York: Modern Library College Paperback Edition, 1983), pp. ix–lv, discussing both the "legend" of the novel and the reality, hidden even from the author herself. For a discussion of the pseudonymous Alcott, "A.M. Barnard," or later, a "No Name" author of

popular melodrama, see Madeleine Stern, *The Hidden Louisa May Alcott* (New York: Avenel Books, 1984). Stern reports Alcott once "confessed her addiction" to the romance:

> "I think my natural ambition is for the lurid style. I indulge in gorgeous fancies and wish that I dared inscribe them upon my pages and set them before the public. . . . How should I dare to interfere with the proper grayness of old Concord? The dear old town has never known a startling hue since the redcoats were there. . . . "

Critical discussion of Alcott as a writer might almost fit Oates:

> Like so many women writers, Alcott began writing as a child, composing stories almost as soon as she was able to put down the characters on a page. . . . She used many styles and techniques: humorous, fanciful, sensational, allegorical, sentimental, realistic: all of them, we suspect, were but masks behind which she could express her defiant, subversive view of love and marriage in the nineteenth century (Bedell, xxxiv–xxxv).

10. Bedell, introduction to *Little Women,* pp. xxvi–xxvii.

11. See Leo Marx, *The Machine in The Garden: Technology and the Pastoral Ideal in America* (London: Oxford University Press, 1964).

12. Such attitudes have been the center of a number of recent studies of Victorian womanhood. Peter T. Caminos, in one of the best of these, "Innocent Femina Sensualis in Unconscious Conflict" (in *Suffer and Be Still,* ed. Martha Vicunis [Bloomington: Indiana University Press, Midland edition, 1973]), describes the prevailing attitude about woman's "depravity":

> Women were classified into polar extremes. They were either sexless ministering angels or sensuously oversexed temptresses of the devil; they were either aids to continence or incontinence; they facilitated or they exacerbated male sexual control.

According to Caminos, there was wide agreement that a desire to be promiscuous was inherent even in the apparent paragon; "unchastity . . . turned a Victorian woman into a prostitute" (pp. 166–67).

Oates both reflects and parodies these Victorian attitudes about women in *A Bloodsmoor Romance* and *Mysteries of Winterthurn.* Her ingenious and subversive imitations thus give form to contemporary feminist concerns. (See for instance the study of women writers and the genres by duPlessis, *Writing Beyond The Ending.* As Oates dramatizes in her portraits of Bloodsmoor narrators, du Plessis suggests nineteenth-century women artists found literary romance a "compensatory social and narrative practice" [p. 2] in a male-dominated society.)

Also see Ehrenreich and English, *For Her Own Good;* and Sarah Stage's fascinating study: *Female Complaints: Lydia Pinkham and the Business of Women's Medicine* (New York: Norton, 1979). In *Mysteries of Winterthurn,* adding further insult to documented injury, Oates has mischievously named her physician "Colney Hatch," for a well-known British lunatic asylum.

13. See Cott "Passionlessness," and Smith-Rosenberg, *Disorderly Conduct,* for excellent discussions of the perverse attitudes toward women's sexuality, and the desire of both men and women—for very different reasons—to promote sexual anesthesia as a feminine model. Both sources include detailed references to popular advice manuals and medical references of the American Victorian age—sources Oates also acknowledges.

Also see Sandra M. Gilbert, "Costumes of the Mind: Transvestism as Metaphor in

Modern Literature," in *Writing and Sexual Difference,* ed. Elizabeth Abel (Chicago: University of Chicago Press, 1982), 193–220.

14. In her essay, first published in 1983, Oates decribes Bronte's masterpiece in terms that are strikingly applicable to her own designs:

> This great novel . . . manages to be a number of things: a romance that brilliantly challenges the basic presumptions of the "romantic"; a "gothic" that evolves—with an absolutely inevitable grace—into its temperamental opposite; a parable of innocence and loss, and childhood's inevitable defeat. . . . Above all, it is a history . . . writ small . . . of civilization itself ("The Magnanimity of *Wuthering Heights,"* in *The Profane Art,* pp. 64–65).

She also praises Bronte's strategy of the "braiding of narrators" no less effective if not as "willfully ingenious" as the fabulation of Nabokov (p. 66). Once again, she displays a deep affinity for a feminine artistic predecessor, welcoming rather than being anxious about lines of connection. At the conclusion of her critical essay, Oates joins her own vision to Bronte's in a characteristic act of triumphant "collaboration": "Though the grave is misjudged by certain persons as a place of fulfillment, the world is not after all phantasmal: it is by daylight that love survives" (p. 81). Such a comment could as easily refer to *Mysteries of Winterthurn,* in which Oates moves her detective out of an eerie and supernatural realm into the "daylight" of ordinary love.

15. Personal communication.

16. Oates, *A Moveable Feast.*

17. Ednah D. Cheney, ed., *Louisa May Alcott: Her Life, Letters, and Journals* (Boston, 1889), p. 296, reprints an entry in Alcott's journal after the completion of one of her detective romances, "Enjoyed doing it, being tired of providing moral pap for the young" (p. 296)!

18. Oates is attempting to bring together two visions of ratiocinative fiction, embodied in her narrator and her hero, in this novel. It is important, then to examine two areas in which she has evidently done a good deal of academic research.

In *A Bloodsmoor Romance,* Oates cites many of the "scribbling females" whose work provided inspiration for both style and content. In *Mysteries of Winterthurn,* she refers to "male" popular literature, not only explicit whodunits, but such now-forgotten but once-influential male "advice" manuals and works of "pop" psychology as *Martyrdom of Man* by Winfield Reade (London: Kegan Paul, Trench, Trubner & Co. Ltd, 22d ed., 1872). Reade's work, at once skeptical and messianic, is a fascinating reflection of the post-Darwinian sensibility. The "martyrdom" he calls for is the surrender of metaphysical belief, born, he claims, "from the fear of ghosts" (p. xxxi). If faith in a life hereafter is abandoned, he predicts an outpouring of amazing invention to improve the human lot. Reade anticipates H. G. Wells in imagining higher forms of technology: "aerial locomotion," a "motive force which will take the place of steam," "synthetic food" and fertilizer. At that point, "the earth being small,"Reade rhapsodizes that "mankind will migrate into space" (pp. 513–15). Again, it is clear that Oates has drawn on such works of popular culture to represent the "mysteries" of Winterthurn; her young detective refers twice to Reade in particular.

For background on "new" theories of detective fiction, see Marjorie Nicholson, "The Professor and the Detective," *The Atlantic,* Apr. 1929, pp. 483–93; Michael Holquist, "Whodunit and Other Questions: Metaphysical Detective Stories in Post-War Fiction," *NLH* 3 (Autumn 1971): 135–56; William V. Spanos, "The Detective and the Boundary: Some Notes on the Postmodern Literary Imagination," *Boundary 2,* 1 (Fall 1972): 147–68; and the excellent monograph by Stefano Tani, *The Doomed Detective: The Contribution of the Detective Novel to Postmodern American and Italian Fiction* (Carbondale: Southern Illinois University Press, 1984).

19. Frank McConnell, *Storytelling and Mythmaking* (New York: Oxford University Press, 1979), pp. 149, 164, 280–83. McConnell sees the detective as a mediating figure whose work is always in danger of being betrayed:

> ... the detective/investigator does not ... institute or incarnate the laws of his culture. He tries to understand them and to apply them creatively in a society that seems half inclined to pervert their original promise (pp. 205–6).

20. Ibid., p. 149.

21. See Gubar and Gilbert, *Madwoman*; see also Oates, "(Woman) Writer," in *First Person Singular,* pp. 190–97.

22. Ildiko de Papp Carrington, "Walls and Labryinths," *The Women's Review of books* 2, 7 (April 1985): 14–15.

23. Doris Lessing, preface to *The Golden Notebook* (New York: Bantam, 1973), p. xv.

24. In her letter to the *Women's Review* 2, 9 (June 1985), Russ calls *Solstice* "another Sadistic Lesbian novel," and claims that "Oates has been long obsessed with this kind of unreal violence" (p. 18). Oates responded in the following issue, "I have never written a Sadistic Lesbian Novel" (*Women's Review* 2, 10 [July 1985]: 18). Characteristically, she also used the occasion to argue her case for nonprogrammatic woman's art: " ... if the (woman) writer is forced to choose between being faithful to what might be called her personal artistic vision and feminist politics, she will always choose the former." From a very different point of view, Christopher Lehmann-Haupt raises a half-angry, half-baffled complaint about *Solstice*:

> It seems to trail off, to disappear into itself. I felt shut out, as if a door had been slammed in my face. I wanted to pound on it and cry, "What happens to Monica's teaching job? What about her health? Is she going to recover?"

Ruefully, he concludes, "But maybe my dissatisfaction is exactly what Miss Oates is aiming for. . . . The door is only closed to those of us unwilling to feel the shape of the story. To which suggestions of failure I can only plead guilty" (*New York Times,* 10 Jan. 1985, p. 19).

25. Nina Auerbach, *Communities of Women* (Cambridge: Harvard University Press, 1978), pp. 5–12.

26. Elaine Showalter, "My Friend Joyce Carol Oates," *Ms,* March 1986, p. 50. In "That Certain Thing Called the Girlfriend" (*New York Times Book Review,* 11 May 1986), Margaret Atwood uses *Solstice* as an example of the subtler and darker representation of friendship in contemporary fiction by and about women. In Atwood's reading, Oates "gives the theme yet another turn of the screw, as she is wont to do with themes," (p. 1), by showing Sheila and Monica as oddly and profoundly "complementary":

> In a relationship that is erotic without being sensual or sexual—this is an eroticism of the psyche only—they slide into intimacy and then toward disaster. . . . Though all this is taking place ostensibly in Pennsylvania, not Transylvania, the inner landscape is one of moors, crags and deserts—Bronte country (pp. 38–39).

Conclusion

1. Roger Shattuck, "Quanta," *New York Review of Books* 31, 4, (15 March 1984), pp. 3–4.

2. Joyce Carol Oates, *Paris Review* interview in *Writers at Work,* ed. G. Plimpton (New York: Penguin, 1981), pp. 365. She adds, "there are pages in recent novels that I've rewritten as many as seventeen times, and a story, 'The Widows,' which I revised both before and after publication in *The Hudson Review,* and then revised slightly again before I included it in my next collection of stories—a fastidiousness that could go on into infinity" (p. 366).

3. Joyce Carol Oates, "Richard Wishnetsky: Joyce Carol Oates Supplies a Missing View," *The Detroit Free Press,* 6 March 1966, pp. 1–2, 12–13. In a recent interview, Oates again discusses the tragic event, and the young student who ended a rabbi's life and then his own:

> He was very brilliant. . . . He was a student of mine. . . . He was very complex, very tortured and really enduring things in his physical self that other people only talk about. I think his problem was that he felt too deeply and too personally, and for a Jew, a young man, learning about the Holocaust and what it had done to his own people, it simply drove him over the edge.

Oates is exasperated at critics who suggest that Wishnetsky-Weinstein-Morgenstern is an inappropriate hero:

> That he is less admirable than somebody else who can read about these things and yawn and go away and have a pizza and not care, I don't agree. While I do not admire people who become murderers and suicides, at the same time their sensitivity sets them apart in some ways from people who are absolutely indifferent *(Chicago Sun-Times,* 3 February 1965, p. 27).

4. Erica Jong, review of *Last Days, New York Times Book Review,* 5 August 1984, p. 7.

5. Denis Donoghue, review of *A Bloodsmoor Romance, New York Review of Books,* 21 October 1982, pp. 12, 14, 17–18.

6. Henry James, "Preface to the Aspern Papers," in *The Art of The Novel* (New York: Scribner's paperback edition, 1962), p. 172.

Afterword

1. Daniel E. Howard, "Joyce Carol Oates," in *The Modern Tradition,* 4th edition (Boston: Little, Brown, 1979), p. 731.

2. Lucy Lippard, *From The Center: Feminist Essays on Women's Art* (New York: Dutton, 1976), p. 49.

3. Julia Stanley and Susan Wolfe Robbins, "Toward a Feminist Aesthetic," *Chrysalis* 6 (1978): 67.

4. Saul Bellow, quoted in "Remaking the City on the Make," review of *Chicago: TriQuarterly 60,* in *Chicago* (Sept. 1984): 148.

5. Joseph Campbell, *The Masks of God: Creative Mythology* (New York: Viking, 1970), p. 90.

6. Frank McConnell, *Storytelling and Mythmaking: Images from Film and Literature* (New York: Oxford University Press, 1979), p. 53.

7. Estella Lauter, *Women as Mythmakers* (Bloomington: Indiana University Press, 1984), p. 212.

8. Joyce Carol Oates, "The Myth of the Isolated Artist," *Psychology Today,* May 1973, p. 74.

Selected Bibliography

Works by Joyce Carol Oates: 1963–1986

Works discussed in this study by Joyce Carol Oates, with
abbreviated citations shown in parentheses:

NOVELS

Angel of Light. 1981, Reprint. New York: Warner, 1982. (*AL*)
The Assassins. New York: Vanguard, 1975. (*A*)
Bellefleur. New York: Dutton, 1980. (*B*)
A Bloodsmoor Romance. New York: Dutton, 1984. (*BR*)
Childwold. New York: Vanguard, 1976. (*C*)
Cybele. Los Angeles: Black Sparrow, 1980. (*Cy*)
Do with Me What You Will. 1973, Reprint. Greenwich, CT: Fawcett, 1974. (*DWM*)
Expensive People. 1968, Reprint. Greenwich, CT: Fawcett, 1968. (*EP*)
A Garden of Earthly Delights. New York: Vanguard, 1967. (*GED*)
Marya: A Life. New York: Dutton, 1986. (*M*)
Mysteries of Winterthurn. New York: Dutton, 1984. (*MW*)
Solstice. New York: Dutton, 1985. (*S*)
Son of the Morning. New York: Vanguard, 1978. (*SM*)
them. 1969, Reprint. Greenwich, CT: Fawcett, 1977. (*t*)
Unholy Loves. New York: Vanguard, 1979. (*UL*)
With Shuddering Fall. 1964, Reprint. Greenwich, CT: Fawcett, 1971. (*WSF*)
Wonderland. New York: Vanguard, 1971.
Wonderland. Greenwich, CT: Fawcett, 1973. (*W*)

SHORT FICTION

By The North Gate. 1963, Reprint. Greenwich, CT: Fawcett, 1971.
The Hungry Ghosts. Los Angeles: Black Sparrow, 1974.
Last Days. New York: Dutton, 1983. (*LD*)
Marriages and Infidelities. New York: Vanguard, 1972. (*MI*)
Night-Side. New York: Vanguard, 1977.
(ed.) *Scenes from American Life.* New York: Random House, 1973. (*Scenes*)
The Wheel of Love. 1970, Reprint. Greenwich, CT: Fawcett, 1972. (*RI*)

COLLECTED CRITICISM

Contraries. New York: Oxford University Press, 1982.
The Edge of Impossibility. New York: Vanguard, 1972. (*EI*)
(ed.) *First Person Singular.* Princeton, NJ: Ontario Review Press, 1982.
New Heaven, New Earth. New York: Vanguard, 1974. (*NHNE*)
The Profane Art. New York: Dutton, 1983.

SELECTED ESSAYS AND REVIEWS

"Art: Therapy and Magic." *American Journal,* 1, viii (3 July 1973): 17–21.

"Article on Yeats." *New York Times Book Review,* 7 Sept. 1969, p. 2.

" 'At Least I Have Made A Woman of Her': Images of Women in Twentieth Century Literature." *The Georgia Review* 37, 1 (Spring 1983); reprinted in *The Profane Art,* pp. 35–62.

"Does The Writer Exist?" *New York Times Book Review,* 22 April 1984, pp. 1, 17.

"The English and Scottish Traditional Ballads." *The Southern Review* 15, 3 (July 1979): 560–66. (*Ballads*)

"Frankenstein's Fallen Angel." Afterword to Mary Shelley's *Frankenstein.* Berkeley: University of California Press, Pennyroyal Edition, 1984.

"How Is Fiction Doing?" *The New York Times Book Review,* 14 Dec. 1980, p. 3.

"An Imperative to Escape the Prison of Gender." *New York Times Book Review,* 15 April 1973, pp. 7, 10, 12.

"Man's Man? Woman-Hater? Our Greatest Writer?" *TV Guide,* 8 Dec. 1984, pp. 5–6.

"The Myth of the Isolated Artist." *Psychology Today,* May 1973, pp. 74–75.

"New Heaven and Earth." *Saturday Review,* 4 Nov. 1972, pp. 51–54. (*NH*)

"Ontological Proof of My Existence," *Partisan Review* 37, 1970, pp. 471–97. (*OP*)

Review of *The Penguin Book of Women Poets. The New Republic,* 21 April 1979, pp. 28–30.

"Richard Wishnetsky: Joyce Carol Oates Supplies a Missing View." *Detroit Free Press,* 6 March 1966, pp. 1–2, 12–13.

"Stories That Define Me." *New York Times Book Review,* 11 July 1982, pp. 1, 15–16. (Stories)

"Whose Side Are You On?" *New York Times Book Review,* 4 June 1972, p. 63.

INTERVIEWS WITH JOYCE CAROL OATES

Abbey, Marilyn R. "Private Lives Don't Beckon to Joyce Carol Oates." *Chicago Sun-Times,* 3 Feb. 1985, pp. 24, 27.

Bellamy, Joe David. "The Dark Lady of American Letters: An Interview with Joyce Carol Oates." *Atlantic Monthly* 229, 2 (Feb. 1972), pp. 63–67.

Frenkiel, Nora. "Joyce Carol Oates: The Quiet Writer of So Many Books." *The Baltimore Sun,* 24 March 1985, pp. 1G–6G.

A Moveable Feast. Interviews and Readings on Audiotape. Columbia, MO: American Audio Prose Library, 1982.

Phillips, Robert. "Joyce Carol Oates: The Art of Fiction." *The Paris Review.* Reprinted in G. Plimpton, ed. *Writers At Work,* 5th series. New York: Penguin, 1981, pp. 359–84.

"Transformations of Self: An Interview with Joyce Carol Oates." *The Ohio Review* 15, 1 (Fall 1973): 51–61.

WORKS BY OTHER AUTHORS

Atwood, Margaret. "That Certain Thing Called the Girlfriend." *New York Times Book Review,* 11 May 1986, pp. 1, 38–39.

Auerbach, Nina. *Communities of Women.* Cambridge: Harvard University Press, 1978.

_____. *Women and the Demon.* Cambridge: Harvard University Press, 1982.

Barth, John. "The Literature of Exhaustion." *Atlantic Monthly* 220, 2 (August 1967), p. 33.

Bedell, Madelon. Introduction to Louisa May Alcott, *Little Women,* pp. ix–lv. New York: Modern Library College Paperback edition, 1983.

Bellow, Saul. *The Dean's December.* New York: Harper, 1982.

Bender, Eileen T. "Autonomy and Influence: Joyce Carol Oates's *Marriages and Infidelities." Soundings* 58, 3 (Fall 1975): 390–406.

_____. "Paedomorphic Art: Joyce Carol Oates's *Childwold."* In *Critical Views of Joyce Carol Oates,* edited by Linda Wagner. Boston: Hall, 1979.

Berets, Ralph. "Joyce Carol Oates' *Wonderland* Seen as a Mythic Rite of Passage." Unpublished essay, presented at 1973 Modern Language Association panel.

Bloom, Harold. *The Anxiety of Influence.* New York: Oxford University Press, 1973.

_____. *A Map of Misreading.* New York: Oxford University Press, 1975.

Burwell, Rose Marie. "The Process of Individuation as Narrative Structure: Joyce Carol Oates's *Do with Me What You Will." Critique* 17, 2 (1976): 93–106.

Caminos, Peter T. "Innocent Femina Sensualis in Unconscious Conflict." In *Suffer and Be Still,* edited by Martha Vicunis. Bloomington: Indiana University Press, 1973.

Carrington, Ildiko de Papp. "Monsters in Wonderland." Unpublished essay, 1973 Modern Language Association session on Oates.

_____. "Walls and Labyrinths." *Women's Review of Books* 2, 7 (April 1985): 14–15.

Chell, Cara. "Un-Tricking the Eye: Joyce Carol Oates and the Feminist Ghost Story." *Arizona Quarterly* 41, 1 (Spring 1985): 5–23.

_____. "Writer as Terrorist." Unpublished essay, 1986.

Clemons, Walter. "Joyce Carol Oates: Love and Violence." *Newsweek,* 11 Dec. 1972, pp. 72–77.

Cott, Nancy. "Passionlessness: An Interpretation of Victorian Sexual Ideology, 1790–1850." *Signs* 1, 2 (1978): 219–36.

Creighton, Joanne. *Joyce Carol Oates.* Boston: Hall, 1979. (Twayne series).

Donoghue, Denis. "Wonder Woman." *New York Review of Books,* 21 October 1982, pp. 12, 14, 17–18.

DuPlessis, Rachel Blau. *Writing Beyond the Ending: Narrative Strategies of Twentieth-Century Women Writers.* Bloomington: Indiana University Press, 1985.

Ehrenreich, Barbara, and Deirdre English. *For Her Own Good: 150 Years of the Experts' Advice to Women.* New York: Doubleday/Anchor, 1978.

Fagles, Robert. "The Serpent and the Eagle." Prefatory essay to *The Oresteia* with W. B. Stanford. New York: Bantam, 1977.

Fossum, Robert H. "Only Control: The Novels of Joyce Carol Oates." *SNNTS* 7, 2 (Summer 1976): 286–96.

Friedman, Ellen. *Joyce Carol Oates.* New York: Ungar, 1980.

Gardner, John. *Mickelsson's Ghosts.* New York: Knopf, 1982.

Gilbert, Sandra. "Costumes of the Mind: Transvestism as Metaphor in Modern Literature." In *Writing and Sexual Difference,* edited by Elizabeth Abel, pp. 193–220. Chicago: University of Chicago Press, 1982.

Gilbert, Sandra, and Susan Gubar. *The Madwoman in the Attic.* New Haven: Yale University Press, 1980.

Graves, Robert. *The Greek Myths.* New York: Braziller, 1957.

Hartman, Geoffrey. *Criticism In The Wilderness.* New Haven: Yale University Press, 1980.

Heilbrun, Carolyn. *Toward a Recognition of Androgyny.* New York: Norton, 1982.

Johnson, Diane. "Balloons and Abductions." *New York Times Book Review,* 5 Sept. 1982, pp. 1, 15–16.

Kazin, Alfred. *Bright Book of Life.* New York: Atlantic/Little Brown, 1973.

_____. "Heroines." *New York Review of Books,* 11 Feb. 1971, p. 32.

_____. "The Literary Sixties, When the World Was Too Much with Us." *New York Times Book Review,* 21 Dec. 1969, pp. 1–3, 18.

_____. "Oates." *Harper's* 243 (August 1971), pp. 78–82.

_____. "The Writer and the University." In *The Inmost Leaf,* pp. 242–52. New York and London: Harbrace/Harvest.

Knowles, John. "A Racing Car is the Symbol of Violence." *New York Times Book Review,* 25 Oct. 1964, p. 5.

_____. "Foreword" to Harold Pinter's screenplay, *The French Lieutenant's Woman.* Boston: Little, Brown, 1981.

Laing, R. D. *The Divided Self: An Existential Study in Sanity and Madness.* London: Pelican/Penguin, 1965.

_____. *The Politics of Experience.* New York: Ballantine, 1967.

Lauter, Estella. *Women as Mythmakers.* Bloomington: Indiana University Press, 1984.

Lawrence, D.H. *Letters.* Edited by Aldous Huxley. London: Heinemann, 1932.

Lessing, Doris. *The Golden Notebook.* New York: Bantam, 1973.

Lifton, Robert J. *Boundaries: Psychological Man in Revolution.* New York: Vintage, 1970.

McConnell, Frank. *Storytelling and Mythmaking: Images from Film and Literature.* New York: Oxford University Press, 1979.

Madden, David. *The Poetic Image in Six Genres.* Carbondale: Southern Illinois University Press, 1969.

Malamud, Bernard. *A New Life.* New York: Farrar, Straus, 1961.

Maslow, A. H. *The Farther Reaches of Human Nature.* New York: Viking, 1971.

Miller, Nancy K. *The Heroine's Text.* New York: Columbia University Press, 1980.

Nietzsche, Friedrich. *The Philosophy of Friedrich Nietzsche.* New York: Random House/Modern Library, 1954.

_____. *Beyond Good and Evil,* trans. R. J. Hollingdale. New York: Penguin, 1973.

Norman, Torburg. *Isolation and Contact: A Study of Character Relationships in Joyce Carol Oates's Short Stories 1963–1980.* Goteborg, Sweden: Gothenburg Studies in English 57, 1984.

Reade, Winfield. *The Martyrdom of Man.* 22d ed. London: Kegan Paul, 1872.

Rubenstein, Charlotte Streifer. *American Women Artists.* New York: Avon, 1982.

Said, Edward. *The World, the Text, and the Critic.* Cambridge: Harvard University Press, 1983.

Scholes, Robert. *The Fabulators.* New York: Oxford University Press, 1973.

Shattuck, Roger. "Quanta." *New York Review of Books* 31, 4 (15 March 1984), pp. 3–4.

Showalter, Elaine. *A Literature of Their Own: British Women Novelists from Bronte to Lessing.* Princeton, NJ: Princeton University Press, 1977.

_____. "My Friend Joyce Carol Oates." *Ms,* March 1986, pp. 44–46, 50.

Smith-Rosenberg, Carroll. *Disorderly Conduct: Visions of Gender in Victorian America.* New York: Knopf, 1985.

Spanos, William V. "The Detective and the Boundary: Some Notes on the Postmodern Literary Imagination." *Boundary* 2, 1 (Fall 1972): 147–68.

Stage, Sarah. *Female Complaints: Lydia Pinkham and the Business of Women's Medicine.* New York: Norton, 1979.

Stern, Madeleine. *The Hidden Louisa May Alcott.* New York: Avenel Books, 1984.

Sullivan, Walter. "The Artificial Demon: Joyce Carol Oates and the Dimensions of the Real." *Hollins Critic* 9, 4 (Dec. 1972): 1–12.

Tani, Stefano. *The Doomed Detective: The Contribution of the Detective Novel to Postmodern American and Italian Fiction.* Carbondale: Southern Illinois University Press, 1984.

Vicinis, Martha, ed. *Suffer and Be Still.* Bloomington: Indiana University Press, 1973.

Wagner, Linda W., ed. *Critical Essays on Joyce Carol Oates.* Boston: Hall, 1979.

Index

Abduction, 71–72, 79–80, 138
Academic characters: "Joyce Carol Oates" in *them*, 102; artist in residence, 152, 154–55, 163, 176; demonic investigators, 134; eccentric pedagogues, 12, 18, 56, 87, 98–99, 105, 126, 135–37, 147–48, 159; egoistic professors, 106, 161–62; English teachers, 45, 64, 91, 102–103, 104; faculty wives, 104–105, 139; frauds, 57; mad scientists, 115, 134; prodigies, 27–28, 53, 115, 120; prom queen, 154; reclusive scholar, 96–97; schoolmistress, 136, 139; women in academe, 8, 107, 158–59, 160–62
Academic metaphor: analogy to detective story, 148; attempts to "gain admission," 102; book burning, 97; course evaluation, 102; disrespectful custodians, 163; disturbing requirements, 126; erotic mentorship, 90–91, 171; feast of books, 161; oral examination in Oates's "The Dead," 103–104; playing school in *them*, 43; romance of teaching, 136; sacred texts, 107–109; schoolroom as sanctuary, 35, 70, 159, 181; terrible lessons, 128; unexamined text of professorial life, 161–62; university as cloister, 170–71
Accident, 17, 20, 22–23, 31, 76, 141, 154
Alcott, Bronson: eccentric pedagogue, 135–36
Alcott, Louisa May, 134–37, 149, 194–95n
Allusions, literary: in *Cybele*, 122–24; in *Marya: A Life*, 163; Irving, Washington, 116; Joyce, James, 98, 127; Lawrence, D. H., 139; Márquez, Gabriel Garcia, 149; Meredith, George, 15; Milton, John, 98; multiple reference in *Unholy Loves*, 104; Shakespearean, 154, 171; to Beckett, in *Unholy Loves*, 108; to Faulkner in *Bellefleur*, 114–15; to George Eliot, in *Do with Me What You Will*, 191n; to Hawthorne in *A Bloodsmoor Romance*, 133; Woolf, Virginia, 138; Wordsworth reference, 21. *See also* Influences; Intertextuality
American themes: adolescence, 173; adolescence as border state, 120; adolescence, in *Cybele*, 121; assassination, 81, 173; caricature of American dream, 29, 41–43; cult of true womanhood, 137–39; flag in *A Garden of Earthly Delights*, 21; history, 121; in *Angel of Light*, 8; in *With Shuddering Fall*, 13; manifest destiny, in *Bellefleur*, 116; outlaw figure, 46; pathfinders and inventors, 133;

pentacostal religion, 93–95; racial conflict, 76; racial violence, 120; romance, 131; transcendental optimism, 136, 148; transcendentalism, Oates's critique, 136; Westering, 70, 99; wilderness, 85
Androgyny, x, 117, 118, 122, 138, 193–94n; hermaphroditic child, in *Cybele*, 123; transvestite, in *A Bloodsmoor Romance*, 135
Art: order of, in *Childwold*, 90
Artist figure: "Joyce Carol Oates" in *them*, 38; artist in residence, 105–10; caricature, in *The Assassins*, 82–83; despairing narrator in *Son of the Morning*, 100; egocentric, 152–53; in *A Garden of Earthly Delights*, 29; in *Solstice*, 8; literary women, 132–33; trickster, in *Wonderland*, 56–57
Automobile, 12–13, 39, 54, 76–77, 159

Barth, John, 38
Barthelme, Donald, viii
Bedell, Madelon, 134
Bellow, Saul, 9; academic fiction, 101
Berets, Ralph: critique of *Wonderland*, 63–64
Blake, William, 14, 50, 125, 159, 160; allusion in *Marya: A Life*, 163; contraries, vii, 124; misquoted, in *Cybele*, 123
Bloom, Harold: anxiety of influence, ix, 185n; on Oates, 3
Borges, Jorge Luis, 5, 52; "Death and The Compass," 149
Bosch, Hieronymous: allusion in *A Garden of Earthly Delights*, 23
Brown, John, 125, 127; in *Angel of Light*, 8
Burwell, Rose Marie: Bosch parallels in Oates, 19; Jungian interpretation of *Do with Me What You Will*, 71

Campbell, Joseph, 182
Campus setting: Harvard, in *Mysteries of Winterthurn*, 148; in "Last Days," 174–76; in *Cybele*, 122–23; in *Marya: A Life*, 160–61; in *Son of the Morning*, 99; in *them*, 43–45; in *Wonderland*, 49
Carroll, Lewis, 114, 189–90n; Looking glass image, 72–73; multiple references in *Wonderland*, 51, 62–63
Cartography, metaphor of: maps, 2, 26, 70, 85–86, 116, 147; maps, charts, graphs, 151; parallels to art, 116
Cinematic metaphor: for deterministic vision, 27–28, 77; for personality, in *them*, 45; for